Guerrilla Guide to Great Graphics with the GIMP

Send Us Your Comments:

To comment on this book or any other PRIMA TECH title, visit PRIMA TECH's reader response page on the Web at **www.prima-tech.com/comments**.

How to Order:

For information on quantity discounts, contact the publisher: Prima Publishing, P.O. Box 1260BK, Rocklin, CA 95677-1260; (916) 787-7000. On your letterhead, include information concerning the intended use of the books and the number of books you wish to purchase. For individual orders, visit PRIMA TECH's Web site at **www.prima-tech.com**.

Guerrilla Guide to Great Graphics with the GIMP

David D. Busch

PRIMA TECH

A Division of Prima Publishing

A Division of Prima Publishing

Prima Publishing and colophon are registered trademarks of Prima Communications, Inc. PRIMA TECH is a trademark of Prima Communications, Inc., Roseville, California 95661.

The GIMP was written by Peter Mattis and Spencer Kimball, and released under the GNU General Public License (GPL).

Linux is a registered trademark of Linus Torvalds. The Linux penguin, Tux, is used with permission from Larry Ewing (**lewing@isc.tamu.edu**). Ewing created this image using The GIMP (**www.gimp.org**). Modifications to Tux were made by Jim Thompson.

Windows and Microsoft are registered trademarks of Microsoft Corporation. Mac and Macintosh are trademarks or registered trademarks of Apple Computer, Inc. Adobe and Adobe Photoshop are registered trademarks of Adobe Systems, Inc. Kai's Power Tools is a registered trademark of MetaCreations, Corp. Sun Microsystems and all Sun-based trademarks and logos are trademarks or registered trademarks of Sun Microsystems, Inc.

Prima Publishing and the authors have attempted throughout this book to distinguish proprietary trademarks from descriptive terms by following the capitalization style used by the manufacturers.

Important: If you experience problems running or installing the GIMP, check the GIMP's Web site at www.gimp.org for support and technical information. Prima Publishing cannot provide software support.

Information contained in this book has been obtained by Prima Publishing from sources believed to be reliable. However, because of the possibility of human or mechanical error by our sources, Prima Publishing, or others, the Publisher does not guarantee the accuracy, adequacy, or completeness of any information and is not responsible for any errors or omissions or the results obtained from the use of such information. Readers should be particularly aware of the fact that the Internet is an ever-changing entity. Some facts may have changed since this book went to press.

ISBN: 0-7615-2407-X

Library of Congress Catalog Card Number: 99-65426

Printed in the United States of America

00 01 02 03 04 II 10 9 8 7 6 5 4 3 2 1

Publisher:
Stacy L. Hiquet

Marketing Manager:
Judi Taylor

Associate Marketing Manager:
Jody Kennen

Managing Editor:
Sandy Doell

Senior Acquisitions Editor:
Kim Spilker

Senior Editor:
Kevin Harreld

Copy Editor:
Chuck Brandstater

Technical Reviewer:
Ryan Palsgaard

Interior Layout:
Shawn Morningstar

Cover Design:
Prima Design Team

Indexer:
Sherry Massey

To Cathy.

   You look great with or without those glasses.

Acknowledgments

Thanks to the folks at Prima, who, despite tight deadlines, gave me the extra time I needed to focus this book on the latest and greatest GIMP, Version 1.2. Among my fellow GIMP guerrillas are Kim Spilker, acquisitions editor, who had the foresight to aggressively develop a book on the GIMP even before Linux had become the Next Big Thing; and Kevin Harreld, senior editor, who gamely kept the project moving and bought into my attempt to bring a light tone to what could have been a heavy topic. Other valiant GIMP warriors include Chuck Brandstater, copy editor, and Ryan Palsgaard, tech editor. My involvement in this project wouldn't have been possible without my agent, Carole McClendon, whose casual question, "Are you familiar with the GIMP?" started the ball rolling. And, finally, I'd like to thank the country of Spain for giving me some beautiful, semi-generic images to transform using my favorite Linux image editor.

About the Author

Two-time Computer Press Association winner David D. Busch has been demystifying arcane computer and imaging technology since the early 1980s. As a writer, photographer, columnist, and contributing editor for 10 leading computer magazines, he has more than 2500 articles to his credit. A specialist in transforming images, his 64 books include eight dealing with scanners and digital photography, and a dozen detailing tips and tricks for getting the most from applications like Adobe Photoshop and Kai's Power Tools.

Contents at a Glance

Contents

Chapter 4: Selection Savvy 93

Will Linux kill off Microsoft Windows? Will the GIMP (*GNU Image Manipulation Program*) replace Adobe Photoshop? Who cares?

If you've picked up this book, you probably don't give a hoot about the operating system wars, and don't know or care how the GIMP compares with its cross-platform rivals. You've made your choices, and don't need to justify them. Your question is not "What can I do?" but "How do I do it?" In fact, your search for a clearly written GIMP manual was probably initiated by an encounter like this one:

"Fran, you know how to use the GIMP, don't you?"

"Uh, I *have* it on my workstation. I haven't really mastered all, er, *any* of its features yet."

"Fine. Sounds like you're our expert, then. Can you dress up this portrait of the boss for our Web site? We don't need it until noon today."

"Umm…what's involved?"

"Just erase a few frown lines. Delete that glare off his glasses. Could you make his bald head look a little less obvious? While you're at it, he thinks he looks awful in that brown suit. Could you make it blue?"

"What?"

"The file should already be in your e-mail box. Give me a nice JPEG file in about 45 minutes, okay?"

"Okay, sure," you reply, wondering exactly what a JPEG file is. You've got BSEE and MBA degrees, and here you are thrown by yet another acronym. You can't tell the boss that you're overqualified for this task—you've got to handle it. What can you do?

If you're really smart, you bought this book and read through it quickly, so you can now spend the next 45 minutes getting up to speed to handle that job. Even if GIMP Guru isn't in your job description, after a few hours with the *Guerrilla Guide to Great Graphics with the GIMP*, you can add that qualification to your résumé.

Never before has a "killer app" been so aptly mated with a "killer OS." The GIMP is an important step in the movement of Linux from the server to the desktop. Individuals and organizations desperate for a lithe, rock-solid operating system that excels as a reliable Web, database, and application server have found Linux the answer to their prayers. The only thing keeping this stellar open-source OS from spreading to desktop workstations has been a suite of applications that equal their counterparts in the Wintel and Macintosh ® worlds. The GIMP is one of the killer apps that is paving the way.

Easily the most sophisticated image application for UNIX and Linux, the GIMP can generate graphics the equal of any competing pixel-pusher, including Adobe Photoshop. However, the most significant difference between Photoshop users and GIMP aficionados is that Linux users are often (but not always) less proficient at image editing. For veteran workers who are more computer-oriented than imaging-oriented, recompiling the GIMP source code for their particular platform, or installing it using a tool like the Red Hat Package Manager, is the easiest part.

The hard part is, how do I get all those cool effects I see in publications, on Web sites, or in presentations? Now what?

Guerrilla Guide to Great Graphics with the GIMP focuses on creative ways to transform ordinary images into triumphant prizewinners, using the advanced features found in this image editor. This book cuts right to the heart of one of the most misunderstood—but easily applied—tools in any serious designer's graphics guerrilla arsenal. It bristles with surprisingly effective examples, simple-to-follow techniques, and tricks that serve as a jumping-off point to spark the reader's own creativity into action.

About the Book

If you're asking yourself "now what?" this book answers the question in the first few chapters, leaping into the fray with the enthusiasm of a guerrilla commando, by showing you how to master your toolkit. A few breathless hours later, anyone using the GIMP with this book will be able to marshal their own platoon of effects, with the ability to do the following:

- Create 3-D type with shadows, cutouts, and perspective. Add a metallic sheen or a neon glow. (You don't need expensive 3-D software to achieve these effects—the same magic can be conjured inside the GIMP using built-in filters and Script-Fu scripts.)

- Make prize Web graphics out of images that aren't even good enough for the shoebox, using the GIMP's enhanced filters and plug-ins. Even if you don't know color correction or gamma correction from brightness-contrast controls, and have been thinking that a histogram is a cold remedy, the GIMP has ways to bring off-color or dull originals to blazing life, ready for use in Web pages and other applications.

- Create impressive images from scratch. Even the best photo may need some sort of object created with painting and drawing tools.

You don't have to be an artist to turn out professional work. *Guerrilla Guide to Great Graphics with the GIMP* is every GIMP professional's dream design guide. This book jumps right in and shows anyone how to create great graphics easily, using step-by-step examples. The impatient, the harried, and those who must use the GIMP in their work—but don't want to make a career of using this application—will love this book. You're the folks who never read the manuals (unless you have to) but instead prefer to ask a colleague who's been there: "just tell me how to do this one thing…" Because so many GIMP users end up being trailblazers, there may not be many colleagues able to serve as mentors. So, *Guerrilla Guide to Great Graphics with the GIMP* steps in to give you exactly the sort of information you are looking for.

Who You Are

You may have some experience with Photoshop, but it's very possible that you do not. At least for the present, full-time graphics professionals will tend to stick with Macs or Windows machines, and with Adobe's flagship imaging product. It's more likely that you spend most of your time with non-imaging tasks. Perhaps you're a programmer or an executive in a technical organization that has settled on Linux, but is finding an increasing need for graphics for Web sites or publications.

Whether you're a Photoshop veteran or not, *Guerrilla Guide to Great Graphics with the GIMP* is intended for everyone from beginners to advanced image designers who already know the basics of creating images, and who now want to spread their wings and learn more. It serves as a tutorial for experienced computer pros and programmers who just lack graphics expertise, and an idea generator for those who want to spice up their work. If you're a typical reader, you probably fall into one of these categories:

- Small business owners who have moved to Linux or UNIX, and want to build a site, create brochures or other publications, or promote their business with images, and who need to know more about using graphics.

- Corporate workers who may or may not have image design in their job descriptions, but who need to learn how to use graphics to beef up or help maintain their company's intranet or Web site or other image-intensive applications.

- Professional Webmasters and designers with strong skills in programming (including Java, JavaScript, HTML, Perl, C++, and so on) but with little or no experience in manipulating or creating graphics.

- Graphic artists and others who already are adept in image editing with Photoshop or another application, and who want to learn how to apply their skills to the best image editor currently available for Linux and UNIX.

- Trainers who need a non-threatening textbook for classes in using the GIMP.

- Potential GIMP users who aren't quite ready to get their feet wet, and want to learn more about what's involved before they jump in.

I kept two things in mind while writing this book. I figured that you want more than just a discussion or tutorial on how the GIMP works. You're looking for tips, tricks, and above all, examples of cool things you can do with images using the GIMP. So, each chapter explains how to use various components and tools—and then follows up with easy-to-duplicate effects. My second assumption is that you're probably not manipulating graphics for pre-press. The real hot area for Linux graphics today is for online or intranet Web sites. Consequently, you'll find that many of the chapters have suggestions for applying the GIMP to Web applications. (I've set aside one chapter to delve into Web topics even more deeply.)

Because a significant number of readers may be former Photoshop users, I'll relate features of the GIMP to their counterparts in Photoshop from time to time. In general, however, you won't find an overabundance of such references. This book is *not* intended to be a GIMP guide for recovering Photoshop workers.

Who I Am

Until I was seduced by the dark side of technology, I was a commercial photographer and writer who'd penned several thousand articles on photographic topics for magazines like *Petersen's PhotoGraphic*, *Professional Photographer*, and *The Rangefinder*. Since then, I've written a clutch of books on image editing, digital photography, and scanning—when not otherwise occupied trying to keeping my Windows and Mac OS systems running. (For some unexplained reason, my Linux box requires little attention: it just keeps chugging along, burping up a core dump every now and then to keep me on my toes.) I've also been a denizen of the online world since July, 1981, so I understand the needs and foibles of Web graphics users. My columns on Web imaging were a long-time feature in *Internet World* magazine.

Because of my background, I bring both a photographer's sensibilities and an imaging end-user's sensitivities to the party. And, as an old Xenix user, I was delighted when Linux began to gain popularity and usability, as GUIs like GNOME and KDE were matched with applications like the GIMP.

A final warning: I first came to national attention for a book called *Sorry About the Explosion!* This book earned the first (and only) Computer Press Association award presented to a book of computer humor. Since then, my rise from oblivion to obscurity has been meteoric—a big flash, followed by a fiery swan dive into the horizon—so each of my books always includes a sprinkling of flippancy scattered among all the dry, factual stuff. You've been duly cautioned.

What You Will Need

All you really need is this book and a working copy of the GIMP. Linux runs on 386 computers with barely enough memory to hold a Windows data link library, but I don't recommend a bare bones system for serious image editing. Unless you like to take a coffee break while the GIMP applies special effects to large images, you're better off with a fast system (if you're in the Intel world, a Pentium II or III or a Celeron 333 Mhz machine or faster would be great), and 64 MB or more of RAM. You'll probably want a gigabyte or so of local free disk space to store your images, although you can get by with less if you're able to offload large files to a server or external storage. You can get by with less muscular hardware if you're willing to spend the time necessary to work around your limitations. One of the machines I used to prepare this book was a Pentium 133 running Red Hat Linux 6.0 on a 2.4 GB hard disk—and it worked great. Of course, I did have 128 MB of RAM. The other computer I used was a Celeron 433 with 96 MB of RAM. It worked great, too. There are some things you just shouldn't skimp on.

I'll assume that you don't need a lot of handholding when it comes to installing the GIMP. Linux users, by necessity, are a little more comfortable with the nuts and bolts of their operating system than the typical "Which key is the *ANY* key I'm supposed to hit?" neophyte on other platforms. You'll find some tips on installation in Appendix A, but the body of the book concentrates on hitting the ground running with great GIMP graphics.

Which GIMP I Will Be Covering

GIMP version control became very interesting in the latter part of the last millennium, but the bottom line is that this book covers both the most recent version of the GIMP and the most commonly used version, 1.0.4 (which is included with many Linux distributions). Because the new version has an overwhelming number of new and enhanced features, you'll find that a great deal of this book is devoted to covering them. So, if you're using GIMP 1.0.4, an upgrade to the new release is a good idea. This book will help you make the transition to all the cool new stuff.

And what, you may ask, is the "new release?" When I wrote this book, the GIMP had entered the final stages of debugging for a feature-frozen version called 1.1.9, later upgraded to the version 1.1.11 I used for most of the book, and version 1.1.13 by the time the book was finished. The scuttlebutt was that a stable version to be called 1.2 would be available by the time *Guerilla Guide* hit the bookshelves, expected to be early in 2000. If everything has gone well, one of the following scenarios will now apply:

- GIMP 1.2 and this book are available at the same time, and vast numbers of happy graphics guerrillas are wildly happy with both.

- Somebody noticed what a huge upgrade the new GIMP is and successfully arranged to have its name changed to GIMP 2.0 or GIMP 2000, or something equally confusing. Even so, the happy throngs continue to celebrate the Year 2000 reading this book by kerosene lamp as they run their workstations from portable generators.
- GIMP is still stuck in version 1.1.13, in which case this book, which covers version 1.1.13, too, does its job even though grumbling GIMPers grudgingly anticipate a long-awaited one-hundredth of a percentage point release upgrade.

In short, whether you're using GIMP 1.0.4, 1.1.9, 1.2, 2.0, 2000, or GIMP Office Deluxe Special Edition, I've got you covered. When a *really* new, even cooler, version of the GIMP is available, I'll update this book with a new edition.

About Those Screen Shots...

I used the GNOME desktop environment and the Enlightenment Window manager to prepare this book, with the Default theme activated. If you're using GNOME with another theme or a different desktop management environment (such as KDE), your screen may look a bit different from my screen shots, particularly in the title bar area icons and the dialog box buttons. I usually hear from a few neophytes who find these differences disturbing, but for you old hands this warning should be enough, or superfluous.

What's GNU with You?

If you're already a GIMP user, you may have—quite rightly—purchased this book to get up to speed on that GNU... er... new version. Although I'll point out spiffy new features as you explore them in the book, the following is a quick summary of what is *probably* included in the latest release. These are only the highlights. Some enhancements have been around awhile in the developer's version, so if you're using any version later than 1.0.4, you may already have them.

Hardware

- Better control over pressure-sensitive devices.
- Wheel-mouse support in many GIMP dialog boxes.

New Tools

- Dodge, Burn, and Smudge tools for editing your images.
- A new Path tool with a combination of Bézier, Spline, and Intelligent Scissors tools.

- Image Pipe, a new brush you can create from a list of pixel maps.
- A new measuring tool for calculating distances and angles.
- Quick Mask (Yes!) for painting selections.

Enhanced Tools

- The Crop and Resize tool (formerly called just Crop), which can be used with layers or an image. (Look for AutoCrop capabilities, too.)
- The Curve dialog box, interactive now, so that you can see how your changes are working.
- Spiral gradients.
- Editable brushes.

Functions

- Improved dithering to let you customize your palettes.
- Preview image for saving JPEGs.
- Enhanced cubic interpolation.
- Conversion of selection to path.
- User-defined measuring units (so you can go from pixels to parsecs if you like).

Interface

- Resizable toolbox, which now shows the current brush, gradient, and pattern.
- Brushes scaled to fit in the Brush Palette's preview thumbnails.
- Pop-up navigation window.
- Drag and Drop features for files, brushes, patterns, layers, and other functions.
- Tear-off menus you can place anywhere on your workspace.
- Ability to toggle many tools by holding down the Shift key.
- Ability to hide dialog boxes by pressing Tab.
- The New Image dialog box, which lets you specify measurements, such as inches or centimeters, along with pixels.

Plug-Ins

Slated for inclusion in the latest distributions are great plug-ins, many of which were available separately. These include GIMPressionist, Sample Colorize, Curve Bend, ImageMap, GFlare, Pyimp, AlienMap2, Color Enhance, Warp, Rotate ColorMap,

GdynText (dynamic, editable text), the GIMP Animation Plug-in, WaterSelect, NewsPrint, and Sphere Designer. No guarantees that they'll be in all distributions, but look for them.

How to Use This Book

Computer books invariably begin with incredible insights, such as a suggestion to read the book from front to back, skim over boring parts, and then review any portions you don't understand until the information finally sinks in. I don't think that *Guerrilla Guide to Great Graphics with the GIMP* must read like an instruction manual, and I've relegated all the boring parts to the bit-bin long before the book hit the printing press. The icons used to point out tips, notes, and cautions should be self-explanatory. I don't care if you read the odd-numbered pages first, as long as you get busy having fun with the GIMP.

Finally, don't be upset if, like most of the available literature, the book sometimes plays fast and loose with the GIMP acronym. Sometimes I'll call it *GIMP*, particularly when using the word as an adjective. Other times I'll refer to it as *the GIMP*. When I'm being formal or stern, I'll call it the *GNU Image Manipulation Program*. If you can handle Linux, you should be able to figure out what I mean.

How to Reach the Author

While I'm not your one-stop source for toll-free technical support, I'm always glad to answer reader questions that relate to this book. Sometimes I can get you pointed in the right direction to resolve peripheral queries I can't answer. You can write to me at gimp@dbusch.com.

Your first stop, however, probably should be my GIMP Web page, at http://www.dbusch.com/gimp. I'll have an errata page with corrections for the one or two typos I've inserted in this book intentionally to see if you're paying attention. You'll also find links to other Linux and GIMP sites, free clip art, and a few tips and tricks that didn't make it into this book.

Organization

Part I: GIMP and Imaging Basics

Chapter 1: Images, Images, Images

In this chapter, you'll learn about the differences between different kinds of artwork, what resolution is, what kind of file formats are available, and a little about grayscales and color.

Chapter 2: Attacking the GIMP Toolbar and User Interface

This chapter introduces you to the GIMP interface, main menus, and tools. You'll also find a brief introduction to layers and channels, and some tips on how to customize the GIMP using the program's Preferences dialog boxes.

Chapter 3: Painting Your Canvas

In case you like to draw or paint, or find yourself needing to create images from scratch, you'll find a comprehensive discussion of GIMP painting tools here.

Chapter 4: Selection Savvy

When it comes to modifying images, making precise selections is crucial. You're going to spend a full chapter learning all the tricks of selecting portions of your graphics.

Chapter 5: Using Layers, Channels, and Masks

Layers, channels, and masks are some of the trickiest aspects of using any image editing program, but you'll find these features less daunting after you've learned to create effective layers and masks the easy way.

Chapter 6: Introduction to Color

Getting good color is not as easy as it looks, nor as difficult as the color gurus make it out to be! Don't panic—once you've absorbed some simple background information, you'll be ready to correct color, change hues, and work with cool color effects alongside the best of them.

Chapter 7: Refining and Modifying Color

You figured that levels and curves belonged in video games, and that histograms sounded like an over-the-counter medicine? You'll be able to enhance the color of your images after working through this chapter.

Chapter 8: Transformations

What good is an image if you can't tear it apart, crop it, or slice it to bits? You'll find great image transformation tools in the GIMP, and this chapter shows you how to use them.

Part II: Putting the GIMP to Work

Chapter 9: Compositing and Photo Restoration

Interested in sending Elvis out on a date with Pamela Anderson? The King will be forever grateful after you learn some nifty techniques for combining photos, removing defects (like those embarrassing sideburns), and restoring damaged images.

Chapter 10: GIMP on the Web

It's easy to add images to your Web pages—but where do you get them? This chapter shows you ways to build better buttons, create rules that rock, generate 3-D effects, and choose the right file format before optimizing your colors for the Web.

Chapter 11: Great Text Effects

A good-looking headline can be the key to having your Web page be an attraction, rather than a distraction. There are lots of text effects here, including glowing text, backlit text, text with perspective, and wrapped text.

Chapter 12: Filter, Plug-In and Extension Arsenal

Filters and Plug-ins are one of my favorite topics (I've written two books devoted exclusively to these wonderful add-ons). The GIMP does not come up short when it comes to filter and plug-in tools you can work with. Discover the best of them, and some of the wonderful things you can do with them.

Chapter 13: Scanning

Now that scanner prices have taken a nosedive below the $100 mark, you'll want to read this chapter for the information you need to put this invaluable peripheral to work.

Chapter 14: Introducing Script-Fu

Learn what's involved in becoming adept in the Way of the Intercepting Macro in this introduction to the GIMP's built-in scripting facility. Why re-invent the wheel?

Appendix A

Here are a bunch of GIMP installation tips for the hurried and harried.

Appendix B

Frequently asked questions for inquisitive minds.

Glossary

All the jargon, tricky words in this book—and many that aren't—are explained in this comprehensive graphics lexicon.

PART I

GIMP and Imaging Basics

Chapter 1: Images, Images, Images

Welcome to the war zone! I didn't name this book *Guerrilla Guide to Great Graphics with the GIMP* because I have an obsession with alliteration. Each of the words in the title (except, maybe, the prepositions) represents an important concern of GIMP users like you. You want *Great Graphics*, need a *Guide* to help you along the path to imaging excellence, and have, obviously, made the *GIMP* your tool of choice. But where does the *Guerrilla* part come in?

If you think about it, one of the coolest things about the GIMP is its in-your-face, guerrilla-band nature. Like a squad of commandos, the GIMP is lean, tough, and flexible, and it has a broad range of capabilities that may surprise you. As you'll learn, it was built by a loose team of programmers working independently and cooperatively. But, most of all, the GIMP is a freedom fighter in every sense of the phrase. It's not only *free* software in terms of cost, but also *free* in terms of how it can be distributed or modified. Even the GIMP's basic documentation is available free from **www.gimp.org**, although beginning GIMP users are likely to find it too technical to use as a get-started manual.

And if that weren't belaboring the guerrilla analogy enough, keep in mind that the GIMP is the Linux user's major weapon in the war against the computer: a collection of silicon, conductive metals, glass, plastic, and other inorganic matter that has been designed from the ground up to make working with graphics difficult. Think about it: for someone working with light and color, a tool that understands only numbers is a formidable handicap, indeed. Yet, in our war zone, the GIMP is a powerful armory all on its own.

This chapter will provide you with an introduction to the GIMP and the basic information about imaging that you need to know to successfully meddle with graphics. You'll learn about bitmapped (*raster*) and line-oriented (*vector*) artwork, and a little about resolution, file formats, grayscales, and color. You'll look at most of these in more detail later in the book; this chapter is intended for graphics tyros who have been dumped kicking and screaming into the world of imaging. You don't really need to understand internal combustion to drive a car, but it does help to know enough about the laws of gravity to understand why your SUV flipped over during that sharp turn.

Enter the GIMP

Bruce Lee, arguably one of the finest choreographers who ever lived, made his *Jeet Kune Do* ballet antics look easy. A craftily designed computer, a decent operating system like Linux, and a stellar image editor like the GIMP can make working with graphics look easy, too. But whether you're creating a spinning back-kick or a spinning Web logo, there's a lot more behind the scenes than the flashy stuff you see. In truth, for your computer, handling images is an extremely complex task.

The visual information your eye can absorb at a glance requires a sophisticated peripheral, such as a scanner or digital camera, and a lot of processing power to convert it to machine-readable form. And while your brain can process uncounted pieces of visual data every second, even a powerful Linux box must have images translated into the strings of 1s and 0s before it can do anything with them. That's why when it comes to manipulating images with the GIMP, guerrilla tactics are in order. Until very recently, images and technology were at war with each other. Every step forward in technology over the last half-millennium seemed to move us a step or two backwards in terms of imaging.

For example, moveable type and mass-produced books replaced handwritten manuscripts and their beautiful illuminated images. As simple as they were to reproduce, early books and newspapers were unattractive masses of black text, punctuated by an occasional engraving. Photographic technology simplified capturing pictures, but took a long time to catch up to the realism possible with painted portraits. It was only in the 20th Century that pictures could be reproduced and transmitted electronically.

If you have used text-only user interfaces with UNIX/Linux-style operating systems (or, perhaps, MS-DOS), you know well how difficult it is to represent image information using only the 1s and 0s that computers handle well. As recently as about 1980, it was quite common for a computer user to generate dot matrix printouts of human faces and other images created using only the ASCII characters, and to display them with pride; if you squinted real hard, you could actually see a picture in there.

It is really only in the 1990s that the majority of personal computers and workstations have finally become fast enough and powerful enough to address each pixel on a computer display in real time, making pixel-oriented—or bitmapped—graphics possible. As you enter the fracas, and struggle to convince your highly sophisticated computer system to capture and modify and output images in the way you'd like, the GIMP may be your main ally. This pixel-pusher has been designed to help you handle images smoothly, despite the obstacles thrown in your way.

The GIMP began as a student project by Peter Mattis and Spencer Kimball in 1995, and was initially entirely the work of those two pioneering programmers. To put the feat into perspective, keep in mind that Photoshop's splash screen lists no less than 30 core programmers for the program and something more than 100 other team members (I lost count at credits for logo designer). One of the nicest things about the genesis of the GIMP is that when an application is initially developed by only two dedicated souls, it's safe to assume they won't be voluntarily padding the program out with 10 million lines of redundant code.

The GIMP started small, and has remained refreshingly lithe. If you look at the GIMP 1.0.4 interface, shown in Figure 1-1, you can see that it's a compact piece of work, unencumbered by clutter and confusing features. The interface for the latest version, which you'll begin exploring in the next chapter, is almost identical.

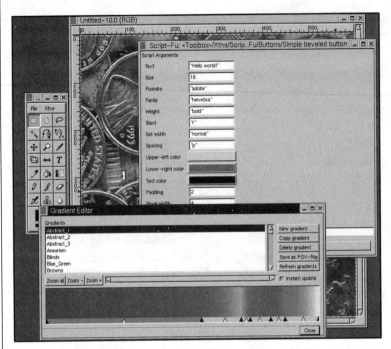

Figure 1-1 *The GIMP may not be "Photoshop for Free" but it has an amazing array of features packed into its compact interface.*

The goal of Mattis and Kimball, as stated on their University of California/Berkeley Web site, was to create a program "that would provide the features missing from the other X painting and imaging tools. A program that would help maintain the long tradition of excellent and free UNIX applications." The GIMP was designed to provide an intuitive graphical interface for a broad range of image editing operations; as you'll see in the chapters that follow, its features fall into several categories:

- Viewing an image in multiple sizes (zooming) to allow editing and previewing.
- Selecting portions of the image to allow them to be manipulated separately, without affecting other portions of the image.
- Cropping an image to exclude portions that you don't want.
- Painting on an image to add new pixels, colors, or shades for editing and retouching operations.
- Combining images and portions of images to create new pictures.
- Changing the colors of images to modify the color balance or to add new hues.
- Transforming images to rotate, scale, shear, and flip pictures or selections.

- Filtering images with plug-ins that add special effects without tedious manual steps.
- Undoing actions that you've changed your mind about, and redoing actions you decide to reapply.
- Extending the GIMP with new features and capabilities, through either plug-ins or changes to the program's code.
- Automating repetitive tasks using the GIMP's scripting language, Script-Fu.

As you might guess, a product as cool as the GIMP could never remain a two-person project. Eventually, the source code was released to the public under the GNU GPL (*General Public License*) as an Open Source software product. This method of distribution allows anyone to revise or improve the source code, remove bugs, or create entirely new products that interface smoothly with the original. Enhancements that truly advance a product—including Linux or the GIMP—can be incorporated into the "official" distributions and thus become an integral part of the program itself. Even better, the GIMP has an open architecture that lets you add plug-in features through a programmer-friendly API (*application programming interface*) without messing with the main source code itself.

So, since its release, many programmers working with thousands of beta testers have expanded the GIMP, enhanced it with plug-ins and scripts, and given it features that, finally, begin to approach those of commercial image editing programs.

Because the source code is available to anyone, it can be recompiled for use on a variety of platforms, including UNIX and UNIX-like operating systems such as Linux, HP-UX, IRIX, Solaris, SunOS, and FreeBSD. If you look carefully, you can find versions for Microsoft Windows and for OS/2. (I have the former operating under Windows NT right now, but it still needs a lot of work; a breaking-glass sound effect to let me know when it's about to crash would be nice.)

What does the future hold for the GIMP? Given that so many individuals are working on it, each tenaciously laboring over his or her particular agenda of dream features, it's difficult to predict what will happen. One way to find out is to visit the GIMP Web site at **www.gimp.org** and download the developer's version that is always tucked away somewhere. This beta software always contains some surprises, cool new features, and a host of untamed bugs hiding out and waiting to bite you. (As I explained in the Introduction, I used the feature-frozen, only-slightly-buggy version 1.1.11 developer's version to write this book—and lived to tell about it.)

Here are some things you can bet on finding in future versions of the GIMP. First, look for support for more and more features found in Adobe Photoshop. One of the prime reasons for the continual development of the GIMP has been that there is no other Photoshop-equivalent application available for platforms like Linux. So, it's only natural that features like Photoshop's History (a near-infinite number of

Undos), very cool mask-making features (like the Extract command added to Photoshop 5.5), and Web optimization tools have been or will be incorporated into the GIMP. (In case you don't know what these features are, you'll be looking at them later in the book.)

Will the GIMP become the color-correction champion that Photoshop is in the prepress world? I doubt that this will happen for a while, as prepress and production applications for the GIMP are probably not going to be a priority among users for a while yet. Will the GIMP add support for additional file formats? Count on it. Although it started with two programmers, the GIMP has, in effect, the largest programming staff in the world at its beck and call.

With all this background behind us, you're ready to look at the GIMP and some of the concepts underlying it. To begin your basic training, it will be helpful to gain an understanding of the different kinds of images.

Understanding Vector Graphics versus Raster Graphics

At its core, the GIMP is a picture element-based, or pixel-based, visual editor. It operates by adding, subtracting, moving, and changing the color or density of the individual picture elements of a photograph or other graphic. Today, virtually everyone, including my grandmother, knows what a pixel is—or thinks they do. Think quickly: are pixels square or rectangular? Are they dots? Are they a triad of dots on an RGB monitor? Do scanners and printers have pixels? Exactly what was that pixel-dust that Tinkerbell used to sprinkle around the Lost Boys?

To use pixels, you need to understand non-pixels. Many programs, particularly drawing applications and computer-assisted drafting and design tools, work with line-based, object-oriented images. These, usually called vector graphics, are the easiest kind of graphics for computers to work with, but, paradoxically, the most difficult to display. A vector (a quantity that can be represented by a magnitude, or length, and a direction) presents a particularly number-friendly way to represent an image. List a few coordinates, specify whether the lines joining them are straight or curved, and presto: you have an image. (Figure 1-2 shows a wire-frame model, one kind of vector graphic image.)

Of course, computers generally don't display vector images as lines alone. The information must be translated into rows of pixels: the raster images that computer monitors and printers, like televisions, use to generate graphics. So, while a computer can manipulate vector graphics at great speed, they must be converted to pixels for display. This process can be quite slow, especially in the case of complex 3-D images.

In the computer world, vector graphics are most easily seen at work in plotters, which draw images much the way people do when operating an Etch-A-Sketch, combining

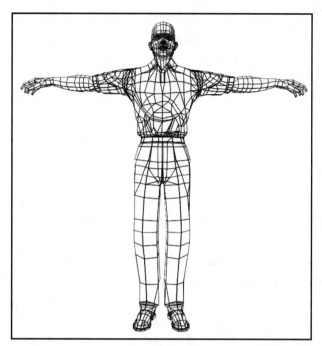

Figure 1-2 *Three–dimensional wire frames use vector lines and curves to represent complex objects.*

lines into shapes. There are a number of advantages to working with images in this way. First, it's fairly easy to treat each of the individual components in a drawing distinctly. The four lines you use to draw a square can be grouped together as one object, even if you happen to draw a second object, such as a circle, that overlaps the first.

In addition, the amount of storage space required for vector graphics is related directly to the complexity of the image. A drawing that consists of a single straight line can be stored as the start and end coordinates. The very cool aspect of this method of representing images is that a vector-based image can be scaled up or down as much as you like, without turning fuzzy like a photograph that's been blown up too far. It doesn't matter whether points A, B, C, and D are two inches apart or are located in different states; the quadrangle they describe can be represented as precisely as their distances apart have been measured.

Raster images like the one in Figure 1-3, on the other hand, are divided up into a series of parallel lines, usually laid out horizontally. Each line is in turn divided into individual squares, dots, or rectangles. Raster graphics are also called bitmaps, because every pixel on each line is mapped to the picture element at the same position in the original image.

Pixels can be dots (they are, in fact, converted to dot-shapes when sent to your printer), but are more commonly rectangles or squares. Both shapes can be butted up smoothly against adjacent pixels with only minimal space between them, but squares have the added advantage of having the same orientation when turned 90 degrees. With rectangular pixels, when a graphic is turned on its side, it can appear taller than it was wide. A 100 x 100-pixel graphic with square picture elements looks the same in either orientation.

Of course, the best results are produced when the graphic is rotated in 90-degree increments. Turn a pixel at a 45-degree angle, as if you were balancing it on one corner, and you're looking for problems. The reason why this appalling condition isn't obvious to the eye is that pixels are very small and it takes many of them to build something you actually can see in an image. (Figure 1-3 gives you a close-up of some pixels in a raster image.)

Like the pattern of dots in a halftoned photograph printed in the newspaper, pixels are used to build an image. A pixel can be either black or white, have some gray value in between, and, in the case of a color image, have a hue associated with its lightness or darkness. The eye merges this array of pixels into a recognizable image. Computers, too, can work with bitmapped images, because the black/white, gray, or color image can be conveniently represented by 1s and 0s in a bitmap.

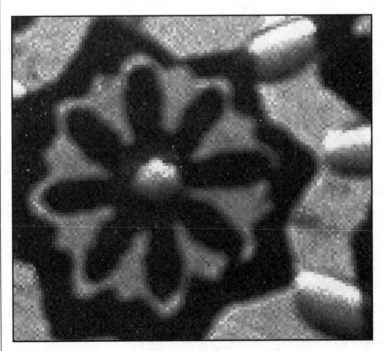

Figure 1-3 *The pixels in a raster image, up close and personal.*

To a computer, the only difference between a pure black or white pixel, a gray pixel, or one with a full range of color is the length of the string of digits that must be used to represent that pixel. For example, where a bit (with a value of either 0 or 1) can represent either black or white, a full 8-bit byte is needed to represent shades or colors with values ranging from 00000000 to 11111111 (0 to 255 in decimal). The length of the string of numbers required to represent a pixel's visual appearance is called *bit depth* (you'll look at that topic in more detail later on). The GIMP can handle anything from 1-bit, black/white images up through 24-bit, full-color graphics.

In many cases, bitmaps are not as efficient in storing images as vector graphics; a simple vector image requires only a few numbers to represent its shape, perhaps a list of coordinates, direction of the lines, and their curve, if any.

However, the state of every single pixel in a bitmapped image must be accounted for, whether the image is filled with detail or consists only of a tiny shape in the center. (In practice, a bitmapped image with that much redundant information is likely to be compressed; image processing software uses algorithms that reduce the amount of numbers needed to represent the entire graphic.)

Finally, while vector images can be smoothly scaled up or down without losing sharpness, bitmaps look their best at the size at which they were created. Scaling up or down, particularly when uneven increments are used, produces an effect called staircasing, as pixels are created or removed in an attempt to portray the image at its new size. (You can see an example of staircasing in Figure 1-4.)

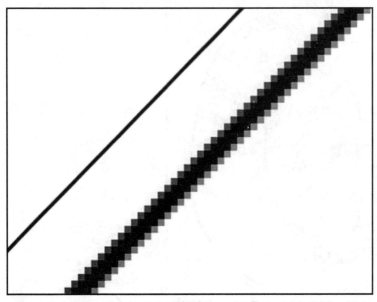

Figure 1-4 *Scaling an image up or down can create or remove so many pixels as to cause "jaggies" or staircasing.*

Differentiating Types of Artwork

In this book, you're going to deal almost exclusively with bitmapped images, although the GIMP can deal with a particular kind of line-oriented artwork called *paths*. Even within the raster realm, there are different kinds of images: line art, continuous tone grayscale and color images, and the faux continuous-tone images we call halftones.

Line Art

Don't confuse line art with line-oriented, vector art. Bitmapped line art is a raster image like any other bitmapped graphic. Line art is any piece of artwork that consists only of black and white areas. We usually think of line art only in terms of illustrations that don't use special techniques to simulate a continuous scale of gray tones. So, a pen-and-ink sketch of a landscape is line art. A cartoon drawn in pencil is also line art. Architectural plans, mechanical drawings, and electrical schematics are another sort of line art. The key idea is that a line of only one density is used to outline the art (the color of the line can be black or dark blue or any other color). (A sample line art illustration is shown in Figure 1-5.)

Because a single density is used to draw line art, computers can represent such images as single-bit, binary images. Of course, the appearance of the image isn't limited to

Figure 1-5 *Line art consists of one color (usually black) drawn on a background of one other color (usually white).*

black-and-white. Line art can include patterns or fills, such as the cross-hatching and other effects used to differentiate between adjacent areas. Pattern fills, for example, are often used on bar charts. Because the regular patterns alternate black and white lines, our eyes blur the two to provide a grayish image. Line art may contain only lines of the same density, but still appear to have gray.

With line art, the higher the resolution, the sharper the image will appear to be. That's because many more pixels are available to represent the edges of the lines without producing a staircased look. Of course, the higher the resolution, the larger the image will be. That's something that often surprises neophytes, who may scan an image at 150 dpi (dots per inch), print it out, then scan it again at 300 dpi. They expect the second image to be the same size, only sharper.

What really happens is that four times as many pixels are used to capture an image at the higher resolution (300 x 300 per square inch, or 90,000 pixels, compared to 150 x 150 per square inch, or 22,500 pixels). So, on a monitor with 72 dpi to display an image, a one-inch square at 150 dpi will require a square about two inches per side on your screen, while the same shape at 300 dpi will demand four-inch sides at the higher resolution. You can tell an application what size you want a printed image to be, regardless of original resolution, but your computer has to recalculate the image to fit it into a larger or smaller space.

Continuous Tone Images

Another kind of image is called continuous tone, because it appears to have a continuous scale of shades from pure white to black, with all the grays in between. A black-and-white photograph is a typical continuous tone image. Color images can also have continuous tones, with the added component of hue. For now, it's simpler just to consider the gray tones or grayscale of monochrome pictures as continuous tone images. (You'll look at what makes up a color image later in this book; this chapter is just basic training, remember.)

Even though continuous tone images may have smooth gradations through all the different shades of gray, it is convenient to think of such images in terms of individual steps or gray levels. Photographers do this all the time when they use one of the various Zone systems of exposure. When you use photographs and other continuous tone images for desktop publishing, you'll need to think of gray levels too. (Figure 1-6 shows an image that is truly continuous tone above one that has been divided into levels of gray, as must be done to manipulate an image with the GIMP.)

Figure 1-6 *Top: A continuous tone grayscale. Bottom: The same grayscale divided into discrete gray levels.*

Halftone Images

Halftoning is a technique that allows printing presses and laser printers to reproduce continuous tone images. Halftones convert the various gray values to black dots of different sizes. The eye merges these black dots with the surrounding white area to produce the perception of a gray tone.

While you'll want to learn more about converting images to halftones than is covered in this book, you'll also need to consider getting images from halftones when using them as original input for scanning. Why would you want to do this? At times, you may discover that an image that has already been halftoned must be recaptured for a publication or Web page. Generally, you'll obtain poor results in capturing such images. Scanning halftones as the continuous tone images they may appear to be works only until you try to apply your own halftone effect to the image. The extra set of dots usually results in an objectionable effect called *moiré*. Scanning an existing halftone as line art or a continuous tone grayscale image may be your only choice, and even that won't reproduce the original halftone well.

What Is Resolution?

Resolution is the number of elements per inch used to represent an image. But, things are far from that simple. When you realize that the resolution of a single image can involve the resolution of the scanner that grabs it, the resolution of the display device that shows the image on your monitor, and the resolution of the output device, such as a printer or imagesetter, you can see some of the cause of confusion.

Things get even better: resolution is measured *differently* for each kind of device you work with. Printer and imagesetter resolution is measured in *dots per inch*, the number of actual spots that the device is able to place on a piece of paper or film. Even if the device is able to vary the size of the dots, the number of them in a linear inch remains the same at a given resolution. These dots are usually round, elliptical, or oval in shape. However, halftoned images, which also consist of dots, are usually represented by the number of lines of dots—the fineness of the halftone screen—used to create them. So halftones are measured in *lines per inch* or, simply, lines; a 133-line screen yields 133 lines per inch.

Your computer display's resolution is measured in *pixels per inch*. The resolution of your screen increases as the screen size is enlarged, so you might have 72 pixels per inch resolution in a 15-inch monitor, up through 96 to 120 ppi in 17-inch and larger models. The tricky part here is that each pixel you work with is created by sets of three red, green, and blue dots or slits on the front surface of the CRT. (You'll look at RGB color in Chapter 6.) Finally, a scanner resolution is measured in *samples per inch*, although you'll see the inaccurate but widely used dots per inch applied to scanners as often as not. (Figure 1-7 shows an image at 100 and 300 dpi/ppi/spi resolution.)

Sorting Out File Formats

GIMP users should become familiar with the various graphics file formats so you'll know which are compatible with your software. The GIMP's flexibility comes from its ability to load an image in one file format and save in another, so you'll be able to convert from one type to another. This is often necessary when you are sharing files with others, particularly those with non-Linux/UNIX platforms.

The next few pages discuss several of the most common file formats. The issue is complicated by the fact that it is becoming more common to exchange graphic files between unlike computer systems, particularly between Linux/Macintosh and Windows-type systems. (Despite the disdain you may have for other platforms, you'll still need to learn to work and play well with them.)

Figure 1-7 *At left, an image at 100 dpi resolution. At right, the same image at 300 dpi resolution. They have been adjusted to provide the same size image in the illustration.*

The GIMP native file format is called XCF; it supports all of the GIMP's special features, including layers. You should always store working files in this format to preserve the effects you create using the program's advanced features; then, when you're ready to save a final copy, you can use one of the other supported file formats if necessary. (Table 1-1 shows all the currently supported file formats that the GIMP can handle; I'll explain a little more about the most important formats, too.)

Table 1-1 File Formats Supported by the GIMP

File Format	Write	Read	Type
BMP	Yes	Yes	Windows graphics format
BZIP	Yes	Yes	Bzip-compressed files
CEL	Yes	Yes	Format used by KISS Software International programs
FAXG3	No	Yes	Fax format
FITS	Yes	Yes	Flexible Image Transport System, or FITS, is the format adopted by the astronomical community for data interchange and archival storage
FLI/FLC	Yes	No	Animation formats, 320 x 320 pixels at 64 colors and 64K x 64K pixels at 256 colors
GBR	Yes	Yes	Format used by the GIMP to store brushes
GICON	Yes	Yes	Format used by the GIMP to store Toolbox icons
GIF	Yes	Yes	Graphics Interchange Format, limited to 256 colors and has a lossless compression scheme
GZIP	Yes	Yes	Gzip-compressed files
HEADER	Yes	No	Used for embedding images in C program files
HRZ	Yes	Yes	Older 256 x 240-pixel slow scan TV format
JPEG	Yes	Yes	Joint Photographic Experts Group, usable at up to 24-bit color, with a lossy compression scheme
MPEG	No	Yes	Motion Picture Experts Group, used for animations and movies
PAT	Yes	Yes	Format used by the GIMP to store patterns
PCX	Yes	Yes	A 24-bit format widely used by Windows painting programs
PIX	Yes	Yes	Format used by Alias/Wavefront on Silicon Graphics workstations
PNG	Yes	Yes	Portable Network Graphics, a newer format especially suitable for Web graphics, with good compression and a lossless compression scheme
PNM	Yes	Yes	Portable aNyMap, used by PBM programs

Table 1-1 File Formats Supported by the GIMP   (continued...)

File Format	Write	Read	Type
PSD	No	Yes	Native format used by Adobe Photoshop
PostScript	Yes	Yes	A page description language used by printers
SGI	Yes	Yes	Graphics format used by Silicon Graphics
SNP	No	Yes	Animation format used by MicroEyes
SunRas	Yes	Yes	Sun rasterfiles, used by Sun workstations
Targa	Yes	Yes	Graphics format developed by TrueVision
TIFF	Yes	Yes	Standard graphics program used by many different applications
XCF	Yes	Yes	Native file format of the GIMP
XWD	Yes	Yes	X Window Dump, format used by X Windows *screendump* utility
XPM	Yes	Yes	X PixMap, format used by X Windows icons
URL	Yes	Yes	Uniform Resource Locator, makes it possible to download Web images directly into the GIMP

TIFF

TIFF (*Tagged Image File Format*) files, which generally have the file extension .TIF, are in the most common of the standard non-proprietary file formats. If a software program is able to load a format other than its own specialized file type, that other format is probably TIFF. Keep in mind that there are various types of TIFF files, including compressed TIFF, uncompressed TIFF and TIFF PackBits. Not all software supports all the TIFF types, but the versions used by the GIMP can generally be read by anyone.

The TIFF format specifications were first developed in 1986. It is so called because each file includes collections of information, called tags, which describe the file type. A tag can provide information on resolution, number of bits used per pixel, and many other descriptors. The basic data needed to handle a file is included in a standardized set of tags that can be interpreted by any application.

However, an application can create its own tags, with information that the application wants to store with the file. A simple example would be a longer descriptive name or caption that is displayed when the file is loaded. These special tags are ignored by applications that don't understand how to read them, which means that you can exchange TIFF files between older versions of an application and newer, enhanced versions of the same software. Totally different programs can also read many TIFF files created by other applications. (Problems arise when new types of tags include important information that must be understood by the application to reconstruct the image; for that reason, you'll sometimes find TIFF files that can't be read by other software easily.)

Four standardized TIFF formats are used by many applications. They are classified as B (black-and-white or binary information only), G (gray scale), P (palette, or a number of different colors), and R (RGB, or red, green, blue). These classes can be compressed or uncompressed.

The trickiest part about TIFF these days is remembering to store the files using the correct byte order. Windows machines put the least significant bit of a byte first, while Macs put the most significant bit first. If you're a programmer, you understand well the concepts of little-endian and big-endian bytes; many programs, including the GIMP, can read both.

PCX

PCX is even older than TIFF. It was developed by a now-defunct company called ZSoft for their line of graphics products, which included PC Paintbrush IV, Publisher's Paintbrush, and Publisher's Type Foundry. PCX was originally a 1-bit binary file format. Grayscale and color capabilities were added later. Because loading files created with one application in TIFF formats can be problematic, particularly with older software, PCX is sometimes used as a fail-safe exchange format.

PSD

Photoshop's proprietary PSD file format has become something of a standard; Adobe's flagship offering has become the de facto standard image editing program for the Windows and Macintosh platforms. Today, many non-Adobe applications can read or write files in PSD format. This format supports all of Photoshop's special functions, including layers, channels, masks, and file information annotations. It includes lossless compression, that is, no image information is discarded as an image is squeezed. The GIMP is able to read files created by Photoshop in PSD format (and can properly import Photoshop layers), but can't write them out for transport in the other direction; you'll have to use one of the other file formats that the two programs have in common.

GIF

GIF (*Graphics Interchange Format*) is a truly venerable graphics format, a popular way of letting users view images made available online. Limited to 256 colors, GIF doesn't provide the best color rendition, but it provides a decent amount of lossless image compression. That allows relatively speedy downloads, without sacrificing image quality significantly.

There are two kinds of GIF files: GIF87a, which allows only opaque pixels, and GIF89a, which allows one color in an image to be transparent, making it possible to overlay the image on a background. GIFs can also be interlaced, so that graphics appear in coarse format while being downloaded from a Web page, and gain sharpness as the download proceeds. Because of some copyright issues (GIF uses an algorithm copyrighted by Unisys), GIF is used today primarily in certain Web graphics settings. Figure 1-8 shows an example a GIF image.

JPEG

The JPEG (*Joint Photographic Experts Group*) format was developed to allow creating full-color, 24-bit images that are significantly compressed for more efficient storage and faster downloading on the 'Net. JPEG is a lossy compression scheme, that is, some image information is discarded. When you save a JPEG file with the GIMP, a dialog box (the GIMP 1.0.4 version is shown in Figure 1-9) pops up with controls for specifying quality and smoothing in a range from 0 to 100 percent.

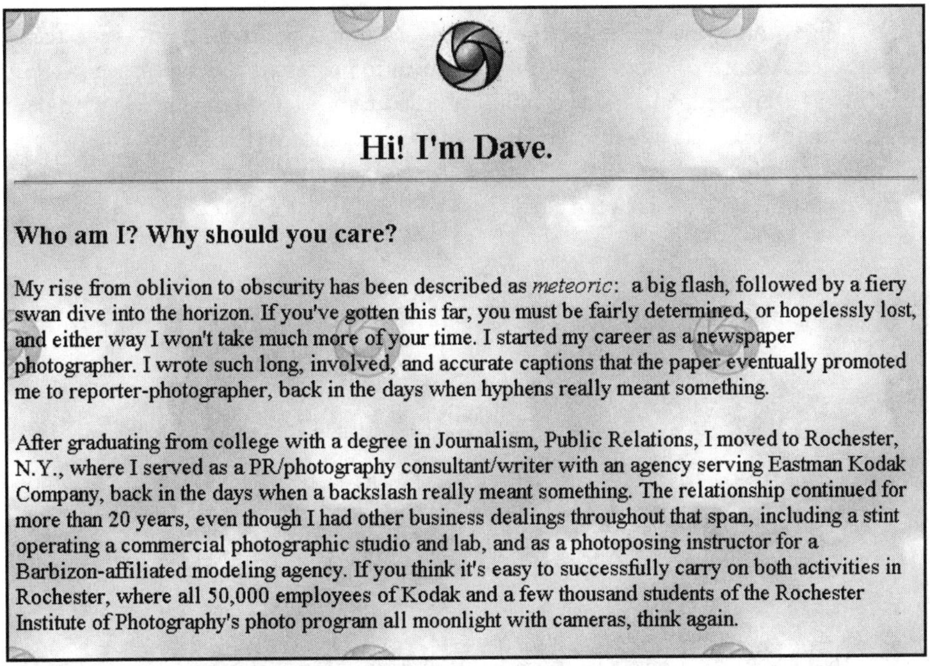

Hi! I'm Dave.

Who am I? Why should you care?

My rise from oblivion to obscurity has been described as *meteoric*: a big flash, followed by a fiery swan dive into the horizon. If you've gotten this far, you must be fairly determined, or hopelessly lost, and either way I won't take much more of your time. I started my career as a newspaper photographer. I wrote such long, involved, and accurate captions that the paper eventually promoted me to reporter-photographer, back in the days when hyphens really meant something.

After graduating from college with a degree in Journalism, Public Relations, I moved to Rochester, N.Y., where I served as a PR/photography consultant/writer with an agency serving Eastman Kodak Company, back in the days when a backslash really meant something. The relationship continued for more than 20 years, even though I had other business dealings throughout that span, including a stint operating a commercial photographic studio and lab, and as a photoposing instructor for a Barbizon-affiliated modeling agency. If you think it's easy to successfully carry on both activities in Rochester, where all 50,000 employees of Kodak and a few thousand students of the Rochester Institute of Photography's photo program all moonlight with cameras, think again.

Figure 1-8 *A GIF on a Web page can use transparency to allow the background to show through.*

Figure 1·9 *The GIMP's Save as JPEG dialog box includes quality and smoothing settings.*

The quality and smoothing settings determine how much image information is discarded. Keep in mind that once the information is gone, it's gone forever. If you're using JPEG, you might want to store at the maximum quality setting until you're sure a lower setting will do the job.

JPEG's algorithms divide your image into blocks of 8 x 8 pixels, then uses a technique called Adaptive Discrete Cosine Transform to process the image. Each pixel in the block is examined, and average values are used to replace the real pixels with new ones. As many pixels as possible are set to a value of 0, meaning that they will be represented by the average value for that block. If you look at a highly compressed JPEG image closely, it will appear very blocky, as shown in Figure 1-10.

Figure 1·10 *Highly compressed JPEG images take on a blocky look when examined closely.*

On the upside, JPEG files can be 8 to 100 times smaller than the equivalent TIFF file. Because of their true color and small file size, JPEG files are a favorite for Web graphics. (Keep in mind when using JPEG that these files are reprocessed and recompressed each time you save them; repeatedly saving a JPEG file through multiple sessions can seriously degrade an image.)

PNG

The PNG (*Portable Network Graphics*) file format was developed as an alternative for Web graphics that eliminates some of the pesky aspects of JPEG and GIF. Unlike JPEG, PNG produces decent compression without losing data; unlike GIF, it can reproduce 24-bit and 48-bit color without upsetting copyright holders (PNG can be used without restriction by anyone). PNG also has built-in features for transparency (allowing up to 256 different shades to be transparent, instead of just one) and progressive (interlaced) display. The other feature of PNG you should keep in mind is that an underwhelming number of browsers support it, so it's been difficult to justify using this format for its intended purpose. The GIMP supports only compression and interlacing at this time.

XCF

As the GIMP's native file format, XCF should be your best choice as the default format for active files. It can save GIMP layers, selections, and other information you probably don't want to lose between sessions.

What's Next

Like it or not, you've now absorbed the basics about the GIMP (where it came from, what it does, and where it's going), the bitmapped graphics that the GIMP can push, jostle, shove, and transform, as well as the file formats you end up with. Basic training is over. Now it's time to enroll in Officer Candidate School.

A good guerrilla needs a Swiss Army knife, and you'll find the cutting-edge tools you're looking for in the GIMP's versatile Toolbar. It includes all the basic implements you need to perform every imaginable manipulation on an image. But most of them remain tucked away out of sight until you need them. The Toolbar isn't bogged down with impressive-looking features that are never used by the vast majority of workers. That approach has a double benefit for you. By working with a smaller set of tools, you'll become more proficient with each of them very quickly. In addition, you won't find yourself racking your brains trying to remember how to use an esoteric gizmo you haven't deployed in six months. The GIMP is a lean, mean editing machine.

This chapter will serve as your introduction to the main tools at your disposal. You'll find that these few pages will be all you need to get started creating and editing your own images.

The GIMP Interface

If you're new to the GIMP, your first clue that this image editor isn't another one of those anti-intuitive, feature-bloated applications will come when you launch the program for the first time. Surprise! The GIMP doesn't monopolize your screen space with a huge window of its own, laden with dozens of toolbars, palettes, and menus.

Instead, the only artifact that appears on your screen (after the opening Startup/ Progress indicator splash screen and GIMP mascot Wilber's tip of the day) is a non-threatening Toolbar that has 26 buttons and two menus. Everything else, including your picture-editing window, is hidden until you need it. Figure 2-1 shows the minimalist GIMP working screen as you'll encounter it the first time you open a file.

You don't always need the Toolbar, as all its features are available by right-clicking on the image window and choosing a tool from the pop-up context menu, like the one shown in Figure 2-2, that appears. You may find it faster to click on a tool in the Toolbar, or choose the tool from the context menu. The choice is up to you. More features and dialog boxes appear as you use the tools. You'll look at each tool later in this chapter.

Accessing the Main Menus

The GIMP has two main menus, each with an eclectic collection of features that don't necessarily reflect the name of the menu itself. For example, the *File* menu, which does include commands to manipulate files, is also your gateway to dialog boxes that set your preferences or that lead to additional GIMP features, such as brushes or patterns. Because there are only a few File menu items, it makes a twisted

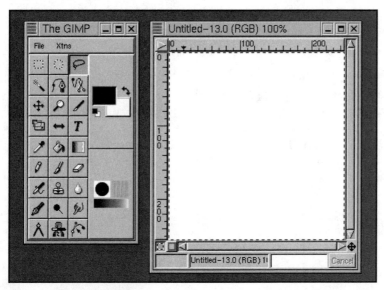

Figure 2-1 *The basic GIMP working area includes a single Toolbar and the image-editing window.*

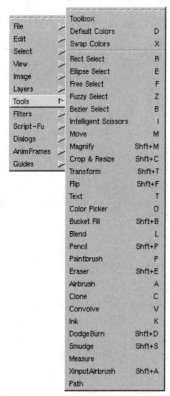

Figure 2-2 *Pop-up context menus appear when you right-click in the image.*

sort of sense to include the unrelated additional commands there even though first-time users may be confused. The *Xtns* (extensions) menu has commands for reviewing GIMP plug-ins and other features.

Notice that in the newest versions of the GIMP, you can tear off a menu by clicking on the dotted line that separates the menu from the menu bar. You can use this feature to make frequently used menus available all the time. Position the torn-off menus wherever you like on your workspace. To learn quickly about these basic menus, take the time now to follow through the simple exercise which follows, creating your first image document with the GIMP (although the particular graphic you're creating has about as much substance as a vice-presidential candidate).

Creating a New File

Let's create a new, empty file first to see how it's done in the GIMP.

1. In the GIMP Toolbar, choose New from the file menu. The New Image dialog box appears.

2. In the image size area at the top of the dialog box, you can type the size of the image you'd like to create. (This dialog box is shown in Figure 2-3.)

   - **Enter a width and height in pixels.** The default value is 256 x 256 pixels, but you can change this in the Preferences dialog box, as you'll discover later. You may enter width and height separately.

   - **Choose RGB (full-color) or grayscale image.** You can always change an RGB image to grayscale later on, so click the RGB button in the Image Type area of the dialog box. The only advantage to working with a grayscale image from the start is that grayscale files are smaller. However, some GIMP features are available only with a full-color image.

   - **Specify a background in the blank image.** This determines the color of the "canvas" you'll be working with. You can choose from the GIMP's foreground or background colors (which are black and white, respectively, by default, but can be any pair of colors you may have set earlier in your session), white, or transparent. (Transparent is displayed on your screen as a gray-and-white checkerboard pattern.) Click the White button.

   These three options were the only ones available with GIMP 1.0.4. Newer versions have these additional choices:

   - **Enter a width and height in inches or some other unit of measurement.** Instead of specifying the pixel measurement, you can enter the width and height using inches, millimeters, points, or some other unit. As you might expect, the pixel equivalents of your entries are reflected in the box above.

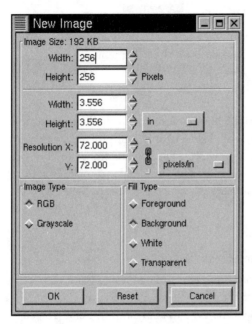

Figure 2-3 *The New Image dialog box lets you define basic parameters for your blank image.*

- **Choose a resolution for the image.** The default resolution for a new image is 72 pixels per inch, which corresponds to the screen resolution of smaller monitors. You can change this to another value, such as 96 ppi (another common monitor resolution), to ensure that the screen display will be closer to the size when printed. That is, at 96 ppi, an inch-wide object will occupy 96 pixels on a 96 ppi monitor. As with the other parameters, you can change the unit of measurement to something other than inches.

The size of the image file using the current parameters is always shown and updated at the top of the dialog box as you alter the dimensions of the image. For this exercise, choose 600 x 600 pixels for the image size, and leave the other sizing specifications as they are.

3. Click OK to create the new image. The GIMP will automatically give it a numbered Untitled file name, which you can change when you save the image.

After at least one file has been opened, you can open or create additional images by right-clicking on the image and choosing from the File menu that appears in the pop-up context menu. (You'll learn about this right-click menu in depth shortly.)

4. Move the new image you just created to the side of the screen, by dragging on its title bar; you'll come back to it in a few minutes, but you can take some time out now to learn about other commands on the File menu.

Saving Files

You may have used other programs that place Save commands in the File menu (for example, the GNOME *gnotepad* application). There is only one problem with this method: if you have several images open at once, you have to remember to click on the file, or in the case of an application like gnotepad, on its tab, to make it active. Then you have to venture over to the menu bar and choose the Save or Save As commands.

With the GIMP, this action is much easier.

1. Right-click on the window of the image you want to save.

2. Choose Save or Save As from the pop-up menu. If you choose Save, the GIMP will use the current name for the file, which will be the numbered Untitled file name unless you've taken the time to apply a new name. You can specify a name for an image by choosing Save As.

3. Type in a file name in the Save Image dialog box, shown in Figure 2-4, when it pops up.

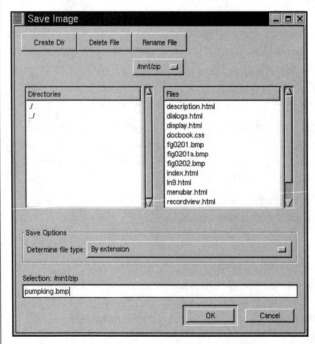

Figure 2-4 *Apply a new name to a file using the Save As command and this dialog box.*

The dialog box has several functions and a few options. At the top of the dialog box are three buttons: Create Dir, Delete File, and Rename File. You can use these to create a new directory to save a file in, remove a file from the Files window at the right of the dialog box, or rename a file highlighted in the Files window.

The box below the buttons can be used to navigate from the current directory upwards to the root, or you can navigate using the Directories window at the left of the Save As dialog box. The Save Options area makes it easy to choose the file format the file will be saved in. If you select Determine file type: By extension, the GIMP will look at the extension you type for the file, and if it is a known extension (for example, .jpg or .tif), it will save the file in that format. You can also choose a file format by clicking the Save Options button and selecting a format from the list that pops up. For a list of file types that the GIMP can read and write, see the Table 1-1 in Chapter 1. Finally, the Selection box at the bottom of the dialog shows the currently selected directory, and provides space for you to type in a file name.

4. Save the new file you created.

5. Make sure By extension is selected in the Save Options area, then type **firstfile.tif** in the Selection box. The Save as Tif dialog box, shown in Figure 2-5, pops up.

   You can choose a compression scheme, and byte (fill) order. You can also add a comment to the file. Note that each type of file format you save may have different options appropriate to that format. For example, if you save as a GIF file, the GIMP will let you choose whether or not to interlace the GIF (display alternating lines first) or—if the image has layers—to create an animated GIF. The JPEG and PNG dialog boxes let you choose a compression level. (You'll learn more about these options later in the book.)

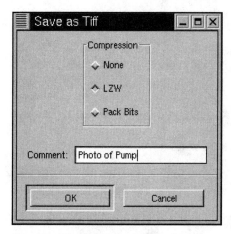

Figure 2-5 *The GIMP uses dialog boxes appropriate for each file type when saving a file for the first time under a particular file name.*

Opening Existing Files

You can work with existing files, including those created by you as well as files that originate from another application, as long as the file format is supported by the GIMP. To open an existing file:

1. Choose Open from the File menu to access the Load Image dialog box. There you'll find Directories and Files lists that you can use to navigate to the file you want to load.

2. Locate the firstfile.tif file you saved in the previous exercise, and highlight the file by clicking on its file name. (See Figure 2-6.)

In most cases, you'll want the GIMP to determine what kind of file it is, by leaving the Open Options Determine file type setting at Automatic. If you need to try and open a file that the GIMP cannot identify, you can select a file format from the button's drop-down list. The chosen file appears in the Selection box. If a preview of the image has been saved with it, the thumbnail will appear in the window at the right side of the dialog box. Click OK to open the file.

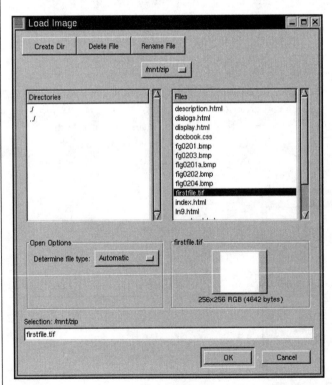

Figure 2-6 *You can locate the file you want to open in the Load Image dialog box.*

Other File Menu Commands

The File menu has the following additional commands, each of which you'll look at in more detail later in the book.

- **About**. A dialog box that provides the version number and other information about this release of the GIMP.
- **Preferences**. A dialog box you can use to control the GIMP's defaults. You'll find out how to change the GIMP's preferences at the end of this chapter.
- **Tip of the day**. Useful advice from Wilber, the GIMP mascot.
- **Dialogs**. Offers access to additional GIMP dialog boxes, such as Brushes, Patterns, Palette, or Gradients.
- **Quit**. Used to close all open image windows and exit the GIMP.

Using the Xtns Menu

The Xtns menu is the home for plug-ins and Script-Fu scripts. While you probably have the common complement of extensions in your version of the GIMP, you should be aware that these add-ons are created by different programmers and folded into the GIMP mix as they are debugged and become "standard" features. (You'll look at these add-ons in Chapter 12.) Figure 2-7 shows some typical extensions that reside in your Xtns menu.

Figure 2-7 *The Xtns menu is the home for add-ons which increase the flexibility and power of the GIMP.*

Introducing the GIMP Toolbar

The GIMP Toolbar is a floating palette of buttons arranged in eight rows of three buttons, with the Foreground/Background Color Selector at the bottom. You can resize the Toolbar, increasing or decreasing the size of the buttons, but you cannot change their order or position. Although I showed you the Toolbar in Figure 2-1, you'll want to take another look at the annotated version shown in Figure 2-8.

Painting Tools

I like to call the group of 12 tools in the second four rows above the Color Selector (plus the Natural Airbrush in the center of the bottom row) the Painting Tools, although they don't all "paint." Some are used to sample colors from your image, erase pixels, or make them darker or lighter. All are deployed, however, to one extent or another, as you create, paint, or modify pixels. You'll use each of these tools in later chapters, but for now I'm sure you'd like a quick introduction to what each one can do.

Keep in mind that each tool has options, which you can access by double-clicking on that tool's button. For now, I'll mention a few (but not necessarily all) key options in these descriptions; you'll look at the options in depth in the next chapter. When you've changed options, you can restore them to the original values by clicking the Reset button in each tool's options dialog box.

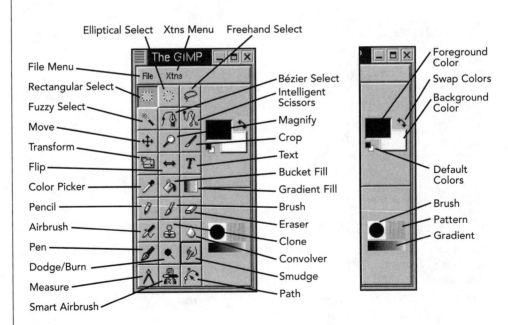

Figure 2-8   *The GIMP Toolbar*

- **Color Selector**. The two overlapping boxes at the bottom of the Toolbar are used to select the color of the foreground (the top-left box) and the background (the bottom-right box). Double-click in either box, and use the Color Selection dialog box to choose a color. Click the double-headed arrow to the upper right of the pair to swap colors. Click the small black and white squares at the lower left to return to the default black foreground/white background colors. (The Color Selection dialog box is shown in Figure 2-9.)

  Note that this dialog box has four tabs, one for each of four different Color Selection modes. (For now, I'll talk about the GIMP selector; you'll learn more about the other three later in this book.)

- **Color Picker.** Choose either the Foreground or Background boxes in the Color Selector, then use the Color Picker tool to click in a portion of an image to change the foreground or background to that color. This is a good way to transfer colors from one open image to another. **Key Options**: Specify whether the Color Picker should sample colors from only the current active layer or all the layers in an image, as if merged, and the size of the area being sampled. You can also vary the radius of the pixels sampled using a slider.

- **Bucket Fill.** Bucket Fill fills an image or selected area with a color or pattern. **Key Options:** Set Threshold (how close a color must be to the selected color to be filled), and whether to fill with foreground color, background color, or a pattern.

- **Blend (Gradient) Fill.** Blend Fill fills an image or selected area with a gradient. **Key Options**: Type of blend (e.g., foreground to transparent, foreground to background) and kind of gradient (linear, radial, and so on) used.

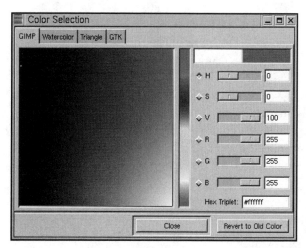

Figure 2-9 *The GIMP's Color Selector allows you to select any color.*

- **Pencil.** Pencil draws a single pixel line. **Key Options:** Whether to use incremental pencil strokes, and pressure sensitive tablet settings.

- **Paintbrush.** Paintbrush lays down color using a brush shape and size you choose. **Key Options:** Amount of fade-out for the brush, and the gradient used, and pressure sensitivity.

- **Eraser.** Eraser removes pixels. **Key Options:** Hardness of edge of eraser, eraser mode, and pressure sensitivity.

- **Airbrush.** Airbrush sprays paint on an image. **Key Options:** Spray rate, pressure (strength of spray).

- **Clone.** Clone paints over an image from a source you specify, either another portion of an image or a pattern. **Key Options:** Source of cloned area, whether cloning source moves around source to match your painting movements.

- **Convolver (Blur/Sharpen).** Convolver blurs or sharpens areas of an image by increasing or decreasing the contrast between adjacent pixels. **Key Options:** Blur or sharpen mode, pressure/strength of the blurring/sharpening effect.

- **Ink.** Ink lets you draw as if with a pen. **Key Options:** Size of point, shape of point.

- **Dodge/Burn.** This tool darkens or lightens portions of an image. **Key Options:** Strength of effect, whether it operates on highlights, mid-tones, or shadows.

- **Smudge.** Smudge smears pixels around. **Key Options:** Strength of effect.

- **Natural Airbrush.** New to the GIMP, this tool provides a more realistic airbrush effect. **Key Options:** Size of airbrush, tilt and angle adjustments.

Selection Tools

Selection tools mark the boundaries of the area of an image that you will be working with. When a portion of an image is selected, any of the tools and effects you apply will affect only the selected area. The rest of the image is "protected" from modification. So, if you wish to fill only a particular area with color, you'll want to select it first. Selections may be regular or odd shapes, or include only pixels of a particular brightness or color, so the GIMP gives you six different tools to use to make your selections. Because selecting is such a powerful capability, I devote all of Chapter 4 to its finer points. Here's a quick introduction to the GIMP's selection tools.

- **Rectangular Select.** Chooses a rectangular or square area of an image.

- **Elliptical Select.** Chooses an elliptical or circular area of an image.

- **Freehand Select.** Commonly called the Lasso, this tool selects an irregular area that you draw freehand (Figure 2-10 shows this tool at work).

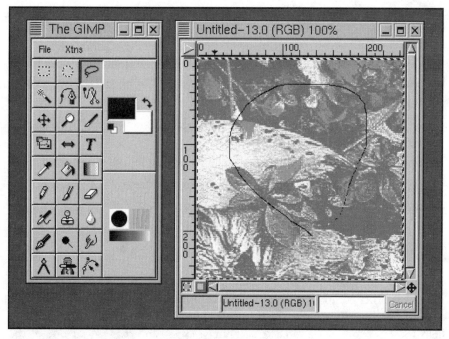

Figure 2-10 *The Freehand Select tool marks irregular areas.*

- **Fuzzy Select.** Better known as the Magic Wand, this tool selects adjacent pixels based on their brightness, choosing pixels that fall within a specified brightness "tolerance" range.
- **Bézier Select.** Creates selections using Bézier curves.
- **Intelligent Scissors.** Does its best to find the edges of objects you mark with it, "clinging" to those edges as you draw.

Transformation Tools

Transformation tools change the position, size, shape, or orientation of an image or selection.

- **Move.** Changes the position of an image or selection.
- **Crop and Resize.** Cuts out portions of an image you don't want, or scales the image larger or smaller.
- **Transform.** Rotates, scales, changes perspective, and performs other transformations on an image or selection.
- **Flip.** Reverses the image horizontally or vertically.

Other Tools

The remaining tools don't quite fit into any of the other categories, although the Text tool could be considered a kind of "painting" tool or even a selection tool, and Magnify is a transformation tool in that it changes the image visually even though it doesn't alter any pixels.

- **Text**. Used to enter type into an image (Figure 2-11 shows some of the kinds of text you can create with this tool).
- **Magnify (Zoom)**. Enlarges or reduces the view of an image.
- **Measure**. A new tool for GIMP, allows you to measure areas of your image.
- **Path**. Another new tool for manipulating Bézier paths.

Other Interface Features

You can see by now that the GIMP's interface is quite easy to master. In fact, there are only a few other components that you need to learn about before you can begin working efficiently with images. You'll want to know about *rulers* and *guides*, which can help you create and select objects accurately. *Layers* and *channels* are one of the most important keys to the GIMP's power. And you'll certainly want to learn how to save time with the GIMP's keyboard *shortcuts*.

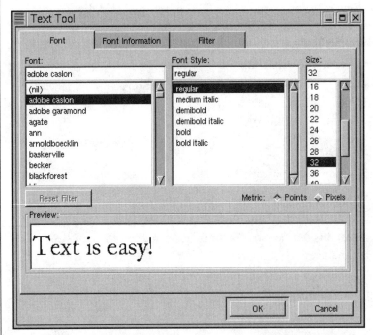

Figure 2-11 *The Text tool creates basic text that you can modify extensively using the GIMP's image-editing features.*

Measuring and Positioning with Rulers and Guides

The GIMP's rulers are placed at the top and left sides of the image window; by default, they measure in pixels. You can change this value to inches or millimeters using the GIMP preferences file (see "Setting Preferences" later in this chapter), although the GIMP doesn't use those measurements when working with a file until the file is printed. A pair of triangular markers appear in the rulers to mark the current cursor position, making it easy to begin drawing or to make a selection at a particular point in an image. You can turn the rulers on or off by right-clicking in an image and choosing View | Toggle Rulers.

Guides are horizontal and vertical reference lines you can place on an image to use for positioning or aligning objects. Guides don't print along with the image, nor are they visible on a final image. Try this quick exercise to see exactly how guides work.

1. In a new, blank image (you can use the one you created earlier in this chapter), position the cursor anywhere in the vertical ruler. (If rulers aren't visible, right-click in the image area, and choose View | Toggle Rulers from the pop-up menu.)

2. Hold down the mouse button and drag toward the right. A vertical line appears. Place it somewhere in the left half of the image.

3. Move the cursor to the horizontal ruler, hold down the mouse button, and drag a horizontal line down onto the image. Drop it somewhere in the upper half of the graphic. Your image should look like Figure 2-12 at this point.

4. Click the Move tool in the Toolbar, and reposition one of the guides. Once you have initially placed a guide, it can only be relocated with the Move tool.

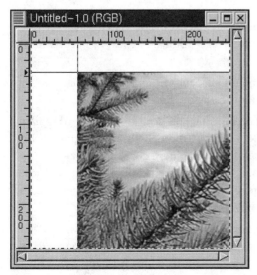

Figure 2-12 *Drag guides from the rulers down into your image.*

5. Right-click on the image area, choose View, and make sure the Snap to Guides button is selected. This is the default, so it should be active (unless you've turned the feature off).

6. Choose the Rectangular Selection tool from the Toolbar, and position the cursor 20 to 30 pixels away from both guides. Hold down the mouse button, and drag a rectangular selection. Notice that the selection appears exactly at the position where you started to drag.

7. Now, using the same selection tool, place the cursor a short distance from the vertical guide. Hold down the mouse button, and notice how the selection snaps to the guide. As you drag, you create a selection positioned exactly on the guide.

8. Use the selection tool to place the cursor near the intersection of the two guides. The selection will snap to both, aligning itself with the corner produced where the guides meet.

9. With the Move tool, drag a guide off the image. To remove any guide, just drag it to any edge of the image window.

Viewing Your Image

The GIMP provides some useful options for viewing your image, letting you choose to examine the image window at several sizes, from 6 percent of original size to 1600 percent, or even to view the graphic in more than one size simultaneously. Here are the basics.

Zooming

- To zoom in on an image, press the plus/equals key. The GIMP enlarges your view while keeping the same window size. Scroll bars appear as needed to let you view the whole image.

- To zoom out on an image, press the underscore/minus key. The image is reduced in size, but the image window remains the same.

- To make the image window grow or shrink to fit, double-click the Magnify tool's icon in the Toolbar, and make sure the Allow Window Resizing button is marked in the options dialog box shown in Figure 2-13. The image window will shrink as you zoom out, and grow as you zoom in, but will never grow larger than your available screen space. When this feature is activated, it applies to all the images you may open.

- To resize just one window automatically, click in the image window, and choose View | Shrink Wrap. The window shrinks to fit around the image at its current size, and stays that size if you zoom in or out further.

Figure 2-13 *The GIMP allows viewing of a single image in several windows at different magnifications.*

- You can also use the Magnify tool to zoom in and out. Click in the image to zoom in, hold down the Shift key and click to zoom out. To zoom in on a specific area of the image, click with the Magnify tool, and drag to choose the area you want to enlarge.

Changing Views

To view a second copy of a single image, right-click in the image and choose View | New View. A second image window appears. You can zoom in tightly on one copy, and zoom out on the other to provide an overall look at the image. Any changes you make in one view are instantly reflected in the other. (Figure 2-14 shows a single image in two different views.)

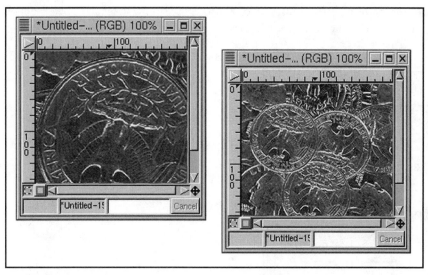

Figure 2-14 *The GIMP allows viewing of a single image in several windows at different magnifications.*

To work on a second copy of an image, select the image and press Ctrl-D; a new, independent copy of the image appears, and either image can be edited and saved separately. To move quickly between open windows, including the toolbar and any image windows you may have, press Ctrl-Tab.

Brief Introduction to Layers and Channels

The ability to work with layers is one of the most significant new features of the GIMP. You'll soon find that many of the effects discussed in upcoming chapters can be enhanced or performed in new ways, simply by dividing your actions among separate, flexible layers.

To understand layers, it helps to think about how a basic document image is arranged. When you open a blank document with the New command, you probably think of it as empty: just a plain white canvas ready for your manipulations. In truth, the document is already filled with something: an opaque layer colored with the foreground, background, or white colors you can select when the image is first created. You also could have checked off the Transparent option. It's hard to show "transparent," or at least to differentiate it from white, so the GIMP represents it with a translucent checkerboard pattern, as shown in Figure 2-15.

The main layer is the foundation of your image; as you add more layers, they are placed on top of this background, and on top of each other. Layers, then, are like transparent sheets of acetate that you lay on top of the background. When you draw something or paste an image on one of those transparent sheets, it covers up or obscures part of what lies underneath, either completely or partially, depending on

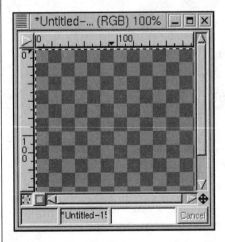

Figure 2-15 *The GIMP represents transparency with a translucent checkerboard pattern.*

whether the new image is fully opaque or transparent. When you create yet another new layer, it goes on top of the background and first transparent layer, perhaps obscuring part of what exists "below."

The *order* of individual layers is the next concept you need to understand. As you work with layers, you may need to change the order in which layers are arranged so that some objects are "in front of" or "behind" others. The GIMP lets you work with layers individually, save documents with the layers preserved, and even print out individual layers if you desire. The GIMP makes it easy to control the opacity of individual layers, and how the layers are blended together when you're finished working with them. When you are done working with a document, you "flatten" the layers together, merging them into a final, background-only image that is your finished work; of course, there is nothing to keep you from saving the "final" version under a new name, keeping the layered document for additional manipulations later on.

A *channel* is a kind of layer used to represent the separate red, green, and blue components of an image. If the image is a full-color one, it is possible to divide that layer into separate red, green, and blue channels. You can also create and add more channels. When you are done working with an image's channels, they can be combined as a finished RGB document.

The chief limitation of a channel is that it is essentially a *grayscale* image. You can paint on a channel, or modify the brightness and contrast or other grayscale characteristics of a channel, but cannot add or remove any color to the channel itself. It's conceivable you might have a picture of a taxicab in one channel and a tree in another, then combine them into a single image—but either object could be represented only in tones of gray. This type of layering would work if your final image were grayscale, but would be of little use for combining full-color images.

Layers, in contrast, each can be a complete *full-color image* of its own, as shown in Figure 2-16. You could paste a picture of Big Ben in one layer and windmill in a second layer, clouds in a third layer, and then combine them in flexible ways. Each layer is in many ways like a separate document, with color channels of its own. If you can think of layers as a kind of full-color "channel" with many of the properties of the channels you already have used, you'll be halfway to understanding this feature.

To see how layers and channels work, try this exercise:

1. Double-click on the black box that overlaps a white one at the bottom of the Toolbar, shown in Figure 2-17. This is the Foreground Selector.

2. Choose a red color from the Color Picker that pops up (click the GIMP tab if it isn't visible). Just click in the red portion of the vertical spectrum bar. The exact color doesn't matter. (The Color Picker is shown in Figure 2-18.)

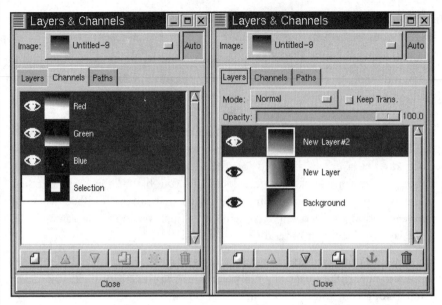

Figure 2-16 *Channels are grayscale images; layers are full-color images stacked on top of one another.*

Figure 2-17 *Click the GIMP Foreground Selector to choose a color.*

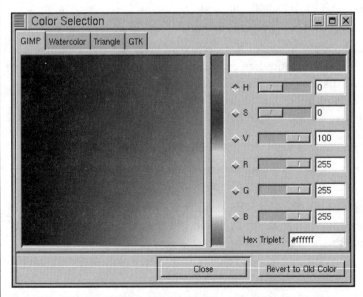

Figure 2-18 *The GIMP's Color Picker is used to select hues for the foreground and background.*

3. Click the Paintbrush icon in the Toolbar, and draw a squiggly line in the image window. (The shape of the line doesn't matter.)

4. Repeat Steps 1-3, choosing a blue color from the Color Picker, and then once more, choosing a green color.

5. Right-click in the image area, and choose Layers | Layers and Channels from the pop-up menu, shown in Figure 2-19.

6. Click the Channels tab to view the separate layers for the red, green, and blue lines you drew. Depending on how close the colors you chose were to pure red, green, or blue, some or all of each line will be invisible on the other channels, as you can see in Figure 2-20.

7. Click the Layers tab, shown in Figure 2-21, to view the single layer you have created so far.

8. Right-click in the layer, and select New Layer from the menu that pops up. Click OK to create the layer, and then confirm that two layers now appear in the Layers tab.

9. Right-click in the first layer you drew, and choose Duplicate Layer from the pop-up menu. A copy of the original layer will appear.

That's all you need to know to view and create layers and channels. You'll explore what you can do with this capability in Chapter 5. (Figure 2-22 shows what your Layers dialog box will look like now.)

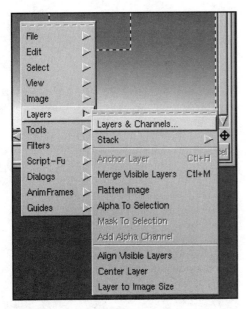

Figure 2-19 *Right-click in the image area and choose the Layers | Layers and Channels menu choice.*

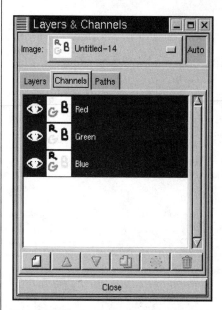

Figure 2-20   *Each of the red, green, and blue color channels are separate.*

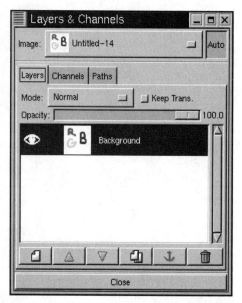

Figure 2-21   *The Layers tab shows the layer created so far.*

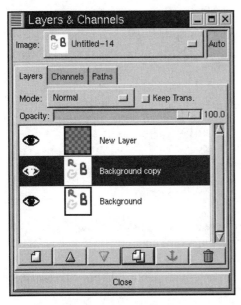

Figure 2-22 *The Layers dialog box with several layers included*

Saving Time with Shortcuts

Shortcut keys, *hotkeys*, or *dynamic key bindings* (depending on how techie you're feeling) can potentially save you time by activating commands—often nested a few levels down in the menu structure—at the press of a few keys. There are two ways of thinking about shortcut keys versus menus. Menus are easy to learn: if you know what kind of function you want, you can usually wend your way down the menus to find the command. For example, if you want to move one layer above another and don't quite remember the command to do that, you can right-click on an image, choose the Layers menu item, find the Stack item in the submenu, then view the list of commands for rearranging layers. However, menus are time-consuming to use, because you must drill down through all those menus each and every time you want to use a command.

Shortcut keys are the exact reverse. They're difficult to learn, because you must memorize all the key combinations you want to use. That's not too hard if you need only a couple shortcuts, such as Ctrl-N to open a new file, or Ctrl-S to save a file. If you want to learn a dozen or more shortcuts it can take some serious study, especially for non-mnemonic combinations (such as Ctrl-V for Paste) or complex sets of keystrokes. Shift-PageUp and Ctrl-PageUp move a layer up one level or to the top of a stack—but which is which? Still, shortcut keys are incredibly speedy once you've learned them.

As you can see, the choice to use menu commands or shortcut keys is a decision you must make on your own. The GIMP complicates things a little, in that you can assign shortcuts yourself—which really can make learning the combinations tricky. To create your own shortcut key definition, use the mouse to access the menu item you'd like to define, then press the key combination to be used. The key assignment is made immediately, and you'll actually see the shortcut definition show up next to the menu item.

Some Photoshop users redefine the keyboard shortcuts of the GIMP to correspond to their counterparts in Photoshop. I don't recommend doing that. You'll only lengthen the time needed for your "conversion" to the GIMP, and others who happen to use your computer with your customized definitions are likely to be confused, or worse.

You must be careful to press keys when a menu command is selected only when you mean to assign a shortcut key; accidentally pressing a key while a menu item is selected may have unintended results. (I once assigned the New File choice to the letter Z, so every time I typed Z within the GIMP I got a new file!) Table 2-1 shows the default shortcut definitions in the GIMP.

Table 2-1 Default GIMP Shortcut Keys

Key	Result
Tools	
R	Rectangular Selection Tool
E	Elliptical Selection Tool
B	Bézier Tool
Z	Fuzzy Select Tool
F	Freehand Select Tool
I	Intelligent Scissors Tool
M	Move Tool
Shift-M	Magnify Tool
Shift-C	Crop Tool
T	Text Tool
O	Color Picker Tool
Shift-T	Transform Tool
Shift-B	Bucket Fill Tool
L	Blend Tool
Shift-P	Pencil Tool
A	Airbrush Tool
Shift-E	Eraser Tool
C	Clone Tool
V	Convolver Tool
X	Swap Foreground/Background Colors

Table 2-1 Default GIMP Shortcut Keys   (continued...)

Menu Commands

File Menu

Ctrl-N	New File
Ctrl-O	Open File
Ctrl-W	Close File
Ctrl-Q	Quit GIMP

Dialogs Menu

Shift-Ctrl-B	Brushes
Shift-Ctrl-P	Patterns
Ctrl-P	Palette
Ctrl-G	Gradient Editor
Shift-Ctrl-T	Tool Options
Ctrl-L	Layers and Channels

Edit Menu

Ctrl-X	Cut
Ctrl-C	Copy
Ctrl-V	Paste
Ctrl-K	Clear
Ctrl-. (period)	Fill
Ctrl-Z	Undo
Ctrl-R	Redo
Shift-Ctrl-X	Cut Named
Shift-Ctrl-C	Copy Named
Shift-Ctrl-V	Paste Named

Filter Menu

Alt-F	Repeat Last Filter
Shift-Alt-F	Re-show Last Filter

Select Menu

Ctrl-T	Toggle
Ctrl-I	Invert Selection
Ctrl-A	Select All
Shift-Ctrl-A	Select None
Shift-Ctrl-L	Float Selection
Shift-Ctrl-H	Sharpen
Shift-Ctrl-F	Feather Selection

Table 2-1 Default GIMP Shortcut Keys [continued...]

View Menu

= (Equals sign)	Zoom in
- (Minus sign)	Zoom out
1	Zoom to 1:1
Shift-Ctrl-I	Window Information
Shift-Ctrl-T	Toggle Guides
Shift-Ctrl-R	Toggle Rulers
Ctrl-E	Shrink Wrap

Image Menu

Ctrl-D	Duplicate Channel
Shift-Ctrl-O	Offset Channel

Layers Menu

Ctrl-L	Dialog
Ctrl-F	Raise Layer
Ctrl-B	Lower Layer
Ctrl-M	Merge Visible Layers

Selecting Preferences in GIMP 1.0.4

As you work with the GIMP, you'll want to configure the program to work and appear the way you prefer; many options can be set in a dialog box you can access by choosing Preferences from the File menu. The available preferences for GIMP 1.0.4 are quite different from those for later versions, so I'm going to explain the former first. In the GIMP 1.0.4 Preferences dialog, there are four tabs: Display, Interface, Environment, and Directories, each bristling with parameters you can set. You may access the tabs in any order and enter preferences in any order, but when you're finished, you must click the Save button at the bottom of the dialog box. Your changes will be activated the next time you start up the GIMP. (See Figure 2-23.)

Display

You can set several defaults dealing with how your image is shown on the Display tab:

- In the Display Settings area, you can specify the image size that will be used as the default when you create a new file. You can also select whether you want an RGB or a grayscale image by default.

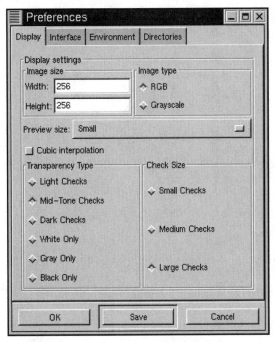

Figure 2-23 *Set your GIMP preferences for Version 1.0.4 using this dialog box.*

- You can set Preview Size of the preview thumbnails shown in the Layers dialog box to None, Small, Medium, or Large, depending on how fast your computer is and how large a screen you have.

- While the GIMP uses *bilinear* interpolation by default when resizing images, this doesn't always produce the best results, as the algorithm takes into account only the pixels on either side of the one being processed. If your machine is fast and you don't mind the performance hit of a more sophisticated interpolation algorithm, or you want the best possible image at all times, you can choose *cubic* interpolation. This algorithm examines the pixels on all sides of the one being processed, and can make a better "guess" about how to create new pixels during resizing.

- At the bottom of the dialog box, you can choose the shade used for the checkerboard that represents transparency (light, mid-tone, dark, white, and so on), and the size of the checkerboard squares.

Interface

You can modify several of the GIMP's appearance settings in the Interface tab. The settings include undo levels, window resizing, and other options. (See Figure 2-24.)

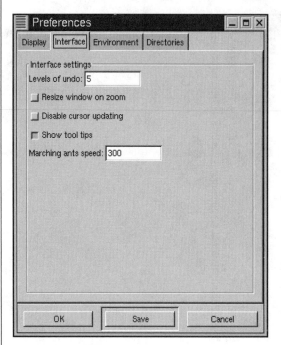

Figure 2-24 *Make changes to the GIMP's appearance in the Interface tab*

- The GIMP can store copies of an image on your hard disk, so you can undo a series of tasks and restore the image to the way it was before you performed that task. If you're working with images that are several megabytes in size, having a large number of Undo levels (say, 40 to 50) can quickly eat up a significant amount of your hard disk. If you have a capacious drive, or want to be able to backtrack significantly, go ahead and use a large number. The GIMP's default value of 5 may be the best option for anyone without extensive resources.

- The Resize window on zoom box permanently sets the automatic window resizing described above. Activate this only if you always want to use this feature, and can't be bothered with setting it from within the GIMP.

- The GIMP changes the cursor to match the tool you are using, which can be a time-saver when you get distracted and forget what you were doing. If you have a slow machine, you can disable cursor update to squeeze out a little more performance.

- If you feel like you've memorized all the tools available in the GIMP, you can turn off the Tool Tips function, which many people like but others find annoying.

- *Marching ants* is a common term for the blinking pixels that represent a selection. You can lower this number to decrease the frequency of the flashing produced by these digital insects, or increase the number to slow down the flashing.

Environment

The main settings on the Environment tab are used to determine how the GIMP handles your precious memory. By default, the program will eat up as much RAM as it thinks it can get away with, in order to speed up memory-dependent operations; if you don't have much memory to spare, you can activate the Conservative memory usage option. The GIMP also uses memory for its Tile cache, which is used for swapping data from RAM to virtual memory on your disk. The larger the number, the more RAM is used and, consequently, the faster the GIMP operates during these swaps; again, if you're short on RAM, you can decrease this figure. (See Figure 2-25.)

Using the Install colormap option is a good idea if you're forced to use the GIMP with a 256-color display (there are reportedly several of these in use in several rural towns in the Midwest); the Colormap ensures that the GIMP has enough colors to provide a decent display of your image. Colormap cycling is another option for those using 8-bit, 256-color displays; it replaces the "marching ant" selection border with a line that toggles from light to dark as you drag and release it. (This option reduces the number of colors required in 8-bit mode.)

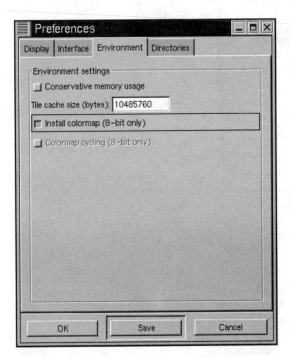

Figure 2-25 *The Environment tab can help you manage memory more efficiently.*

Directories

The Directories tab lets you specify which directories the GIMP uses for temporary files and its virtual memory swap files. You can also specify directories for brushes, gradients, patterns, palettes and other files. Keeping each type of file in its own directory makes it easier to manage particular categories. (Figure 2-26 shows the Directories tab.)

Modifying the *gimprc* Preferences File

GIMP 1.0.4 doesn't have quite as many preferences to set within the program itself as later versions. While you can set most of the defaults GIMP 1.0.4 uses in the Preferences dialog box, there are a few that you cannot modify unless you edit the *gimprc* preferences file.

Actually, your system will have at least two copies of this file, the system-wide preferences file and a personal file located in your own *gimp* directory. Your own file supersedes the settings in the system-wide file, so you can make your changes in your own file. You'll need to modify the file in an editor such as *emacs*. Following are some (but not all) of the settings you can change that aren't available from the Preferences dialog box:

- Default brush to be used, from among the brush files available in your *gimp* directory's brush path; use the form (default-brush "*brushname*.gbr")

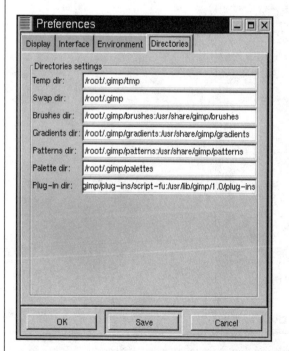

Figure 2-26 *You can specify the directories used to store files used by the GIMP.*

- Default pattern from your pattern directory, in the form (default-pattern "*patternname.pat*")
- Default palette from your palette directory, in the form (default-palette "*palettename*")
- Default gradient from your gradient directory, in the form (default-gradient "*gradientname*")
- Script-fu path, in the form (script-fu-path "*path*")
- Change ruler default from *on* to *off*, in the form (dont-show-rulers)
- Change ruler units from pixels to inches or centimeters, in the form (ruler-units centimeters) or (ruler-units inches)
- Disable confirmation when closing an image that needs to be saved, in the form (dont-confirm-on-close)

Setting Preferences in Later Versions

GIMP users gained great gobs of flexibility when a new, more comprehensive Preferences dialog box was introduced in the most recent version. Instead of four measly tabs of information, there are no less than nine different Preferences boxes you can play with, many offering defaults you were not able to set with GIMP 1.0.4. Although you might not know why some of these parameters may be worth using until you've read later chapters in this book, here they are for your entertainment. As with previous versions of the GIMP, you can access the Preferences dialogs from the File menu. Click Save to update any of these preferences.

New File Settings

You can use the New File Settings dialog box to change the default image size from the factory setting of 256 x 256 pixels, just as you could with GIMP 1.0.4's Display tab. However, you can now enter values in inches, points, millimeters, picas, and a few units you may not have heard of. You can also set the default resolution of a new image, the units used to measure the pixels (inch, millimeter, and so on), and the image type (either RGB or grayscale). (See Figure 2-27.)

Display Settings

The Display Settings dialog box corresponds to some of the settings in the Display tab in the earlier version. At the bottom of the dialog box, you can choose the shade used for the checkerboard that represents transparency (light, mid-tone, dark, white, and so on) and the size of the checkerboard squares. Instead of the bilinear interpolation the GIMP uses by default, you can switch to cubic interpolation, which bases its calculations on the pixels on all sides of the one being processed. (See Figure 2-28.)

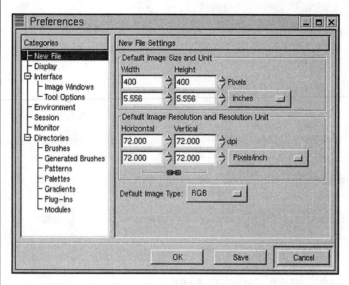

Figure 2-27 *The New File Settings preferences dialog box*

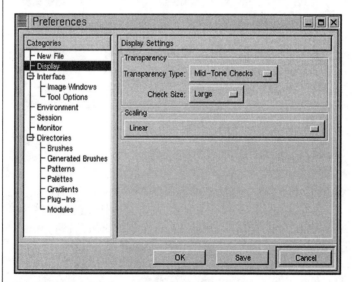

Figure 2-28 *The Display Settings dialog box*

Interface Settings-General

In the Interface Settings-General dialog box, you can set the size of the preview thumbnails shown in the Layers dialog box to None, Small, Medium, or Large, depending on how fast your computer is and how large a screen you have. You can also set the size of the Navigation Preview (which appears when you click on the four-headed arrow at the bottom right corner of an image window). You can control the number of levels of Undo (and thus how much hard disk space the GIMP uses to store copies of a file for undo operations, from the default of 5 up to a highly impractical 255 levels). The GIMP can now store the names of the most recent files you've worked on at the bottom of the File menu, and you can specify the number of images to list here. Finally, you can turn on or off display of the tool tips that pop up when the cursor passes over a tool. (See Figure 2-29.)

Interface Settings-Image Windows

The Interface Settings-Image Windows dialog box is used to specify how windows appear on your screen. You can make these settings, shown in Figure 2-30:

- Have the GIMP automatically resize a window during zooms, so the window is as close as possible to the size of the new image.
- Display Rulers by default.
- Display the status bar at the bottom of the window by default. The status bar displays the name of the image, the current coordinates (in pixels) of the cursor, and other information.
- Interval between flashes produced by the selection tools' "marching ants" display. Lower numbers decrease the speed; higher numbers increase it.
- Specify Image Title format, using one of the default values from the drop-down list, or your custom format using the following variables: %f (filename); %p (consecutive image number); %i (copy number of the image); %t (image type—RGB or grayscale); %z (zoom percentage); %d:%s (zoom ratio, e.g. 1:2).
- Mouse pointer movement feedback, from perfect (but slow) to fast (with some time lag), either with or without rapid updating.

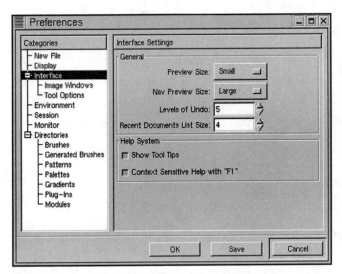

Figure 2-29 *The Interface Settings–General dialog box*

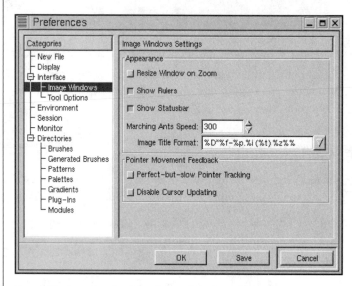

Figure 2-30 *Interface Settings–Image Windows dialog box*

Interface Settings-Tool Options

Not many choices here. You can specify whether settings you make in a session for one painting tool should apply to all of them globally. You can also toggle the brush and pattern indicators in the Toolbar. The dialog box is shown in Figure 2-31.

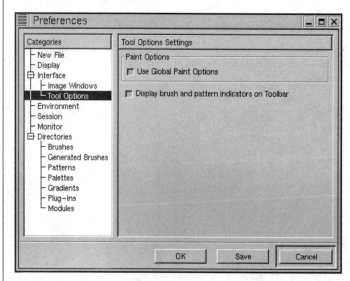

Figure 2-31 *The Interface Settings–Tool Options dialog box*

Environment

As I mentioned earlier, the GIMP can eat up your RAM at an alarming rate, as a way to speed up some of its functions. If you don't have much memory to spare, you can activate the Conservative Memory Usage option in this dialog box, shown in Figure 2-32.

The program also uses memory for its Tile cache, a RAM area used for swapping data from RAM to your hard disk. The larger the number, the more RAM used and, consequently, the faster the GIMP operates during these swaps. Again, if you're short on RAM, you can decrease this figure.

You can use the Maximum Image Size setting to control how large a single image can be before the GIMP calls a halt. The default value of 32 MB is a good choice unless you have a great deal of hard disk space, or very little.

If you're using an 8-bit, 256-color display, using the Install Colormap option is a good idea. This option ensures that the GIMP has enough colors to provide a decent display of your image. Colormap Cycling is another option for those using 8-bit, 256-color displays. It replaces the "marching ant" selection border with a line that toggles from light to dark as you drag and release it, reducing the number of colors needed in hue-challenged mode.

Finally, you can choose to create thumbnails that can be used to preview files before opening. Select Always, and the GIMP will automatically save a preview with the file. Choose Never, and you'll have to hope a picture isn't worth a thousand words.

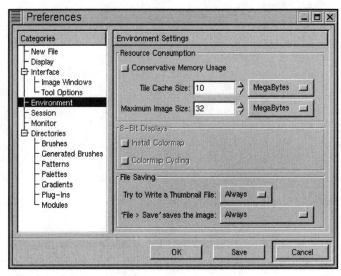

Figure 2-32 *Environment Settings dialog box*

Session Management

The Session Management dialog box controls how the GIMP acts when you exit the program. It can save the position of your windows, restore the previous session when you next launch the program, and "remember" the status of devices when you return. If you want to remove stored window positions, click the Clear Saved Window Positions button. (See Figure 2-33.)

Monitor Information

Here you can instruct the GIMP to get its monitor resolution information from the X Windows server, or use values that you enter manually. Values can be set in pixels per inch, or using another measurement unit. (See Figure 2-34.)

Directories

As with earlier versions of the GIMP, the new Directories dialog box lets you specify which directories the GIMP uses for temporary files and its virtual memory swap files, as well as those for brushes, gradients, patterns, palettes and other files. (You can see the Directories dialog box in Figure 2-35.)

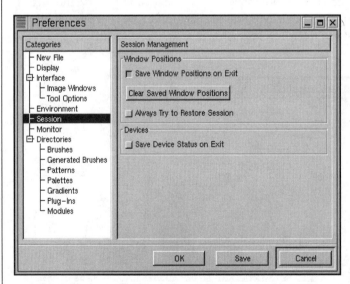

Figure 2-33 *The Session Management dialog box*

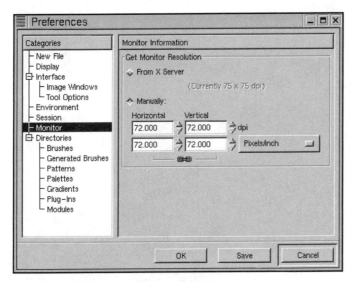

Figure 2·34 *Monitor Information dialog box*

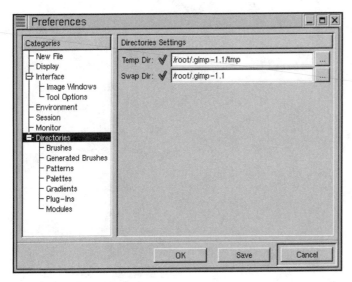

Figure 2·35 *Directories dialog box*

What's Next

This chapter provided you with a quick overview of the GIMP's Toolbar and interface, and some tips on how to customize everything with your own preferences. You can start putting these implements to work in the next chapter, when you take a more in-depth look at the image editor's painting tools.

A GIMP Guerrilla doesn't need to have an artistic bent to paint using the GIMP's brush and filling tools. In fact, the editor's painting tools have so many cool features that even a neophyte artist can create images from scratch that look good. However, if you do have artistic skills, you'll find that the GIMP lets you apply as much of your talent as you can muster.

This chapter looks at choosing colors, drawing with tools like the Paintbrush and Airbrush, creating your own custom colors, applying fills and patterns, and working with the Eraser, Clone Tool, and other utensils. Drawing on a computer screen using an input device shaped like a block of soap may not be a breeze, but the GIMP gives you the tools to make the most of your abilities and ideas.

The GIMP gives you millions of brushes in one! They are very adaptable tools. You can use them to paint freeform or draw straight lines, with a smooth or fuzzy or rough-edged appearance. Brush shapes can be round, oval, or calligraphic, or you can use a brush tip that you create. The paint can be applied continuously or intermittently as a dotted line, and the paint can range from opaque to completely transparent. It can fade or blend between shades should you desire. If you multiply the number of different brush shapes furnished with the GIMP by the options you can apply yourself, it's evident there may be millions of brush effects you can use to express your latent creativity.

Choosing Colors

Before you can paint, you'll need to use the Foreground/Background Color Selector to choose a color to paint with. (Although my personal favorite color is Clear, painting with a totally transparent layer is counterproductive.) See Figure 3-1.

If you want to use the current *foreground* color, shown in the upper-left square in the Foreground/Background Color Selector, you're all set; choose the Paintbrush tool, and begin painting. However, you'll often want to paint with a different color than the default value; you'll need to choose a hue or graytone using one of several different methods. You can also override the default *background* color.

Beginners can easily become confused by the terminology "foreground" and "background," because the GIMP uses them in several different ways; here's how to understand the difference.

When I'm talking about different layers of a document (which I'm not, in this chapter), the foreground and background can refer to the bottom and upper layers of an image. I'm concerned with foreground and background colors, here.

NOTE

Figure 3-1 *The Foreground/Background Color Selector is your starting point for choosing colors.*

The current foreground color—the color the Paintbrush and some other tools use to make their strokes—is represented by the upper-left square. The foreground color is also used to fill an image or selections when you use the Paint Bucket tool with the FG Color Fill option selected.

The background color, represented by the lower-right square, is the color that will be used when you cut or erase a portion of your image, or fill an image or selection when you use the Paint Bucket tool with the BG Color Fill option selected.

However, to make things interesting, the latter statement is completely true *only* if you're working with a solid color layer. If you're painting on a transparent area, the foreground color is still used by the painting tool, and the background color can be used to fill using the Paint Bucket tool and the BG Color Fill option. However, the background color is ignored when you cut or erase a portion of an image. The removed or erased portion becomes transparent, rather than the same color as the background hue. Check it out for yourself:

1. Create two new empty documents, as you learned to do in Chapter 2. Give one a white background, and let the other have a transparent background. The transparent image will have a gray checkerboard pattern to show it is transparent.

2. Click the small black/white squares in the lower left of the Foreground/Background Color Selector. This returns the GIMP's default foreground and background colors to black and white, respectively.

3. Click the Paintbrush tool in the Toolbox, and draw a few lines in each image.

4. Click the Eraser tool, and erase a portion of each of the lines you've drawn. In the image with the white background, the line will be replaced with white, but in the transparent image, the portion you erase will return to transparent.

5. Double-click the background square in the Foreground/Background Color Selector to make it active.

6. Click anywhere in the Color Selection dialog box that appears to choose a new background color that isn't white.

7. Use the Eraser tool again to erase more of the lines you've drawn in each of the two images. Notice how the Eraser now paints with your new background color in the first image, but still just erases to transparency in the second? You can see the effect in Figure 3-2.

Figure 3-2 *The Eraser paints with the background color in an image or layer with a background (lower examples), but erases to transparency in an image or layer that is transparent (upper examples).*

You can exchange the foreground color and background color at any time by clicking the arc with arrowheads at either end located to the upper-right of the Foreground/Background Color Selector. To return the colors to their default black foreground/white background, click the smaller set of black/white boxes in the lower-left corner.

Choosing from the Color Selection Dialog Box

The Color Selection dialog box lets you choose any color in the rainbow for your foreground or background colors. Just double-click the Foreground or Background squares, respectively. Click on the GIMP tab, if necessary, to bring the default Color Selection dialog (shown in Figure 3-3) to the top, and then choose your color.

1. Click in the vertical spectrum bar in the center of the dialog box, to choose the kind of color you're looking for—reds, greens, blues, yellows, and so forth. The palette at the left of the bar changes to show a full range of hues in the color you chose.

2. Click anywhere in the palette. The horizontal and vertical guides will intersect at that position, marking the color you have chosen. This color will be shown at the left side of the before/after box at the top of the dialog. The color on the left is the new color you're specifying. The color on the right is the original color being replaced.

3. You can drag either the horizontal or vertical color guides separately to change the saturation and brightness of a color, respectively. Moving the horizontal guide alone selects the most saturated color (at the top) or least saturated version of that color (at the bottom). Dragging the vertical guide from side to side changes the relative darkness (left side) or brightness (right side).

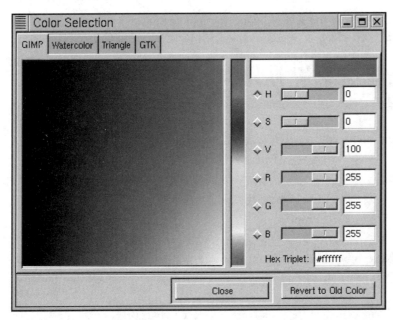

Figure 3-3 *Any color in the spectrum can be chosen from the Color Selection dialog box.*

4. Underneath the before/after box are sliders that change to represent the Hue, Saturation, Value/Brightness of the selected color, as well as the Red, Green, and Blue values of the color. (You'll learn more about HSV/HSB and RGB, as well as saturation, in Chapter 6.)

5. If you know the exact values of the color you want, you can use the sliders, shown in Figure 3-4, to select that color directly, without using the palette.

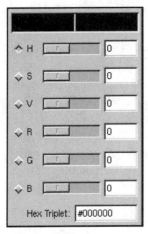

Figure 3-4 *Use the color selection sliders to enter color values precisely.*

6. Click OK to choose the selected color for your foreground or background. To cancel the color selection operation, click on Revert to Old Color.

Choosing with the Color Picker

You can also select colors using the eyedropper-shaped Color Picker tool. You might want to use this method to select an exact color to match. Perhaps you've been painting in your image and want to duplicate that color. Or, you might want to transfer a color from one image to another.

1. Make either the Foreground or Background color active by clicking the appropriate square in the Foreground/Background Color Selector.

2. Click the Color Picker tool.

3. Move the cursor to the color you want to select. Whenever the cursor is over an area that can be chosen, it changes into a crosshair. If you have multiple images open, you can select a color from any of them, except for transparent areas.

4. Click with the center of the crosshairs to select a color precisely.

5. The Color Picker dialog pops up, showing the Red, Green and Blue values for the selected color, along with those values in hexadecimal. (You can use the hex values to specify a color in a Web page; you'll learn how to do this in Chapter 6.) Click the Close button to choose the selected color. (See Figure 3-5.)

SideBar

Notes on the Color Picker

The Color Picker has just a few options, which you can set by double-clicking the Color Picker Tool in the Toolbox, producing the dialog box shown in Figure 3-6.

The Color Picker can sample the *merged* values of the colors of all the visible layers, rather than just the pixels in the currently active layer. (I'll explain about layers in Chapter 5.) Or, it can sample the average of the pixels in an area you can set using the Radius slider. You can also check or uncheck the Update Active Color box. When this button is depressed, the Color Picker updates the currently active color (either foreground or background) with the color you click on. When the button is unmarked, the Color Picker displays the color values for the hue, but doesn't change the active color. You can use this capability to determine the color values for a color without changing an active color.

Figure 3-5 *The Color Picker dialog box shows the values of the color you have chosen.*

Figure 3-6 *The Color Picker can be directed to merge the values of all the colors in every layer of an image.*

Choosing from a Palette

In case you want to choose from a palette of related colors, the GIMP has a rich collection of color swatches you can use. You'll probably find the Color Palette more helpful than the Color Picker or Color Selection dialog boxes, because this feature makes it easy to choose specific colors repeatedly. While the GIMP provides many useful palettes to work from, you can also create your own.

1. Choose File | Dialogs | Palette or press Ctrl-P to produce the Color Palette. The default palette that appears has about a dozen colors, plus a selection of gray values. (See Figure 3-7.)

2. Click in the appropriate box in the Foreground/Background Color Selector to activate the foreground or background colors. Click in any of the colors in the palette to change the foreground or background to that color. (It's not necessary to use the Color Picker; just click.) The name of the color you click is shown in the box below the palette.

3. Click in the zoom icons (magnifying glasses with plus and minus signs in them) to zoom in and out on the Color Palette.

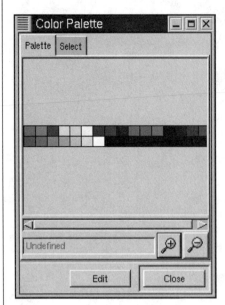

Figure 3-7 *The Color Palette offers access to the GIMP's built-in palettes, plus any custom palettes you create.*

4. Change to a different palette by clicking the Select tab, shown in Figure 3-8, and choosing from the scrolling list. You can select from among the palettes with names like Firecode or China. Click the Palette tab to return to the palette display.

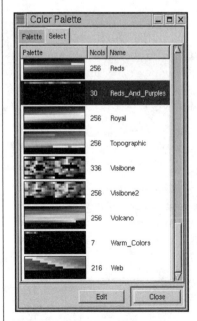

Figure 3-8 *The Select tab provides a scrolling list of palettes to choose from.*

5. Now that the new palette is visible, select any of the new colors you like. Note that each palette has groups of colors that work well with each other. For example, the Kahki palette (yes, that's how it's spelled!) offers various khaki-style shades. The Web palette offers a handy selection of colors that can be reproduced by Web browsers on screens displaying no more than 256 colors.

Creating New Palettes

If the GIMP's selection of palettes isn't enough for you, you can create your own. There are several ways to do this. The easiest way is to convert an existing image to a color palette. You can also pick and choose the exact colors you want in a palette. Here's a quick description of both ways to create palettes.

Creating a Palette from an Existing Image

1. First create the image with all the colors you want to add to your palette. You can load an existing image with the colors, or add them by hand. Just select a color and paint somewhere on the image with it. Repeat until all the colors are added.

2. A fast way to create variations on a single color is to use that color to paint, but vary the opacity between strokes. You'll end up with lighter and darker versions of that color.

3. When you have all the colors you want, press Ctrl-P to produce the Color Palette dialog box, then click the Edit button. The Color Palette Edit dialog box shown in Figure 3-9 appears.

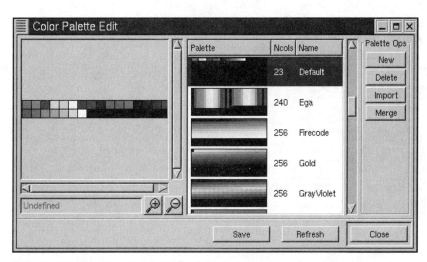

Figure 3-9 *Use the Color Palette Edit dialog box to create custom palettes.*

4. Click the Import button in the Color Palette Edit dialog box. In the Name box of the dialog that appears, type a name for the new palette in the Name box. Then click Import. The colors of the current image will be imported as a palette. If the new palette doesn't appear in the scrolling list, click the Refresh button. (See Figure 3-10.)

Creating a Palette from Colors You Select

1. Press Ctrl-P to produce the Color Palette dialog box. Click Edit to access the Color Palette Edit dialog box.

2. To add colors to an existing palette, choose the palette from the scrolling list. To create an all-new palette, click the New button and enter a name for the new palette.

3. To add colors from an image on the screen, click the Color Picker tool, and click in the color you want. It will appear in the Foreground square on the Foreground/Background Color Selector. To add this color to your palette, right-click in a swatch in the palette, and select New from the context menu that pops up. Repeat until all the colors you want to add are chosen. You can use this method to add new colors, or replace existing swatches in the palette with new colors.

4. To add colors from the Color Selection dialog box, right-click on a swatch, and choose the colors you want.

5. To merge colors from several palettes, select the palettes you want to merge, by clicking in the first palette and then Shift-clicking in the subsequent palettes. Click the Merge button, and enter a name for your merged palette.

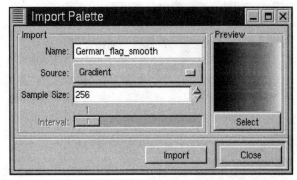

Figure 3-10 *Import an image as a palette using all the colors in the image.*

Selecting Brush Attributes

You can choose from any of the brush shapes the GIMP provides. Later on, I'll show you how to create your own brush shapes, either by adapting an existing shape, or by building one entirely from scratch.

1. Start with a clean, white screen, with black as your foreground color. Make sure your Paintbrush tool is selected in the toolbox.

2. Choose Dialogs | Brushes from the File menu to display the Brush Selection palette, shown in Figure 3-11.

3. You can resize the palette to make all available brushes visible. If a brush tip is too large to view easily in the preview square, click in the thumbnail to see an enlarged version. (Earlier versions of the GIMP would crop over-large brushes to fit in the thumbnail; more recent versions shrink the brush shape to fit.)

4. Click in one of the brush shape boxes to choose the shape of the tip of the Paintbrush. First choose one of the diagonal line brush tips, and sketch some lines. Then choose one of the hard-edged round brush shapes, and draw a few more lines. Finally, choose a soft-edged brush tip, and sketch a little more. Your results should look like Figure 3-12.

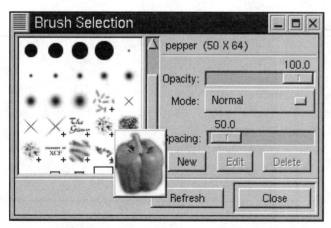

Figure 3-11 *The Brush Selection palette offers an array of brush types to choose from.*

Figure 3-12 *Examples of brush strokes with diagonal line brush tip (top), hard-edged round brush (middle), and soft-edged brush (bottom).*

The diagonal line brushes, called Calligraphic brushes, produce strokes of varying width, depending on how you draw. They can be used to duplicate many effects available with a calligraphic pen. The hard-edged brushes, called Circle brushes in GIMP-speak, produce a line like you might get with a wide paintbrush, giving a fixed-width stroke regardless of which direction you paint. Soft-edged brushes, the so-called Circle Fuzzy tips, give a result similar to what you might get with a spray can of paint or an airbrush. Notice that a status line at the upper-right corner of the dialog box displays the name of the currently active brush, as well as its size in pixels (8 x 8, 10 x 10, and so on).

Sidebar

Meet Undo/Redo

Make a mistake in any of the exercises so far? Use the GIMP's Undo command to backtrack. Just press Ctrl-Z to undo the last command or brushstroke you carried out. Press Ctrl-Z repeatedly (up to five times with the default setting) to remove multiple steps in reverse order. If you want more than five steps available to Undo, change this parameter in the GIMP's Preferences, as explained in Chapter 2. You can reverse an Undo by pressing the Redo key, Ctrl-R.

You can change the way brushes work in several ways. Try the following exercise to see how the options work:

1. Select the 11 x 11-pixel Circle brush. Draw a few lines on an open document, as shown in Figure 3-13.

2. Change the Opacity slider at the right side of the dialog box to roughly the 50-percent mark.

3. Draw a stroke that overlaps other lines on your sketchpad. Note that the stroke not only is lighter (it's a 50-percent gray color now, rather than black), but also is semi-transparent, allowing the pixels underneath to show through, as you can see in Figure 3-14.

4. Change the Opacity slider to 25 percent, and draw a line that overlaps both the 50-percent and 100-percent lines. You'll see how reduced opacity makes a line more transparent. (You can see the results in Figure 3-15.)

Figure 3-13 *First, draw some lines in an open document.*

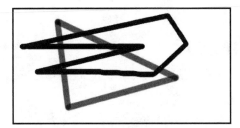

Figure 3-14 *Overlapping lines allow the strokes underneath to show through.*

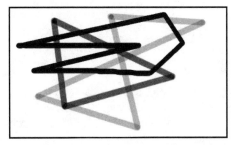

Figure 3-15 *Adjust the transparency of a brush with the Opacity slider to produce semi-opaque lines.*

5. With the 11 x 11-pixel Circle brush still active, change the Spacing slider to a value of 100, then draw a line in a new document. Notice that instead of drawing a continuous line, the brush creates a series of circles, each spaced 100 percent of the width of the brush tip from the last circle. This is a great tool for drawing dotted lines. You can vary the spacing from 0 percent (a continuous line) to 400 percent. (Figure 3-16 shows dotted lines produced with various brushes at different spacing settings.)

Unless you're a Photoshop veteran, you're probably wondering about the Mode control in the dialog box. Modes are various ways that the GIMP can use to merge pixels when you paint over one line with another one, or combine layers. For example, you can apply paint strokes so that either the darker or lighter stroke shows through, at your option, or so that the combined values of both strokes are used where they overlap. The GIMP has 16 different Mode methods; for now, you'll want to stick to the Normal setting. Even Photoshop old hands can get confused by Modes, so you'll look at them in more detail in Chapter 5 when I explain one of the prime reasons to use Modes: blending layers.

Creating Custom Brushes

In case you want to be really creative, the GIMP lets you build your own brushes that have unique brush stroke styles, or that can even serve as "Clone tool" printers. There are several ways to do this, and all of them are ridiculously easy. Try the following methods.

Creating a Brush of a Particular Size

Here's how to build a rectangular, elliptical, round, or irregular brush of a particular size.

1. Access the Brush Selection dialog box as you did before. (Ctrl-Shft-B is a shortcut to this dialog box.)

2. Click the New button. The Brush Editor dialog box, shown in Figure 3-17, will appear.

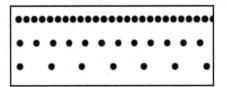

Figure 3-16   *Create dotted lines by adjusting the Spacing slider, set to (top to bottom) values of 125, 250, and 500, using an 11 x 11-pixel brush.*

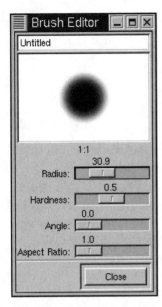

Figure 3-17 *Create or edit brushes using the Brush Editor.*

3. Type in a name for your new brush in the space provided.
4. Choose a Radius (size), Hardness (fuzziness of the edges), Aspect Ratio (how wide the brush is in relation to its height), and angle of rotation.

To create a tall, thin brush, just make a wide, squat one first, and rotate it 90 degrees.

5. Click Close when finished. The new brush is added to your brush palette.

Creating a Brush from a Selection

You can also create a brush from a selection that contains brush strokes you want to use; you can even use it to brush in text (such as a signature). You'll end up with a Clone tool effect.

1. To create a brush from a selection, select the portion of the image you want to convert to a brush, as shown in Figure 3-18.

The image you select can be in color, but it will be converted to grayscale when it becomes a brush.

Figure 3-18 *Choose a portion of an image to be converted into a brush.*

To create a brush that consists of text, click the Type tool, enter the text into your document, and select that.

2. Right-click inside the selection, and choose Script-Fu | Selection | To Brush. When the Script-Fu dialog box pops up, type in a description and a file name for the brush, and type in a value to adjust spacing. If you use narrow spacing, the brush strokes will overlap and blend together as you paint; with a wider spacing (especially useful for Clone tool brushes) each time you click, a distinct brush shape will appear. The value you enter is the default; you can always adjust spacing in the Brush Selection dialog box. (See Figure 3-19.)

3. Click OK to save the selection as a brush. Right-click in the image and choose Dialogs | Brushes, then click the Refresh button. Your new brush will be added to the Brushes Palette.

Figure 3-20 shows some of the brush effects you can get with custom-designed brushes.

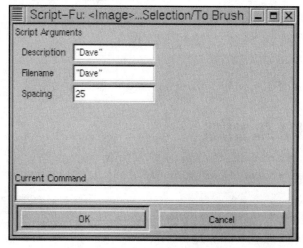

Figure 3-19 *Enter a file name and description into the Script-Fu dialog box.*

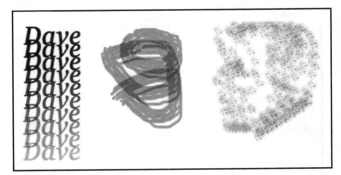

Figure 3-20 *Custom brushes can produce impressive artistic effects.*

What's Script-Fu?

Script-Fu is a way of interacting with the GIMP using a *scripting language*. JavaScript and SCHEME are examples of scripting languages. When a Script-Fu script is invoked, the GIMP follows the instructions therein exactly, producing in a second or two an effect that could take many minutes to achieve if you had to carry out all the effects one at a time manually. Script-Fu is a powerful way of extending and automating the GIMP. If you've used Photoshop, you can think of Script-Fu as a kind of big brother to Photoshop's Actions.

Script-Fu add-ons can be created using the SCHEME language, or other languages, such as Perl, by way of plug-ins that enable the GIMP to interpret those scripts. The Perl plug-in was made part of the latest version of GIMP. (You'll learn more about Script-Fu in Chapter 14.)

Drawing Lines with the Paintbrush

To draw a freehand line, just place the cursor where you want to begin and sketch. To draw a vertical or horizontal straight line, follow these steps:

1. Position the brush at the point where you want the line to begin.
2. Press the Shift key and keep it held down.
3. Click at the position where you want the straight line to begin.
4. With the Shift key still held down, move the cursor to the point you want the straight line to extend to, and click. A line is drawn between the two points.
5. Continue clicking with the Shift key depressed to add straight lines, as shown in Figure 3-21.

Figure 3-21 *Holding the Shift key while clicking draws straight lines.*

Changing Paintbrush Options

The Paintbrush has a cool option you can use to create eye-catching lines with a very different look. You can fade out a line as you draw, so it seems to vanish onto the canvas. Open a blank image document. Double-click the Paintbrush tool icon in the toolbox to access the Tool Options dialog box, and try this effect out.

With the Fade Out effect, your brush stroke gradually blends in with the background. The Fade Out slider lets you set the degree of fadeout. Specify a number of pixels from 0 to 1000. The line you draw will start to fade after the stroke has reached that number of pixels, and will continue for about three times that amount before fading entirely. That is, if you use a value of 100, your line will appear to be normal for the first 100 pixels, then begin to fade out for the next 300 pixels, becoming completely transparent when the line is 400 pixels long. Figure 3-22 shows how the Fade Out effect can be used.

Figure 3-22 *The Fade Out option produces vanishing brush strokes you can use in an artistic way.*

You can also set the Incremental feature in the Brush Tool Options dialog box. When you click the Incremental button while using semi-transparent paint, you can view the incremental position of spaced brush strokes when painting with a brush that is less than fully opaque at slow speed.

Otherwise, the brush strokes all run together. This produces an interesting effect, especially where partially opaque brush strokes cross. (An example of this effect is shown in Figure 3-23.)

In the most recent version of the GIMP, you can also set pressure sensitivity to make the best use of a pressure-sensitive tablet.

Drawing with the Pencil, Airbrush, and Convolver

Now that you've seen what the Paintbrush can do, you'll be able to pick up other drawing tools (so to speak), including the Pencil, Airbrush, and Convolver (blur/sharpen tool) very quickly. They all operate in a similar manner. For example, you can draw straight lines with any of these using the Shift key technique described earlier. These tools have other options and capabilities of their own.

- The Pencil tool is very similar to the Paintbrush. While the Paintbrush can draw both hard- and soft-edged lines, the Pencil can draw only hard-edged lines. You can choose any of the brush tips for the Pencil, including those you've created from selections, but if they include gray or fuzzy tones, they will be converted to black-and-white, hard-edged tips while you're using this tool. The Pencil has only a couple options: pressure sensitivity and the incremental mode. (You can see a comparison of Pencil and Paintbrush strokes using the same tips in Figure 3-24.)

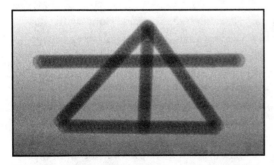

Figure 3-23 *The Incremental effect produces interesting brush strokes when used with semi-transparent paint.*

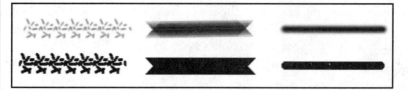

Figure 3-24 *Even though they can use the same brush tips, the Pencil and Paintbrush provide different effects.*

- The *Airbrush* and *Natural Airbrush* tools function a little like the Paintbrush with a fuzzy brush and transparent paint; however, they include more options you can set by double-clicking the tool and manipulating the sliders in the Options dialog box.

- The conventional Airbrush has a *Rate slider* that controls the amount of paint delivered relative to the movement of the mouse. That is, a low value produces a stroke that is the same density no matter how quickly or slowly you paint. If you use a high value, moving the brush more slowly produces a denser stroke.

- The *Pressure slider* controls the amount of paint sprayed. Lower values provide lower-density, irregular strokes, while higher values produce denser, smoother strokes.

- The Natural Airbrush has additional options for tilt and angle of the spray.

  Figure 3-25 shows the spray-paint effect you can get with the airbrush tools.

- The *Convolver* tool uses a particular kind of *convolution* (a set of algorithms applied to pixels in an image, such that the effects are based on the values of surrounding pixels); the pixels are changed depending on their contrast with the pixels around them. When you increase the contrast, an image appears sharper. Decrease the contrast, and the image starts to blur. You can "paint" with the Convolver as you would with other painting tools, but the area beneath your strokes is made sharper or blurrier, depending on whether you've chosen Sharpen or Blur in the Convolve Options dialog box. You can also manipulate the degree of blurring and sharpening by setting the Pressure slider.

The Convolver should be considered a painting tool because the strokes it creates aren't exactly what you might expect from a simple blurring or sharpening effect. For example, it can change colors slightly, and often adds a pixel-like effect when used repeatedly over a particular area. You can vary the effect by using different brush tips while blurring/sharpening. See Figure 3-26 for some effects you can achieve with the Convolver.

NOTE

Figure 3-25   *The Airbrush and Natural Airbrush do an excellent job of simulating sprayed paint.*

Figure 3-26   *The left half of this pumpkin was sharpened using the Convolver tool.*

Removing Strokes with the Eraser

The Eraser is another brush-like tool that removes parts of your image, returning the areas to the background color (or, in the case of an image on a transparent layer, to transparency). You can use any of the brush tips found in the Brush Selection dialog box, and set the opacity of your eraser using the dialog box's slider. You can set the Eraser's options to produce a hard or soft eraser edge, and to perform as an anti-Eraser on transparent layers (that is, it erases to the background color instead of transparency).

Copying Pixels with the Clone Tool

If there is one GIMP tool I couldn't live without, it is the Clone tool. With the humble Clone tool, you can sample one part of an image and paint what you're sampling on another part of the screen. (This is called *cloning*.) You can even clone an image from one image window into another. It's an essential tool for retouching images, as you can clone "good" pixels from one area to cover "bad" (for example, dust-spotted or scratched image areas) in another. (You'll look at uses for the Clone tool in Chapter 9, when I reveal to you the arcane mysteries of retouching and photo restoration.)

Since the Clone tool is officially a painting tool, you can use any of the available brushes, including your own custom brushes. All of the painting modes you'll work with later apply (Lighten, Darken, and so on), and you can control opacity just as you do with the other painting tools. The Clone tool has additional options that control the source for the pixels you're cloning, as well as how the cloned image area is aligned with the source. The best way to learn how to use this tool, often called the Rubber Stamp because of its icon, is to work with it. (See Figure 3-27.)

Rubber-Stamping an Aligned Clone

Most often, you'll be cloning in the aligned mode. That is, you'll start copying, or cloning, from one area of an image to another area, and as you paint in any direction, the copied pixels will correspond to the pixels proceeding in the same direction in the source image. You can create a duplicate of the original image, even if you stop painting and start up again. The source image and target image will remain aligned. Try the following exercise to see how it works:

1. Reset the colors to the black foreground/white background defaults, as you learned how to do in "Choosing Colors" earlier in this chapter. Create a new document, at least 500 x 500 pixels. Give yourself plenty of area to work in.

2. Choose a brush shape to work with from the Brush Selection dialog box. The shape doesn't really matter for this exercise, but will when you're retouching

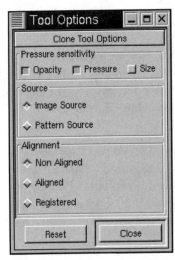

Figure 3-27 *The Clone Tool Options dialog box offers settings for rubber-stamping images.*

photos. In that case, you'll usually want a soft-edged brush of a size that will copy only small sections of the cloned image at a time.

3. You need an image to clone, so draw a star in the lower-right corner using the Paintbrush tool. Remember to keep the Shift key held down to connect the strokes. (See Figure 3-28.)

4. When you're finished drawing the star, select the Clone tool from the toolbox. Double-click on the Clone tool icon to open the Clone Tool Options dialog box.

5. In the Source area, click Image Source. In the Alignment area, click Aligned.

6. Position the Clone tool over the lower-right leg of the star. Press the Ctrl key, and click the mouse button to sample that area. You will notice that the Clone tool cursor turns into a crosshair while the Ctrl key is depressed, showing you exactly which area will be used as the source. It is as though the Clone tool is memorizing the part of the screen from which it will start sampling.

Figure 3-28 *The star you'll be cloning*

7. Move the Clone tool into the upper-left corner of the document, giving yourself some space above and to the left of the star.

8. Holding down only the left mouse button, start painting with the mouse, using small strokes. You'll see the outlines of the star emerging. If you look at your original star, you'll see a small plus sign sampling the image as the copy of the star is made. Stop copying before you finish making the clone, as shown in Figure 3-29.

Try moving the mouse to another place on the image, and try to paint another star. Don't press any keys—just try to paint by clicking and dragging the mouse. Notice that you can't start a new star, but can only continue the old one. That's because the cloning is precisely aligned to where you first started painting. Continue painting until the star is complete.

Rubber-Stamping a Nonaligned Clone

If you want to make multiple copies of all or part of a sampled object, you can use the Nonaligned mode. Unclick the Aligned button in the Clone Tool Options dialog box, then try this exercise:

1. Select the Eraser tool, and erase the cloned star you just made. (Be sure your background color is still white.) Leave the original star alone.

2. Position the mouse on the original star. As before, press the Ctrl key, and click the mouse button, to begin sampling the star.

3. Move the mouse to another location, and begin painting. A star will appear, just as it did the first time. When the first star is finished, move the mouse to another location and try to paint a second one. In the nonaligned mode, you can do this. Note that every time you stop cloning and move to another position, you start cloning a new star. (See Figure 3-30.)

Figure 3-29 *A partially cloned star*

Figure 3-30 *Multiple stars cloned in nonaligned form*

Cloning with a Pattern

You can clone patterns into an image, too. In fact, the Clone tool and Fill tool are the only GIMP tools that can use patterns. Try this to see how to do it (I'll show you how to create your own patterns later in this chapter):

1. Start with a white canvas, white background color, black foreground color.
2. Choose a brush shape from the Brush Selection dialog box.
3. Double-click the Clone tool, and choose Pattern Source in the Source area. You can use Aligned or Nonaligned mode, depending on whether you want to paint a continuous pattern, or different splotches of pattern.
4. Right-click in the image, and choose Dialogs | Patterns to produce the Pattern Selection dialog box (shown in Figure 3-31).
5. Click in a pattern swatch to select it.
6. Paint the pattern onto your image.

Filling an Image with Color, Patterns, and Gradients

The last way of painting an image that you'll look at in this chapter are the various methods for filling images or selections with colors, patterns, or gradients. All three modes work similarly: you select an area to be filled, then click in it to add the color, pattern, or gradient to the area you've chosen. In this section, you'll learn how to use the Bucket Fill tool to fill an area with either a solid color or a pattern (note that solid colors are easiest to apply).

1. Make sure the foreground or background color is set to the color you want to fill with.

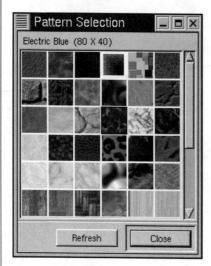

Figure 3-31 *The Pattern Selection dialog box lets you choose from standard or custom patterns.*

2. Double-click the Bucket Fill tool to produce the Bucket Fill Options dialog box (shown in Figure 3-32).

3. Choose either FG (foreground) Color Fill or BG (background) Color Fill.

4. Use the Rectangular selection tool to select the area you want to fill. (You'll look at exactly how to use the GIMP's selection tools in Chapter 4.)

5. Set the Threshold (Tolerance) slider to 15 if it is not already at that value. The Threshold value lets the GIMP determine which pixels to fill; the lower the Threshold, the closer in value to an initial pixel the one that you click in the selection must be to fill the selected pixel with color.

6. Using the Bucket Fill tool, click inside the area to be filled.

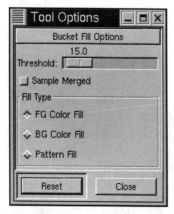

Figure 3-32 *Choose the Bucket Fill Options dialog box to make settings for this tool.*

Say What? Explain Threshold Again

Threshold can mean several things in the GIMP, but here we're talking about what Photoshop users think of as Tolerance. Several tools, including the Bucket Fill tool, select or fill areas based on how close they are in value to a starter or *seed* value determined by the pixel you first click on with the tool. The tool "branches out" from that initial pixel, and acts on all contiguous pixels that fall within the tolerance or threshold you've set, based on a brightness scale from 0 (black) to 255 (white).

For example, if the Threshold is set to 255 (the maximum), all the pixels will fall within the tolerance range, since every pixel will have a value between 0 and 255. If the Threshold is set to 15 (the minimum), pixels must have a value within 15, plus or minus, of the initial pixel to be operated on. So, with the Bucket Fill tool you can choose whether to fill an area completely, or to fill only pixels that match—to a specified degree—the first pixel clicked. Figure 3-33 shows an image with a selection made with a tolerance of 16, 24, and 32, respectively. You'll learn more about tolerance in Chapter 4 when I explain selections.

> If you don't want to use the Threshold slider, you can choose to fill with foreground or background colors, by clicking or Shift-clicking in the area to be filled, respectively.

You can set several options for the Bucket Fill tool, including Mode (which you'll look at later), Fill Opacity, and whether or not the tool should base its Threshold calculations using only the current layer or all the merged layers of your image. You can also use the Bucket Fill tool to add patterns, using the same patterns you worked with in the section on the Clone tool; just click the Pattern Fill button in the Tool Options

Figure 3-33 *Left to right, tolerance of 16, 24, and 32 would fill different areas of the image.*

dialog box, and choose a pattern as you did before, by right-clicking in the image area, and then selecting Dialogs | Patterns to access the Pattern Selection dialog box. A fill made using a pattern is shown in Figure 3-34.

Creating Custom Patterns

You can easily create your own patterns, just by painting in an image and saving it as a GIMP pattern file. Well, it's not exactly that easy. Patterns must be created so they tile seamlessly, that is, combined so that, say, a 32 x 32-pixel pattern can be used to fill a much larger area without the edges of the pattern being apparent. To do that, the edges of one pattern must match the edges of adjacent tiles. (Figure 3-35 shows a tiled pattern.)

So, creating your own pattern consists of three easy steps:

1. Drawing the pattern.
2. Making it seamless.
3. Saving the pattern as a GIMP-compatible pattern file.

OK, so step 1 is easy. The other two aren't as difficult as you might think. The GIMP includes a filter (a kind of automated function, like a Script-Fu script) that changes a nontileable image into the tileable variety. What it actually does is displace the image by an amount equal to half the width and height of the image, so the center of the image is actually the point at which the original four corners now meet. What could be clearer than that?

Figure 3-34 *Fills can be made using a pattern.*

Figure 3-35 *A tiled pattern blends together seamlessly.*

A Better Explanation Could Be Clearer Than That

All right, Figure 3-36 may do a better job of explaining how a tileable image is created. At upper-left is the original image pattern, which measures 64 x 64 pixels. To make the image tileable, it has to be broken into four pieces, which are arranged so they match the corresponding piece of the tile above, below, and to either side (as you can see at upper-right). This is done by moving the image up and to the left by 32 pixels (half the height and width of the original) and wrapping the image around to the opposite edge (as you can see at bottom left). A tiled image is shown at right, with the individual tiles separated slightly so you can see how they fit together.

I thought you'd like to know how seamless tiles become seamless, but there is no need for you to worry about the details when using the GIMP; it includes a feature that automatically turns a pattern or background into a seamless image. When you've finished creating your image, right-click in the image, and choose Filters | Map | Make Seamless; the filter takes care of offsetting and blending your pattern for you. The last step is to save the tileable image to your *.gimp/patterns* directory using a *.pat* extension. Make your new pattern available by clicking Refresh in the Pattern Select dialog box.

Blending with the Gradient Fill Tool

The Gradient Fill tool operates much like the Bucket Fill tool; it has many cool options of its own. Double-click the Gradient Fill tool in the toolbox to produce the Blend Options dialog box (shown in Figure 3-37).

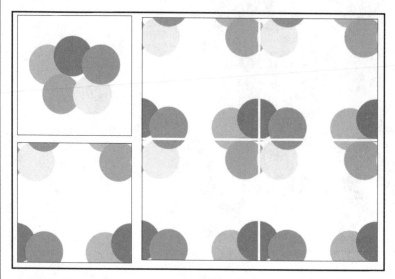

Figure 3-36 *Tiled patterns are created by offsetting the original image.*

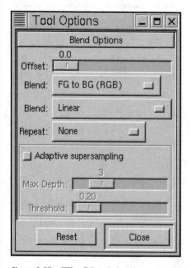

Figure 3-37 *The Blend Options dialog box has settings for the Gradient Fill tool.*

In the *Opacity* option, you can lower the value to increase the degree of transparency of the blend, that is, how much of the background image is allowed to show through. Or you can make the image more opaque.

The *Offset* option determines the smoothness of the blend. A low value provides a gradual, even transition from one color to the other. Higher values emphasize the foreground color, and provide a rougher transition. Note that the Offset slider has no effect on the Linear and Shapeburst blend styles (described next). Figure 3-38 shows two blends using lower and higher offsets.

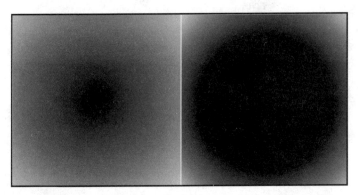

Figure 3-38 *Blend with a low offset (left) and a higher offset (right)*

Here are those pesky blending *Modes* again. You can play with them now or ignore them; for now I'm going to stick to explaining the Gradient Fill tool's basic features. The *Blend* list determines what colors the Gradient Fill tool uses to create its blend. You can choose FG to BG (foreground to background) in either RGB (red, green, blue), or HSV (hue, saturation value/brightness). You can choose FG to Transparent. You can use a custom set of multiple colors that you create from the GIMP's *Gradient Editor*. Choose from the following different gradient types (shown in Figure 3-39):

- Linear: A gradual transition from one color to the other, in a straight line.
- Bilinear: A transition from the background color to the foreground color, and then back to the background color.
- Radial: A transition from the foreground color in the middle of the selection to the background color around the edges.
- Square: Similar to the Radial gradient, but using a rectangular transition from the center of the selection outward.
- Conical: The symmetric and asymmetric provide a gradient as if viewed from above a shaded cone.
- Shapeburst: These gradients give selections a 3-D fill, either smooth and rounded (spherical) or sharper (angular or dimpled).
- Spiral: Both clockwise and counter-clockwise are available.

In the *Repeat* function, three repeating patterns are available for your gradient. You can choose from Sawtooth Wave, Triangular Wave, or None. Instead of stroking across the full selection when using this option, drag for a shorter distance. The shorter the distance, the more times the gradient will be repeated to fill the selection. This option has no effect on conical or shapeburst gradients. (Figure 3-40 shows the Repeat function in action.)

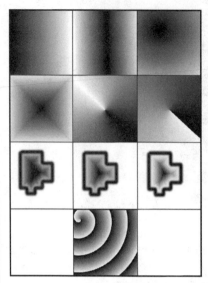

Figure 3-39　*Gradient types: Top row, Linear, Bilinear, Radial; Middle, Square, Conical (Symmetrical), Conical (Asymmetrical); Bottom, Shapeburst (Angular), Shapeburst (Spherical), Shapeburst (Dimpled), Spiral (clockwise)*

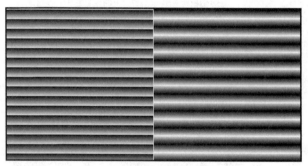

Figure 3-40　*Left, Sawtooth repeat; right, Triangular repeat*

Adaptive Supersampling is one last option, which may enhance the smoothness of a gradient, by adding intermediate colors that fall between the foreground and background colors. You can best understand this option by trying it out to see if you can notice the effect. (As the Vulcan philosopher Spock once observed, "A difference that makes no difference is no difference.")

What's Next

The GIMP's painting tools are one of the basic sets of utensils you must master to use this image editor effectively. Another essential tool is the ability to select portions of an image precisely, and that's what you'll look at in the next chapter.

o, selection services are *not* used to draft unwilling participants into the GIMP Guerrilla army. In truth, the GIMP's selection features are among the most powerful utensils in your image editing field kit, because they make it possible to work on only part of an image, rather than the whole thing. This chapter will arm you with knowledge so that you, too, can be selective when it comes to pushing pixels. Just look at all the things you can do with selections:

- Paint or fill selected areas with color or pattern, using all the painting tools in any of their available modes.
- Edit a selected area using any of the editing tools.
- Fill selections with the contents of other selected areas (e.g., pasting one image into another).
- Mask selected areas to prevent them from being changed.
- Apply a filter to a selected area.
- Edit a selection: scale its size, skew or distort its shape, change its perspective, flip it horizontally or vertically, rotate it, add to or subtract from it, and combine it with another selection.
- Save selections for later use.
- Convert selections to paths.

When you create a selection with the GIMP, you are essentially doing what airbrush artists do when they cut masks out of film. You define an area in which painting (or another process, such as applying a filter) can take place.

GIMP Selection Tools

The GIMP has six different selection tools, which you first learned about in the overview in Chapter 2. (See Figure 4-1.)

- The *Rectangular Select* tool creates selections that are rectangular or square, with their edges parallel to the edges of the image.
- The *Elliptical Select* tool creates elliptical or circular selections.
- The *Freehand Select* tool (also called the Lasso because of its icon) allows you to draw irregularly shaped selections around any part of the image.
- The *Fuzzy Select* tool, usually called the Magic Wand after its icon, selects a group of pixels based on how they compare to the pixels contiguous to the one you click on. You can use Fuzzy Select to select pixels of a certain color or tone.
- The *Bézier Select* tool (known as the Pen tool in Photoshop circles) lets you create selections based on curves and lines rather than individual pixels.

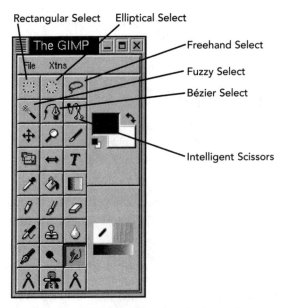

Figure 4-1 *The GIMP has these six selection tools.*

- The *Intelligent Scissors* tool is smart enough to find the edges of portions of your image; you can snip around as closely as you can to the selection you want, and the Intelligent Scissors will hug the edges.

When you create a selection, its border will be marked by a flashing dotted line called, variously, the *selection border* (not a very imaginative term), the *marquee* (a bit more daring), or *marching ants* (somebody must have worked too hard the day they came up with this one). The flashing marquee helps you see exactly what area of the image has been selected, but sometimes can obscure your view of the pixels you're trying to work on. To toggle the marquee on or off, press Ctrl-T. (This is one of those must-know keyboard shortcuts, because your alternative is to right-click on the image and choose Select | Toggle; that's about as convenient as having to open up a cover every time you want to turn a light switch on or off.)

You'll look at some other selection options shortly. Meanwhile, the best way to master these tools is to try them out and see how they work. The following exercises will put you on the fast track to selection proficiency.

Making Rectangular, Elliptical, and Freehand Selections

The easiest way to make rectangular, square, elliptical and circular selections is with the Rectangular Select and Elliptical Select tools. You can also make these shapes with the Freehand Select tool, but the dedicated tools are easier to use (and have added advantages, as you'll see). Create a new window at least 500 x 500 pixels to work with, and then try the following exercises. You'll create simple selections at first, and then look at how they can be added, subtracted, and otherwise modified. (See Figure 4-2.)

Creating a Rectangle or Square Selection

Rectangular selection tools are useful for choosing areas that are roughly rectangular in shape, and for selecting areas that you want to copy as a new image (since new images must be rectangular.) The GIMP's selection tools make choosing these areas as simple as dragging with the cursor.

1. Choose the Rectangular Select tool from the Toolbar. Position the mouse pointer in the window.
2. To create a square, press the Shift key, and hold it down as you drag.
3. Click and drag in a southeasterly direction to produce a rectangle. You will be creating a rectangular selection, which starts at the point you originally click, and proceeds down and to the right to the position of the mouse cursor when you release it. (You can also drag in other directions, using any combination of up/down and left/right.)

Creating an Ellipse or Circle Selection

Objects without sharp corners fit into elliptical and circular selections with less wasted space. Follow the following steps to learn how to use the GIMP's oval-oriented selection tools:

1. Choose the Elliptical Select tool from the Toolbar. Position the mouse pointer in the window.
2. To create a circle, press the Shift key, and hold it down as you drag.
3. Click and drag in any direction to produce an ellipse. One edge of the ellipse remains at the point where you clicked, and the opposite edge follows the mouse pointer as you drag.
4. Release the mouse button when the ellipse is the size and shape you want.

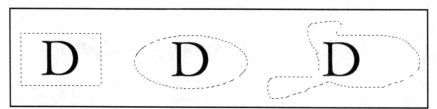

Figure 4-2 *You can select portions of an image in rectangular, elliptical, or freehand mode.*

Creating a Rectangular or Elliptical Selection Centered on a Point

You'll note that in both cases previously, one edge of the selection was placed where you first clicked with the mouse. You can also create a selection centered around the point where you click.

1. Choose either the Rectangular or Elliptical Select tools from the toolbar.
2. Hold down the Ctrl key, and click at the center point of the new selection.
3. Still holding down the Ctrl key, drag in any direction. The selection "grows" from the center point.
4. To create a circle or square centered on a point, drag while holding down both the Ctrl and Shift keys.

Drawing a Freehand Selection

Use of the Freehand Select tool is very straightforward. You might want to draw a figure, such as the star you created in the last chapter, to have something to select.

1. Choose the Freehand Select tool from the toolbar.
2. Position the mouse pointer at the place you want to begin drawing.
3. Drag around the object, following its outline as closely as you like.
4. To finish a selection, either draw back to the point where you began, or release the mouse button. In the latter case, the tool draws a straight line from the point where you release the button back to the origin.

Creating a Selection of a Fixed Size or Aspect Ratio

The GIMP allows you to make a rectangular or elliptical selection of a fixed size or proportion. If you want to select 40 x 50 pixel areas of one or more images repeatedly (say, to extract features that are always about the same size), you can "freeze" the selection at a particular size. Try this:

1. Double-click on either the Rectangular or Elliptical Select tools, to produce the Tool Options dialog box (shown in Figure 4-3).
2. Click the Fixed Size/Aspect Ratio button.
3. To fix a selection at a particular absolute size, click the Unit list and choose from pixels (px), inches, millimeters, or another value; then set the width and height in the Width and Height boxes. Selections will be locked into the exact dimensions you define.

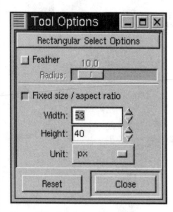

Figure 4-3 *Lock in selections to a particular size or aspect ratio.*

4. To fix a selection at a particular percentage of the image, click the Unit list and choose %. Then set the percentage of the window's width and height in the Width and Height boxes. Selections will then be created in a fixed size, in the relation to the window's width and height according to the values you set.

Making "Fuzzy" Selections

Often, you'll want a selection that is slightly fuzzy, either to provide a smooth transition from the selected object to the background it is pasted into, or to soften rough edges. Selections that gradually fade out are called *feathered*, while selections that have lines that are not diagonal or horizontal smoothed out are called *anti-aliased*. This section will help you get familiar with both types.

Creating Feathered Selections

Feathering can be applied to a selection border to soften the transition between the inside of the border and the background. With feathering, the pixels along the edge are gradually faded out into the background, producing an even smoother edge, although at the loss of some detail. Feathering can be added to any kind of selection. Feathered selections are a good choice when you want to blend an object in with its background. Figure 4-4 shows how feathered selections work.

At top left is a hard-edged circular selection that has been filled with black; at top right, the same selection has been feathered, using a value of 20 pixels, and then filled. Notice how the tone gradually fades out along the edges. At the bottom of the figure, you can see how feathered selections work with an actual image. At lower left is an image of a penny which was selected and copied using a hard-edged circular selection, then pasted down; at lower right is the same penny, copied using a fuzzy selection feathered with a 20-pixel setting. Notice how the image fades out.

Figure 4-4 *Feathered selections can help blend objects in with their backgrounds.*

The GIMP's Rectangular, Elliptical, Magic Wand, Freehand, Bézier, and Intelligent Scissors selection tools all can use feathering. (I'll describe the latter two specialized selection tools later in this chapter.) To see how this feature works, first double-click the tool's icon in the toolbar (to access the Tool Options dialog box); then mark the Feather checkbox, and choose a radius for the effect, from 0 pixels (which sort of defeats the purpose) to 100 pixels (which will blur your selection almost beyond recognition).

To see the difference between a feathered and nonfeathered selection, try this exercise:

1. Start with a clean white screen, using a white background color and black foreground color.

2. Double-click on the Rectangular Select tool to open the Tool Options palette. Make sure the Feather button is unchecked.

3. Select a square shape in the image, then use the Paint Bucket tool to fill it with color. You'll notice that the black fill is solid all the way to the crawling selection border.

4. Press Ctrl-Z to undo the fill, then Shift-Ctrl-A to get rid of the selection.

5. The Tool Options dialog box should still be open on your screen. Click the Feather button, and set the Radius slider to a value of 50.

6. Fill the selection using the Paint Bucket tool. You'll see that the fill doesn't have a hard edge, but feathers softly from inside the border to outside. Figure 4-5 shows the difference between the hard-edged and fuzzy-edged rectangles.

Figure 4-5 *Hard-edged (left) and fuzzy-edged (right) rectangles, produced by varying the feathering of the selection.*

The higher the number you set for a pixel radius, the larger the zone of feathering, and the softer, more blurred the effect. The zone of feathering is actually twice the pixel radius, as you saw in the enlargement. When you set a feather radius of 4 pixels, the border is actually feathered 4 pixels on the outside and 4 pixels on the inside, for a total border width of 8 pixels. The value of 50 that you used feathered the selection by 100 pixels.

Anti-Aliasing a Selection

Anti-aliasing is a process that smoothes the edge of a border by adding pixels of related, lighter tones that the eye can blend into a gradual transition. When you create an anti-aliased selection, the GIMP automatically smoothes out the pixels along the boundary of the selection. Straight lines in horizontal and vertical directions don't need to be anti-aliased, because whole pixels can be used to represent such lines with a sharp edge. Anti-aliasing works on lines that aren't at perfect right angles to an edge of the image, and for that reason, the feature is not available with the Rectangular Select tool.

You can turn anti-aliasing on or off by checking the Antialiasing box in a tool's Tool Options dialog box. (Figure 4-6 shows identical filled selections that were made both without and with anti-aliasing.)

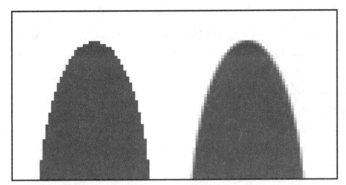

Figure 4-6 *Anti-aliasing (turned on in the example on the right) produces smoother edges in selections.*

Using the Fuzzy Select Tool

The Fuzzy Select tool selects all touching pixels that are similar in hue and value to the pixel you first clicked on. You tell the wand how choosy to be by setting its tolerance. Based on the tolerance set, the tool extends the selection outward until it finds no more pixels with the color values you want. If the tolerance is set to 40 and you click with the wand on a pixel that has a color value of 100, the Fuzzy Select tool will select all pixels with values between 60 and 140. (Both hue and luminance are figured into a special equation that determines which pixels the wand can and cannot select.) A high tolerance will select a wider range of pixels; a low tolerance will select a very narrow range of pixels. Figure 4-7 shows an example of a single image, with the water in the river selected using tolerances of (from left to right) 16, 24, and 32 pixels.

If you want to select a wide range of a color, from bright to dark, set the tolerance higher than the default (15) and then click the wand in the middle of the range of color values. If you click in an area of the color that is very dark or very light, you are giving the wand less latitude. (Remember, color values can range from 0 to 255.)

Figure 4-7 *River selected using tolerances of (left to right) 16, 24, and 32 pixels.*

A gradient is a good example of the simplest kind of area you can select with a Fuzzy Select tool. Try the following exercise to see how Fuzzy Select works. Create a blank image (the size doesn't matter), and fill it with a black-to-white gradient using the Gradient tool.

1. Double-click on the Fuzzy Select tool to open the Fuzzy Select Tool Options dialog box. Turn off Feathering and Antialiasing, and set the Threshold slider to 32, as shown in Figure 4-8.

2. Returning to the image window, click the Fuzzy Select tool once in the center of the gradient. Notice how pixels to the left and right of the point you click are selected.

3. Return to the Tool Options dialog box, and reset the Tolerance slider to 64. Then return to the image window and click in the center of the gradient once again. Notice how the number of pixels has doubled; changing the Tolerance value changes the range of pixels that the Fuzzy Select tool will grab. (Figure 4-9 shows the results you should have gotten.)

Fuzzy Select works like other selection tools: you can feather and anti-alias the selection, and click and drag to include more colors in the same range. Use Shift and Ctrl keys to add or subtract areas. In real life, you won't be selecting pixels from a gradient; instead, you'll be using Fuzzy Select to extract pixels from areas with similar color. (Figure 4-10 shows a typical selection.)

There is one selection tool not covered in this chapter. Select by Color works exclusively with the colors of the pixels, rather than with hue and brightness. I'll save that specialized tool for the discussion on photocompositing in Chapter 9 (in which you'll also use the Fuzzy Select capability extensively).

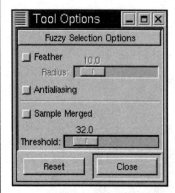

Figure 4-8 *Working with the Fuzzy Select Tool Options.*

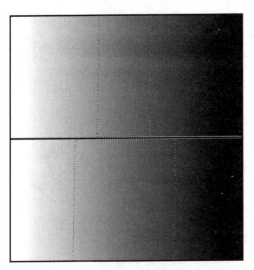

Figure 4-9 *Fuzzy Select is used to grab pixels based on their similarity to other surrounding pixels.*

Figure 4-10 *Fuzzy Select makes it easy to separate objects from their backgrounds.*

Making Selections with the Bézier Select Tool

If you have used an object-oriented illustration program, you will recognize the Bézier Select tool as a Bézier (Bez-ee-ay) curve-drawing device. With this tool, you can create lines and shapes that can be fine-tuned, saved as paths, filled with color or outlined (stroked), and used as the basis for selections. Conversely, you can change selections into paths, and edit them with the new Path tool added to the most recent version of the GIMP.

> The smallest part of a path is a segment—the line connecting two anchor points. Several segments, linked, make a subpath, and subpaths combine to form paths. A path can be a line or a closed shape or a series of lines, a series of shapes or a combination of lines and shapes. You can stroke and fill subpaths as well as paths.

Drawing Straight Lines with the Bézier Select Tool

If you're used to working with vector-based drawing programs, you'll be right at home with the Bézier Select tool. If not, you'll want to work with this exercise to get some practice:

1. Start with a white screen, black foreground color, white background.

2. Choose the Bézier Select tool. Click in the window to set an *anchor point* (so named because it will anchor one end of a line). Release the mouse button. Click again a distance away to create a second anchor point—a line will be drawn between the two.

3. Notice that a new anchor point is white as it is created, indicating that it is selected. At the same time, the previous anchor point darkens, meaning that it is deselected. Release the mouse button, and click to create a third anchor point and second line.

4. Release the mouse button, and move the pen on top of the first anchor point. A small square appears to the side of the Bézier Select cursor, letting you know that clicking will close the triangle. Click on the first anchor point to close the triangle.

5. Click inside the triangle to convert it to a selection.

Be certain that you do not drag the mouse as you create any of these lines. If you do, you will create curved lines, not straight-edged ones. (Figure 4-11 shows what your selection should look like.)

Drawing Curves with the Bézier Select Tool

Curves are what the Bézier Select Tool does best; you can shape smooth curves simply by dragging on the handles the tool creates.

1. Click the pen once in the window to create an anchor point.

2. Click at a second point to set the end point of the curve.

3. Holding down the mouse button, drag at an angle to shape the curve. As soon as you begin dragging, lines with new handles will appear.

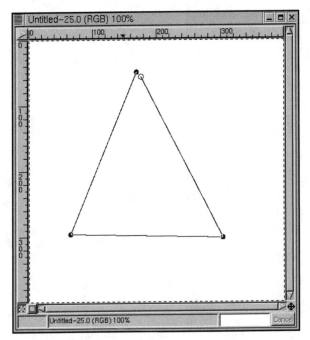

Figure 4-11 *A triangular selection made with Bézier Select*

> The lines that emerge as you drag are called direction lines. The slope of the curve is the same as the slope of its direction lines, and the height of the direction lines determines the height of the curve. There are two white boxes at the end of each direction line; these are direction points.

NOTE

4. When you have the curve shaped as you like, release the mouse button.

5. Position the cursor a short distance from the first line. Click, keeping the mouse button held down. A slightly curved line will form between the two anchor points.

6. Still holding the mouse button down, drag in a direction away from the first anchor point. This action will shape the curve connecting the two anchor points, making it more exaggerated.

7. Click on the first point you created. Another curve is formed, closing the figure. Click inside the shape to convert it to a selection. (Figure 4-12 shows the Bézier Select tool in action.)

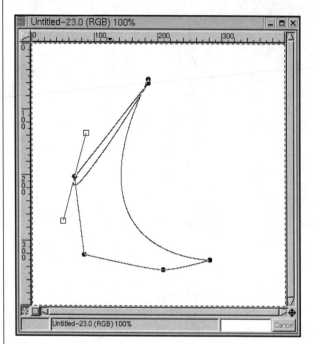

Figure 4-12 *Bézier Select lets you create selections from curves.*

The Bézier tool and the New Path tool (still under development at this writing) both take a lot of practice to master. To get that practice, I will have you use them in Chapter 9, and will introduce some options for fine-tuning (editing and adjusting) at that time.

Making Selections with Intelligent Scissors

The Intelligent Scissors can be a fast way of selecting areas that have a good contrast between adjoining areas. As you draw a selection, it "clings" to the edges of an image area, so you don't have to draw quite as precisely as you would with, say, the Freehand Select tool. Consider it a shortcut to use when you have a suitable image, and not as a replacement for the other selection tools. (Note that, as with the Bézier Select tool, you must click inside the shape you draw to convert it to a selection.) You can use the anti-aliasing and feathe ing settings common to the other selection tools, but Intelligent Scissors has some additional parameters; these include Curve Resolution, Edge Detect Threshold, and Elasticity.

The *Curve Resolution* slider controls the smoothness of the edge of the selection that the Intelligent Scissors produces. A high setting smoothes out the curves used to produce the selection; a low setting creates a more accurate selection that really hugs the

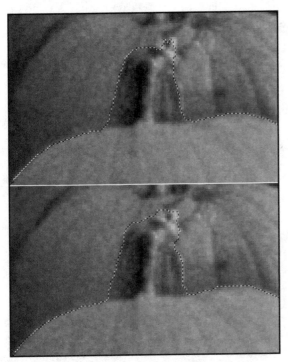

Figure 4-13 *Jaggier but more accurate selection (above) is contrasted with a smoother selection (bottom)*

edges of the image, but with more jaggy lines. If your image has many curves, you'll probably prefer the smoother effect. (Figure 4-13 shows selections made with both low and high curve resolution settings.)

The *Edge Detect Threshold* slider works like the Tolerance control used in the Fuzzy Select tool, and sets the range of colors that will be used to determine where an edge begins. A high value allows more colors to be included in the selection; a low value restricts the selection to a narrower range of hues.

The *Elasticity* slider sets how pliant the selection edge is. With high elasticity, the selection clings loosely to an edge, like a rubber band that is too large for the object it embraces. With a low elasticity setting, the selection will cling tightly to a distinct edge, like a tight rubber band.

Modifying Selections

Once you make a selection, you can modify it in various ways, to select areas more precisely or to fine-tune the selection. The GIMP provides quick techniques for changing a selection to better suit your needs.

Adding or Subtracting Selection Areas

You can add more area to a selection, remove areas you no longer want selected, and create selections based on where several selections overlap. Try these out on the sample image you created earlier.

- To select multiple areas of an image simultaneously, select the first area and release the mouse button. Then hold down the Shift key and select the next area. You can use the same selection tool or a different one. Repeat until all the areas you want are selected. (Figure 4-14 shows an image with multiple selections.)

- To extend the boundaries of a selection, hold down the Shift key and select the additional area, overlapping the original selection. You can use the same selection tool or a different one to add to your selection. You might want to use this capability to select an area that is almost rectangular, but with an extra piece or two sticking out. Figure 4-15 shows how a selection can be extended using the Shift key.

To make a tight-fitting selection around a child's drawing of a house, for example, you could select the lower part of the house with the Rectangular Select tool, then draw around the roof and chimney using the Freehand Select Tool.

- To remove some area from a selection you have already made, hold down the Ctrl key, and drag over the area you want to remove from the selection, using any selection tool. (Figure 4-16 shows a rectangular selection, with a circular section removed from it.)

Figure 4-14 *Holding down the Shift key lets you select multiple portions of an image.*

Figure 4-15 *The Shift key also allows extending the area of a selection.*

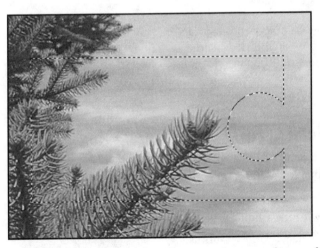

Figure 4-16 *Holding down the Ctrl key removes an area from a selection.*

- To create a selection based on the area where two selections overlap, make the first selection, then hold down the Ctrl and Shift keys, and drag a second selection. Only the area where the two coincide will end up in your selection (as you can see in Figure 4-17).

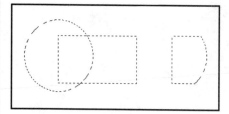

Figure 4-17   *Overlapping circular and rectangular selections (left) and the area produced by their intersection (right)*

Selecting All or None of an Image

You may want to select all of an image (as usual, by pressing Ctrl-A), say, to copy the whole thing to another window; at times, though, you may want to cancel a selection and start over. To deselect any selection at any time, press Shift-Ctrl-A or click any-where on the screen (with a Selection tool) outside the selection border. (If you click outside the border with another tool, this shortcut will not work.)

This technique works only on standard selections, but not on *floating* selec-tions (both described below); if you've moved a selection, turning it into a floating selection, you must *defloat* the selection to deselect it.

Inversing the Selection Border

Inversing reverses what is selected and not selected in the document window. This is an extremely handy technique for drawing on both the inside and outside of a selec-tion border. Try this:

1. Select an oval shape with the Elliptical tool.
2. Choose a paintbrush (select a large, soft brush size).
3. Paint just inside the selection border with a medium color, just to suggest the shape. (See Figure 4-18.)
4. Inverse the selection by pressing Ctrl-I (or by right-clicking in the image and choosing Select | Invert).
5. Change the brush to a darker color, and paint a shadow below the shape. You can still paint only inside the selection border, but by inverting the selection, you've made the inside become the outside (as shown in Figure 4-19).

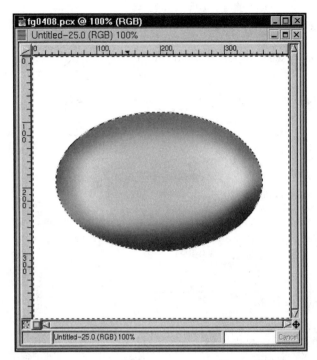

Figure 4-18 *You can paint only inside a selection border.*

Figure 4-19 *Inverting the selection lets you draw "outside" the previous selection border.*

Creating a Picture-Frame Border

The Border control allows you to select a bordering area around a selection border. (It's easier to show than to say.)

1. Make a rectangular shape with the Rectangular Select tool. Fill it with a solid color.

2. Right-click in the image and choose Select | Border.

3. When the Border Selection dialog box pops up, enter the width of the border you'd like to create (you can specify pixels or another unit of measurement), and click OK. (See Figure 4-20.)

You will have chosen a border around the inner rectangle. The border extends both inside and outside the previous selection border line. The Border control can be applied to any selection border, around an object of any shape.

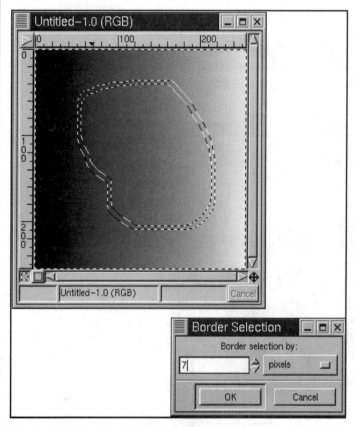

Figure 4-20   *The Border option lets you turn selections into a border.*

Modifying the Edges of Selections

Several other controls allow you to modify the edges of a selection. Some let you feather, sharpen, grow, or shrink the edges.

The *Feather* control is used to feather the edges of any selection, even if the selection was not feathered with a tool when it was created. Create a selection, right-click in the image, and choose Select | Feather. Type in the width of the feathering you want.

While the Feather control expands the edges of a selection as it blurs its border, the *Sharpen* control does the opposite: It creates a smaller selection with sharper edges. Create a selection, right-click in the image, and choose Select | Sharpen. Type in the width of the area around the selection you want sharpened.

Sometimes when you cut an anti-aliased image from one background and paste it into another, you'll see traces of the old background around the very edge of the selection. With the *Shrink* control, those offensive pixels are replaced with pixels that don't contain the background color. Its opposite number, *Grow*, can expand the selected area. Activate either by right-clicking on an image with a selection, and choosing Shrink or Grow from the Select menu.

Moving, Copying, and Cutting Selections

You can relocate a selection to a different part of your image, create clones by copying to another part of the image (or to a completely different image), or cut it to remove it from your image entirely. This section discusses the three options.

Moving Selections

You can move a selection and its contents. The GIMP has two different types of selections, standard and floating. A standard selection becomes part of your image. Any operation you carry out on the selection affects only the image area inside the selection.

Once you move a selection (place the cursor inside the selection, and drag) or right-click on the image and choose Float, it becomes a floating selection; in effect, the selected area is placed on a separate layer. You can move it around "above" the underlying layer. It continues to float until you cancel the selection, or until you right-click and choose Defloat. You can merge a floating selection with a particular layer by choosing Anchor layer from the Layers menu. (You'll learn how to use layers in Chapter 5.) Note that you can move a selection once by dragging with the mouse when a selection tool is activated; after you release the mouse button, you must use the Move tool to relocate it further.

Copying Selections

You can copy a selection in several ways. The simplest is just to press Ctrl-C (Copy) and Ctrl-V (Paste). In that case, the copy of the image would be pasted directly on top of the copied image, in place. You can move it to another location if you like. As long as you don't press Ctrl-C again (to copy a different selection), you can keep pressing Ctrl-V to paste down multiple copies of the selection.

The GIMP lets you paste down a selection inside another selection. You'll want to do this when you need to fit a selection inside a particular area. In that case, make the second selection, right-click in the image, and use Edit | Paste Into. (See Figure 4-21.) In this case I copied the pennies background, then created a selection in the shape of CENTS in a new image. Then, I chose Edit | Paste Into to paste the background down only inside the selection, producing a cookie-cutter effect.

Cutting Selections

To remove a selected area from an image entirely, press Ctrl-X. If you make a mistake, don't panic. The selection has been copied to the clipboard. As long as you haven't pressed Ctrl-X or Ctrl-C, you can press Ctrl-V to paste the cut image back down.

Using Quick Mask

One of the most sensational additions to the most recent version of the GIMP was the Quick Mask tool, similar to Quick Mask found in Photoshop. You can use this tool to paint your selections using any of the painting tools. So, if you find that the

Figure 4-21 *Use Paste Into when you want to put a selection inside another selection.*

Freehand Select or even Bézier Select tools are a bit too clumsy for your needs, Quick Mask can let you create very fine-tuned selections that are as detailed as you can paint.

Activate Quick Mask by clicking in the red-bordered square in the lower-left corner of an image window. When you click, the image changes to a transparent red. The transparent effect will show the area currently available for masking.

If you've worked in the graphic arts, you might remember RubyLith overlays. These were red acetate sheets that were transparent to the eye, but which blocked the kind of light that exposed graphic arts film. By laying a sheet over a page or an image, a worker could cut out the areas that should be exposed to light, making customized "windows."

Quick Mask works in the same way. You can erase portions of the mask to reveal parts of your image (in effect, selecting that part of the image), or use brush tools to cover parts you want to deselect. You can even use selection tools within Quick Mask, to select large areas and fill them with masking color, or to remove color. (Figure 4-22 shows an image being worked on with Quick Mask.)

To change the Quick Mask into a selection, click the Selection icon to the immediate left of the Quick Mask icon. If you double-click on the Quick Mask icon, you can change the opacity of the mask (from the default value of 50 percent), or you can

Figure 4-22 *Quick Mask lets you paint selections.*

choose a color other than red (which can be useful when you're working on a color image that already has a lot of red in it). Just click the color patch, and choose a new hue from the Color Selection dialog box.

Loading and Saving Selections

Selections are cool, right? So, what do you do if you want to reuse them? The most common scenario that you'll run into is when you painstakingly make a selection, copy the portion of the image, and then want to paste it down inside another selection. When you create a new selection in the same image window, the old selection is lost. While in some cases that won't matter, if you want to go back and use the original selection, you won't want to make the selection manually; save it and recall it later instead.

The GIMP allows you to save your selections so that you can use them later in a variety of ways, including copying them to other documents. Selections are saved in mask channels. (They are also commonly called Alpha Channels.) A mask channel is a special 8-bit image attached to the document. It contains only grayscale information: it can be all white, all black, or shades of gray in between (256 levels of gray are possible). In fact, a mask channel can be as simple as a white circle on a black screen, or it can have all the complexity of a grayscale photograph. We'll learn more about masks and channels in Chapter 5, but you can save a selection as a channel right now to get the basics down.

First, in a suitable image window, make a selection. Right-click in that window, then choose Select | Save to Channel. That's all there is to it. Now, if you want to know where your selection went, and how to retrieve it, just try the following steps:

1. Make a selection and save it, by right-clicking and choosing Select | Save to Channel.

2. Deselect the selection by pressing Shift-Ctrl-A, or by clicking outside the selection with a selection tool.

3. Right-click in the image, and choose Layers | Layers and Channels. Click the Channels tab, if necessary, to produce the dialog box shown in Figure 4-23.

4. You'll see at least four channels with an RGB image: one each for red, green, and blue colors, plus the channel you just saved, which will be named Selection Mask copy. Click in the selection channel to highlight it.

5. In the lower right of the dialog box, you'll see an icon that looks like the Elliptical Select tool. You can retrieve the selection by clicking this icon.

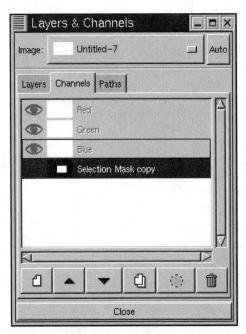

Figure 4-23 *You can save and restore selections that have been saved as channels.*

Here are some ways of manipulating the channel:

- Click to change the channel to an active selection.
- Shift-Click to add the channel to any current active selection.
- Ctrl-Click the icon to subtract the channel from any current active selection.
- Shift-Ctrl-Click the icon to intersect the channel with the current active selection.

The other icons in the dialog box let you create new channels, remove unwanted ones, duplicate channels, and move them up and down in a "stack." I'll save all the gory details on these channel operations for the next chapter.

What's Next

You'll need a lot more work with selections to become one of the Select Few, but I plan on giving you all the experience you need in the upcoming sections. You'll learn more about manipulating selection channels in Chapter 5, and put what you know to work in Chapter 9.

Chapter 5: Using Layers, Channels, and Masks

You got a gimpse…er, glimpse of what layers and channels were all about in the last chapter. Although they have some similarities, and both are accessed through the same GIMP dialog box, layers and channels (and the masks used with both) serve quite different purposes. It's time to clear up this topic, so to speak.

Layers: A Review

As you recall, layers can be thought of as transparent overlays, each containing part of an image. They can be stacked on top of each other in any order you like, placing some objects in front of or behind other objects. You can make layers visible or invisible, combine two or more layers into one, and *flatten* the image down to one layer when the image is finished. The GIMP will let you have as many layers in a single image as you like, but each layer takes up a significant amount of RAM. If your memory is scarce, you'll want to limit the layers in an image to a reasonable number. You need to understand four other key concepts to work with layers.

First, the GIMP's layers each can be a complete *full-color image* of its own if you're working with an RGB image. You could paste a picture of Big Ben in one layer, a rustic windmill in a second layer, and a background of clouds in a third, and then combine them in flexible ways. Each layer is in many ways like a separate document. (Figure 5-1 shows a representation of these three layers.)

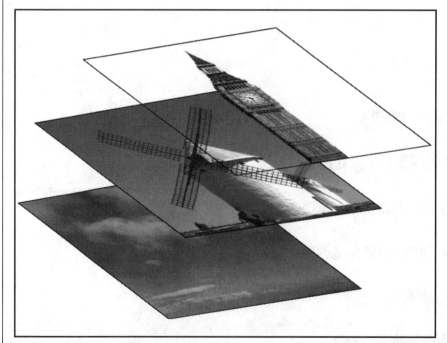

Figure 5-1 *Opaque and transparent layers can be stacked on one another.*

The next concept you need to understand is the idea of *transparency*. In that sense, layers are not like separate documents, since they aren't automatically filled with opaque white. A layer is transparent until you place something on it. Think of a white art board as the base or background of your document. You create that white art board background when you open the document using the File | New command. Layers, then, are a lot like transparent sheets of acetate that you lay on top of the background.

The next concept is *opacity*. When you draw something or paste an image on one of those transparent sheets, it covers up or obscures part of what lies underneath, either completely or partially, depending on whether the new image is fully opaque or somewhat transparent. When you create yet another new layer, it goes on top of the background and first transparent layer, perhaps obscuring part of what exists "below." The image of Big Ben in Figure 5-1 was created on a transparent background, so the windmill can be seen below it (as the composite image in Figure 5-2 shows).

Finally, the *order* of individual layers is the fourth concept you need to understand. As you work with layers, you may need to change the order in which layers are arranged. If you stacked the cloud layer on top of the windmill layer, none of the windmill could be seen. Your picture might look like Figure 5-3 instead.

Taking the idea a step further, you can erase everything in the windmill layer except for the foreground area, and place it on top of the cloud image, but below the layer with Big Ben. You end up with a composite like that shown in Figure 5-4.

Figure 5-2 *Transparent and opaque images can be combined to create a single image.*

Figure 5-3 *Changing the stacking order of layers moves some objects in front of others.*

As you can see, the GIMP lets you work with layers individually, save documents (in the GIMP format only) with the layers preserved, and even print out individual layers if you desire. When you are done working with a document, you "flatten" the layers together, merging them into a final, background-only image that is your finished

Figure 5-4 *Several layers can be composited together to form an entirely new image.*

work. Of course, there is nothing to keep you from saving the "final" version under a new name, keeping the layered document for additional manipulations later on. You can follow along with the following exercise to learn about the basic features of the Layers palette, using some of the files available at `www.dbusch.com/gimp`.

Creating and Editing Layers

As you practice creating and editing layers, you can work with your own image, or go to my Web site at `www.dbusch.com/gimp` and download a compact JPEG version of the same images I used, pennies.jpg and quarters.jpg. If you have a scanner, you can instead spread a few pennies and quarters around on the glass, and scan them in.

Creating, Deleting, Naming, and Duplicating Layers

First off, let's investigate how layers are created, removed, named, and copied.

1. Open the Pennies image file or the file you've chosen to work with.
2. Right-click on the image, and choose Layers | Layers & Channels from the pop-up menu. A dialog box like the one shown in Figure 5-5 appears.

The layer created by default appears in the scrolling window with the default name Background. The eyeball in the left column shows that the layer is currently visible, and the layer's dark background indicates that it is the active layer (the one on which any drawing or other manipulations take place).

NOTE

Every layer has an icon representing a thumbnail image of the information in that layer. You can change the size of this thumbnail. Choose Preferences from the File menu, and click on the Interface entry. In the General area, choose a small (the default), medium, or large Preview Size from the drop-down list.

TIP

---

3. Double-click the layer. The Edit Layer Attributes dialog box appears, and you can enter a new name, such as Pennies Background, for the layer.
4. Click the button at the lower left corner of the Layers & Channels window. This is the New Layer button, which produces the New Layer Options dialog box.
5. Call the layer Empty Layer, and check the Transparent box in the Layer Fill Type area. Click OK to produce the new, transparent layer. Notice that the new layer is now highlighted to indicate that it is active and ready for editing.

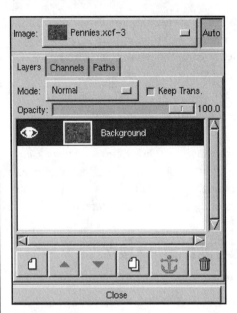

Figure 5-5 *The Layers & Channels dialog box*

6. Make the Pennies Background layer active once more, by clicking on it, and then click the button with the icon that looks like two overlapping pieces of paper. This is the Duplicate Layer button. (No dialog box appears.)

7. When you click the button, a duplicate of the active layer appears; by default, the duplicate's name consists of the active layer's name with the word **copy** appended, but you can rename the new layer if you like, by double-clicking on its name and retyping. (You'll often want to create a duplicate of a layer, so that you can work on the copy without changing the original version.)

To remove a layer, select the layer and click the trash can button (an X in earlier versions of the GIMP) in the button bar at the bottom of the Layers & Channels dialog box. You can also delete a layer by selecting it in the dialog box and pressing Ctrl-X. Or, you can right-click on a layer and choose Delete Layer.

Copying Objects onto Layers

One key to editing images is the ability to copy objects onto different layers so that you can manipulate them separately. Portions of images can easily be copied from one image to another. To use the copied images with your layers, you need to understand about floating selections.

Floating Selections

I didn't mention in the last chapter all the weird things that happen when you make and copy a selection, because I didn't want to scare you. (You'll understand the weirdness that I'm talking about if you happen to be familiar with Photoshop; the GIMP, though, treats selections in a slightly different way than the Adobe product does.) In any event, the discussion belongs here in the chapter on layers.

When you make a selection, it is "removed" from the layer where the selection was made (leaving a hole filled in with the current background color), and it "floats" above the layers of your image. Text that you enter becomes a floating selection, which behaves exactly like any other floating selection. (Photoshop used to work this way, too, but now by default places text in an editable layer that must be merged manually with an image.) See Figure 5-6.

You can move a selection anywhere in your image. It remains floating, and appears (labeled Floating Selection) in the Layers & Channels dialog box as if it were a layer itself. It automatically becomes the active layer, too, and the other layers are grayed out and inaccessible. (This is different from Photoshop, which does not make a selection visible in its Layers palette as if it were a layer.) As you can see at left in Figure 5-7, the floating selection's layer is placed on top of all the other layers in your image. If you like, you can download the XCF format image from my Web site and work with this same image.

Figure 5-6 *When a selection is moved, an empty space filled with the background color is left behind.*

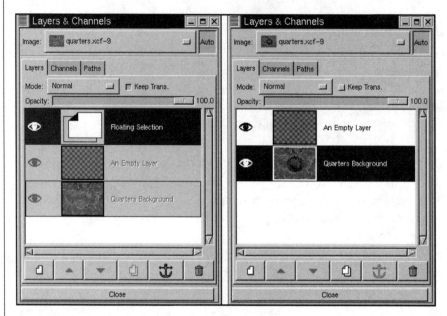

Figure 5-7 *Selections float on top of the other layers.*

When you deselect it, the floating selection merges back with the original layer where the selection was made, even if the target layer is several layers "below" the selection in the dialog box. Deselect a floating selection by clicking outside the selection when a selection tool is active, or by clicking the Anchor button in the Layers & Channels dialog box. (At right in Figure 5-7, you can see how the floating selection merges with the original layer.)

When you paste an object down, it too becomes a floating selection. Make active the layer you want to paste the object into, by clicking it in the Layers & Channels dialog, then paste. When you defloat the selection, it will merge with the layer you had selected. If you'd rather place the selection on a new layer of its own, double-click in the Floating Selection layer in the Layers & Channels dialog box *before* you defloat the selection, and give it a name. If you've gotten confused, try the exercise in the Pasting a Selection subsection, which follows.

When you click in the column between the "eyeball" and the thumbnail, a four-headed arrow appears. That indicates that the layer so marked is linked to the visible layer. If you move the visible layer, any linked layers will move, too, until you unlink them by clicking in the column again.

Pasting a Selection

Next, let's work on pasting the selection down into a layer.

1. Make a circular selection, as you learned in Chapter 4. Use it to select one of the pennies in the pennies.jpg image.

2. Copy the penny by pressing Ctrl-C.

3. Open the image quarters.jpg, or use another image that contrasts with the one you chose to work with first.

4. Press Ctrl-V to paste down the penny image on top of the quarters background.

5. Open the Layers & Channels dialog box if it isn't still visible on your screen. The penny image you pasted will be labeled Floating Selection.

6. Double-click the floating selection's layer, and rename it Penny1. (Your image should now look like Figure 5-8.)

Resizing Image Layers

Let's continue with the same image to create a cool effect and to learn more about working with layers. Use the quarters.jpg file with the penny pasted into it that you created in the last exercise. In this next exercise, you're going to learn an important thing about the GIMP's layers: each layer can be a different size (whereas in Photoshop, all the layers in an image are the size of the image). That is, if your overall

Figure 5-8 *The image with the penny pasted into a new layer*

image measures 400 x 400 pixels and you paste a 200 x 183-pixel object into a new layer, that layer actually measures only 200 x 183 pixels, as you can see in Figure 5-9. When the layer is active, a box appears around it showing the actual size of the layer relative to the entire image. This exercise will show you how to resize the boundaries of a layer (not the image itself, but only the layer that contains it).

1. Select and duplicate the Penny1 layer.

2. The new layer is the exact size of the penny you pasted down; you need to make it larger, because you're going to blur the image, making the edges extend out into an area beyond the current boundaries of the layer. Right-click on the layer (not the image window) and choose Resize Layer. Notice that the menus that pop up are slightly different when you right-click on the layer in the Layers & Channels dialog box, than when you right-click on the image itself.

3. In the dialog box, add 100 pixels to the height and width shown. The exact value doesn't matter, as long as you make the layer at least 10 percent bigger, in both directions, than it was before. The original layer image is moved to the upper-left corner of the new layer, as shown in the preview box at the bottom of the dialog. (See Figure 5-10.)

4. Center the original layer by typing in X and Y offset values that are half the amount you added (for example, 50 pixels if you added 100 to each dimension). The GIMP moves the image down by the number of pixels specified as the Y offset, and to the right by the number of pixels specified as the X offset.

5. Click OK to resize the layer.

6. Make sure that the Keep Transparent box is not marked in the Layers & Channels dialog box. Right-click the image, and choose Filters | Blur | Gaussian Blur IIR. In the dialog box that appears, type **30** as the value for the blurring to be applied. Both the Blur Horizontally and Blur Vertically buttons should be checked.

Figure 5-9 *The box around the penny represents the actual size of the layer the penny is in.*

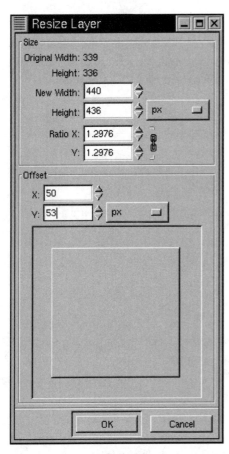

Figure 5-10 *Offset an image to center it in the resized layer.*

7. Now check the Keep Transparent box, and then press Ctrl-A to select everything in the layer.

8. Use the Paintbucket tool to fill the layer with black. Notice that because the Keep Transparent box was checked, only the blurry penny's image area is actually filled; the rest of the layer remains transparent. (You'll want to use the Keep Transparent option any time that you want to apply a coloring effect only to the image area of a layer.) You now have a blurry, black "shadow" of a penny, which you will make more realistic in the next exercise.

Stacking Layers and Changing Opacity

If you used the duplicated copy of the penny layer, your dark shadow is now on top of the layer with the original penny. You need to move it so it is underneath the penny, as a good shadow should be.

1. Click the layer containing the shadow, if it isn't already active.

2. Holding down the mouse button, drag the layer downward in the layers list, so that it is immediately under the original penny layer. Alternatively, you can click the up and down arrows in the button bar at the bottom of the Layers & Channels dialog box.

3. Now use the Move tool to move the shadow layer up and to the left slightly. The shadow is a bit too dark, so move the Opacity slider to 50 percent, making the shadow semi-transparent.

4. To make the image even more interesting, make additional copies of the penny, and give each of them a shadow too.

5. Flatten the image, so that all the layers are merged into a single image: right-click in one of the layers, and choose Flatten Image. (My final image looks like Figure 5-11.)

Other Basic Layer Functions

- The *Merge Visible* option (similar to its counterpart in Photoshop) combines all of the layers that are marked with the eyeball icon; that is, you can see them on the screen. It's especially useful when you're working with multiple layers and then want to join some of them into a single layer.

Suppose that you have been working on several image components of a building, and now want to merge them into an image of the completed edifice. Make all the other layers invisible, then right-click in the image and choose Layers | Merge Visible Layers, or right-click in the Layers & Channels dialog box and choose Merge Visible Layers, or simply press Ctrl-M.

Figure 5-11 *Finished image with multiple floating pennies*

- Any time that you merge visible layers, a small Layer Merge Options dialog box appears with three sub-options. The *Expand as Necessary* sub-option makes the merged layer large enough to include all the component layers; that is, as large as the largest layer you are merging. The *Clipped to Image* sub-option removes any areas outside the merged image area, making the final layer the same size as the merged image. The *Clipped to Bottom Layer* sub-option makes the merged layer the same size as the bottom layer of the layers being merged.

Figure 5-12 deserves some explaining. At upper-left is an image with three visible layers; here, the outlines of the layers for all three are visible (ordinarily, only the outline for the active layer could be seen). At right is the result when all three layers are merged; the size of the layer is just big enough to encompass all three. At bottom is an example of the merged layers that have been clipped to the size of the bottom layer (which in this case was the layer containing the "tree branches").

NOTE

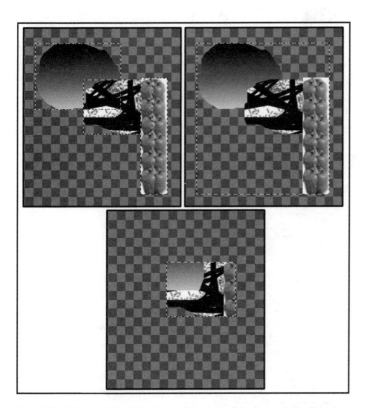

Figure 5-12 *Upper-left, three-layered image with sizes of all of the layers visible; upper-right, layers merged into one, expanded to include all of the image area; bottom, layers merged, but clipped to the image area of the bottom layer.*

- You may want to merge a layer only with the layer beneath it. You can do this by highlighting the upper layer, then right-clicking in the Layers & Channels dialog and choosing Merge Down, or simply by pressing Shift-Ctrl-M.

- You've already used the Flatten Image capability. You must flatten an image before you can save it in a format other than .xcf. If you think you'll want to work on an image later, save both an .xcf copy and a version in your target format.

- Advanced users can get some extra precision in lining up their layers by using the Align Visible Layers dialog box, right-clicking on the image, and then choosing this option from the Layers menu. You can elect to align all the visible layers by t/p or side edges, and use other parameters to align them automatically.

  The Layers menu also has choices for centering a layer within the boundaries of the image size, and filling the image area with a particular layer. (See Figure 5-13.)

Creating a Layer Mask

You can modify how a layer is combined with other layers by creating a separate layer that masks off part of an image, as if it were a stencil. Not surprisingly, this tool is called a layer mask. Like a stencil, a layer mask hides the portion of the layer it covers; unlike a stencil, though, a layer mask doesn't have to be pure black with transparent openings.

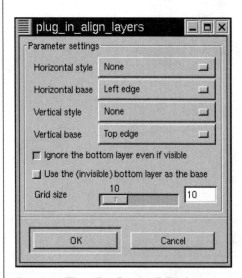

Figure 5-13 *The Align Layers dialog box*

Instead, a layer mask can contain black areas (completely transparent), white areas (completely opaque), and various shades of gray (which are translucent). So, a layer mask can be a gradient or have other shades of gray, to mask different portions of an image to differing extents. To see how this works, follow these steps, using any file with a background layer and an object pasted into a separate layer.

1. Load or create an image like the one you worked with earlier in this chapter, with a background consisting of quarters, and a transparent layer above with an image of a penny floating on it. With both layers visible, the image will look like Figure 5-14.

2. Right-click in the quarters background layer and choose Add Layer Mask from the menu; the Add Mask Options dialog box will appear. Choose White (Full Opacity) as the option. The background layer now has a fully opaque mask, meaning that the quarters layer itself has no transparency. The mask is shown by a new, all-white thumbnail image that appears to the right of the layer's original thumbnail.

3. You can switch back and forth between editing the layer itself and its layer mask by clicking in either the layer thumbnail or the layer mask thumbnail. Make sure the layer mask is active, by clicking in its thumbnail.

4. Using the default black and white foreground and background colors, apply a white-to-black gradient to the layer mask; apply it from the bottom of the image to the top. The layer mask thumbnail will change to show the new gradient as dark on the bottom and white at the top. At the same time, the image of the background changes: the background layer is now fully opaque

Figure 5-14 *Existing layer with layer mask applied*

only at the top (white) of the gradient, and fully transparent at the bottom (black). Under the transparent parts of the image, the checkerboard pattern that the GIMP uses to represent transparency should be visible, as in Figure 5-15.

5. Apply the mask to the layer, by right-clicking the layer in the Layers & Channels palette and choosing Apply Layer Mask. Click Apply in the dialog box that appears.

6. Flatten the image, by right-clicking within it and choosing Layers | Flatten Image, to produce the final version shown in Figure 5-16.

Figure 5-15 *Checkerboard pattern visible under the layer mask*

Figure 5-16 *Flattened image with layer mask applied*

Creating a Layer Mask in a New Layer

You can also create a new layer, and use that as a layer mask to hide or reveal parts of the layers underneath it, by following these steps:

1. Open the same image as the one you used in the last exercise: a penny layer on top of a background layer consisting of quarters.

2. Right-click in the pennies layer and choose New Layer. Select white as the new layer's background color. Notice that the new white layer totally obscures the layers underneath.

3. Right-click in the new layer and choose Add Layer Mask. Click in the layer mask thumbnail to make it active.

4. In the Layers and Channels dialog box, move the Opacity slider to about 75 percent. You'll be able to see the underlying layers again as a "ghost" image.

5. Using a textured brush and black paint, create an outline or design on the layer mask, revealing a portion of the image underneath, as shown in Figure 5-17.

6. Make the mask layer opaque again. Only the portions that you've painted on the mask will allow the underlying layers to show through, as you can see in Figure 5-18.

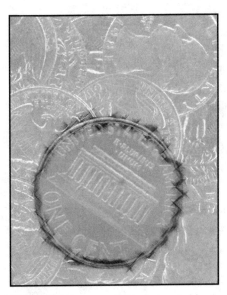

Figure 5-17 *A layer mask can be created in a new layer.*

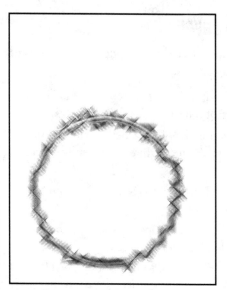

Figure 5-18   *Final flattened image*

Working with Channels

Every image layer is composed of channels. For example, an RGB image is composed of three color channels, plus any additional channels you add. Those extra channels, often called alpha or mask channels, are 8-bit grayscale images in which selections (masks) are stored. Each of these additional channels adds to the size of your overall file. Each channel is in perfect registration with every other channel—all channels for a particular layer have the same size and resolution.

Alpha channels can operate much like the layer masks you worked with earlier in this chapter. A *masked* area is an area that you cannot paint on, edit, filter, or manipulate in any way. A masked area is protected by a mask, which, by default, is represented by the black area in the channel.

A *selected* area is an area that you can paint on, edit, fill, filter, flip, or rotate, or one to which you can apply effects. A selection, by default, is represented by the white area in the channel.

Viewing Color Channels

Open any RGB color image, right-click in the image, and choose Layers | Layers & Channels to produce the familiar dialog box. Click on the Channels tab. You'll view something like what is shown in Figure 5-19.

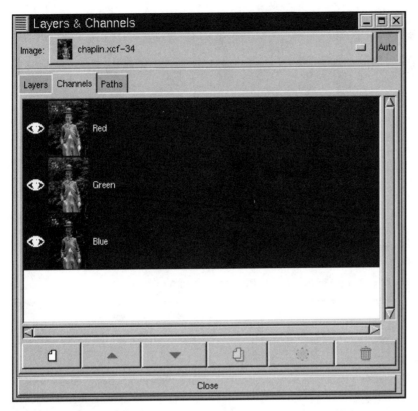

Figure 5-19 *RGB channels*

Notice that there are three channels (which look rather like layers), one each for the red, green, and blue components of the image. Each channel has a grayscale image (with brightness values ranging from 0 to 255, as with any grayscale image) that represents how much of a color is included in that channel. For example, the red channel will be very light in areas where there is a lot of red, and very dark in areas where there is little red; the same is true of the green and blue channels. Because a channel need not contain pure red, pure green, or pure blue, it will appear to be a grayscale image ranging from a strong amount of a color (white) through medium tones (gray) to none of that color at all (black).

Channels have eyeball icons that you can switch on and off, just like layers. Using them, you can view any one channel or any combination of them. Figure 5-20 shows what the red, green, and blue channels of a typical image look like when viewed alone.

Figure 5-20 *Left to right: red, green, and blue channels*

You can manipulate images by changing the brightness and contrast of the RGB channels, and you might want to do so for special effects, but for most GIMP users, there is little need to fiddle with the color channels.

Working with Alpha Channels

Alpha channels are your way of working directly with selections. Alpha channels are grayscale images. Like the color channels, they use values ranging from 0 to 255. However, the grayscale values don't represent the amount of a particular color, as with the RGB channels. With alpha channels, the grayscale represents the degree of transparency of a particular pixel. A pixel with a value of 0 is completely transparent, while one with a value of 255 is completely opaque. This means that alpha channels operate like the masks you used earlier in this chapter, and like the selections you worked with in Chapter 4. In fact, every selection you make can be represented by an alpha channel. Try this exercise to see what I mean.

1. Open any image and make a feathered selection, as you learned to do in Chapter 4.

2. Right-click on the selection in the image window, and choose Select | Save to Channel.

3. Open the Layers & Channels dialog box, and click the Channels tab. The selection you've saved appears as an alpha channel, as shown in Figure 5-21.

4. Click in your image outside your selection, so that the selection vanishes.

5. Go back to the Channels tab, and right-click on the alpha channel you just created. Choose Channel to Selection (you can also click the Channel to Selection button in the button bar, at the bottom of the dialog box); your original selection appears again in the image window. You can save multiple selections as channels, and recall them at any time with a click.

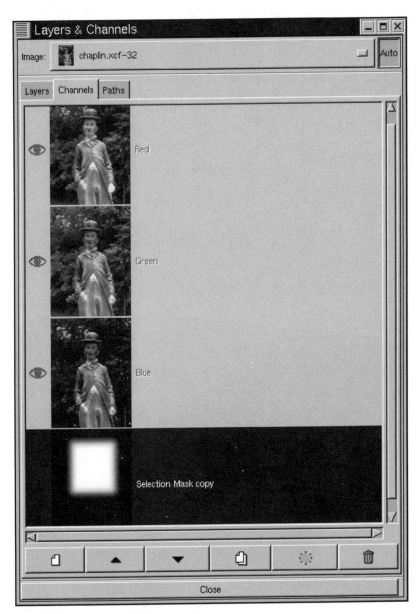

Figure 5-21 *Selections are actually alpha channels.*

What's Next

The discussion of color channels has broached the topic of how colors are created and manipulated. There's nothing worse than a topic that's been broached to death. So, in the next chapter, you'll look at how color works and what the GIMP does with it.

Chapter 6: Introduction to Color

ovies and magazines rarely used color until the middle of the 20th century. It must have been bleak indeed in the stark black-and-white world of Charlie Chaplin and Life Magazine. In the media, at least, there wasn't a lot of color to be seen for an extended period of time.

Today, technology has finally caught up with the spectrum, and color is all around us. The GIMP is your first line of offense for tweaking, enhancing, and transforming the colors of your images. This chapter will explain what you need to know about color from a digital standpoint, so you can work more easily with your photographs, Web graphics, and other images.

What's "Good" Color

Anyone who's tried to select a sofa knows that good color is a deeply subjective thing, residing very much in the eye of the beholder, reflecting both the intended purpose of the color image and the pattern in the purchaser's drapery. Good color doesn't necessarily mean accurate color by any means. If you snapped a photo of a fall landscape on an overcast day, the sky and foliage would probably look dull and lifeless. Instead of an accurate portrayal of what you saw that day, you'd probably welcome a richer, more saturated image: one with vibrant greens, glowing reds, and resonant blues that corresponded to the ideal colors for such a scenic view.

On the other hand, if you were reproducing a photo for advertising purposes (say, a picture of some articles of clothing), you'd want the colors to represent the appearance of the product very closely. In this case, an idealized image could be the same as false advertising. In the same vein, photographs of a painting and images that use a corporation's trade dress colors (e.g., Kodak yellow, IBM blue) must meet exacting specifications.

When it comes to human faces, color rendition is even more complicated, because while we all have a firm picture in our minds of how human flesh should appear, our brains allow a surprising amount of latitude. A face rendered with more red or more magenta than is present in real life may look healthy and flattering to the subject; however, even a tiny amount of blue or green cast can add a deathly pallor to a portrait.

Good color can involve technological considerations, too. If an image will be used on a Web page, shown as an overhead projection slide, printed in a magazine, transferred to video, or used in any of a myriad of other display mediums, the way that color is represented can be important. The phosphors in computer displays and televisions don't show all colors in the same way, and magazine reproduction can vary even more widely.

You're going to look at how color is produced before moving on, in the next chapter, to studying how it can be fine-tuned. I'll explain how the most common color models differ, and give you a sense of how they can affect your scanner, video display, and printer.

How Colors Are Produced

You probably dimly remember that stuff from grade school about rods and cones and retinas, and perhaps you also learned early on about the importance of cleaning your eyeglasses or contact lenses. That's all that many of us remember about how human vision works. If your computer geekdom was preceded by a more broad-based scientific nerdship, you may remember even more, such as the fact that our eyes are able to detect only a relatively narrow band of wavelengths of light. These range from 400 nanometers (4 ten-millionths of an inch) at the short (violet) end of the visible spectrum to 700 nanometers (7 ten-millionths of an inch) at the long (red) end. You see certain frequencies as violet/blue, while longer wavelengths are perceived as red. All the colors in between have wavelengths that are shorter than red, but longer than blue—a continuous spectrum of hues.

However, humans don't really see a continuous spectrum of color. We have three different types of cone cells in our eyes, each of which respond to different wavelengths of light—red, green, and blue. Our brains combine the three colors into the near-infinite combination we think we see. All color systems, from computer monitors through the printing press, try to reproduce those three combinations of colors, using different kinds of technology. Just keep in mind that the RGB basis for our sight is the key component of every different way of representing color—the so-called *color models*. If we happened to possess cells that were individually sensitive to yellow, purple, and blue-green, computer color systems would probably be based on that model.

The colors that can be represented by a model constitute its *color space*. The color space is defined by three different parameters; you can plot it using x, y, and z coordinates as a three-dimensional *color gamut*, or range of colors. Note, though, that a color gamut isn't a continuous spectrum of colors; every color model has gaps and shortcomings, and individual colors that it can't represent.

> There is one scientific model that can define all the colors that humans see; it was defined in 1931 by the CIE (*Commission International de l'Eclairage*). It isn't used by computers, because the hardware you use isn't up to the task. Like computers, printing presses and color printers and other devices still use one of several other color models, which are more practical, in that they have been developed around the limitations of the hardware to be used for color reproduction.

NOTE

A simple way to envision color is through a color wheel. The color wheel places each of the primary colors at points of a triangle, with the nominal intermediate colors halfway between them. Colors directly opposite each other are known as complements; that is, the complement of blue is yellow, and vice versa. This representation is impossibly simplified, in that it includes only pure colors; actual colors can be bright or dark, saturated or unsaturated, or some combination. (Notice that I didn't say which are the primary colors and which are secondary; you'll learn why in the sections that follow.) See Figure 6-1 and the color insert of this book.

Additive Color

The primary colors of light are red, green, and blue; for us to perceive color, beams of light (or waves/particles of light, in case you're heavy into quantum electrodynamics) must reach our eyes and be separated into those red, green, and blue colors. One way to generate color is to use rays of colored light, generated by a light source such as a color television or computer display screen. Color monitors produce color by aiming three electronic guns at sets of red, green, and blue phosphors (compounds which give off photons when struck by beams of electrons), coated on the screen of your display. The guns excite the phosphors in proportion to the amount of red, green, or blue light in a given pixel of the image.

The phosphors glow, and your eyes add their illumination together, perceiving a color image. If none of the phosphors glows, you see a black pixel. If all three glow in equal proportions, you see a neutral color—gray or white, depending on the intensity.

To produce a pure red, green, or blue color, those hues of light can be used alone. Colors other than black, gray, or white result when the red, green, and blue phosphors are used in uneven amounts. Mixing red and blue together produces magenta, blue-green is called cyan, and red and green mixed together produce yellow (strange but true). Because these colors are added together, they are referred to as the additive primary colors of light. This color model is known as RGB. You've probably seen diagrams with the overlapping circles (as shown in Figure 6-2 and in the color insert), which are meant to represent the colors of the RGB model.

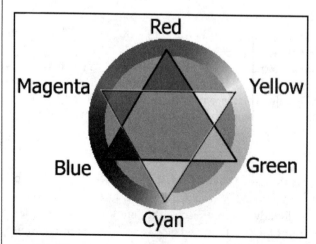

Figure 6-1 *The color wheel*

Figure 6-2 *The additive color model*

The largest circles represent beams of light in red, green, and blue. Where the beams overlap, they produce other colors. For example, red and green combine to produce yellow. Red and blue add up to magenta, and green and blue produce cyan. The center portion, in which all three colors overlap, is black.

Unfortunately, no light source or electron gun, or other light-dispensing gadget (other than lasers) can emit pure red, green, or blue light. The purity of the color you view on your computer monitor is determined by the accuracy of the three colors produced. For that reason, color representations of a monitor differ from brand to brand and even among displays within the same brand. In addition, the characteristics of a monitor can vary as it ages; the phosphors in a monitor can "wear out," so even if an image editor supplies exact color information, it's likely to appear differently on different monitors, or even the same monitor, at different times.

Subtractive Color

Although color starts with beams of light, sometimes that light doesn't take a direct route to our eyes. The illumination may strike a surface, such as a printed sheet of paper, which absorbs part of the light and reflects the rest back to our eyes. Indeed, pigments and inks work quite differently than beams of colored light in their effect on color vision.

Pure red pigment reflects only red light, and absorbs blue and green. Green pigment reflects only green light and absorbs red and blue. Can you see what happens when pigments overlap? Superimpose red pigment on top of green, and the red absorbs the green (and blue), and the green absorbs the red (and blue). The net result is that all colors are absorbed, and nothing reaches your eyes. You see black.

Because pigments subtract colors from the light that reflects from them, this type of color is called *subtractive color*. So, when you add red and blue beams of light, you get magenta. When you add red and blue pigments, you get black. How is it possible to see printed colors at all? The answer is that the subtractive color model uses a different set of primary colors: cyan, magenta and yellow. These work much better for reproducing color, as each subtractive primary absorbs only one of the additive primary colors, and reflects the other two back.

For example, magenta ink on a white piece of paper absorbs some green light, reflecting the red and blue, and producing the magenta color that you see. Similarly, yellow ink absorbs blue light, and reflects both red and green, producing a yellow color. Cyan ink absorbs red light, and reflects blue and green to produce red. In each of these simplified cases, one RGB primary color is subtracted, and you see the color produced by the two that remain in the reflected light. (Figure 6-3 and the color insert show a simplified rendition of this model.)

As with the additive color model, real-world imperfections mean that mixtures of the three colors (in the form of ink, toner, or pigment) don't always produce the color you

Figure 6-3 *The subtractive color model*

expect. Equal amounts of cyan, magenta, and yellow ink usually generate a muddy brown rather than a true gray or black. This imperfect black is often called composite black, because it is produced using nothing but the composite of cyan, magenta, and yellow pigments.

So, printers use a fourth color, black, to fill in the neutral color missing when the subtractive colors are combined. The black pigment can replace equal amounts of the other three colors, to produce the same effect with less ink and at a lower cost. This is especially true in the case of portions of an image that are usually nothing but black, such as text. Because "b" has already been applied to the RGB primary color blue, black is represented by its terminal letter ("k"), and the color model is known as CMYK. While the GIMP doesn't work with CMYK images at present, you need to understand this color model to work effectively with images intended for reproduction.

Other Color Models

Other color models that have been developed include HSB (*hue-saturation-brightness*), HLS (*hue-lightness-saturation*), and HSV (*hue-lightness-value*). You'll see HSV represented in the GIMP's Color Selection dialogs. You'll also find references to LAB color.

> The LAB scheme was developed by the CIE as a device-independent, international standard. LAB colors look exactly the same when output to different, but correctly calibrated, monitors and printers. The LAB acronym comes from the three channels used to represent all colors in this model; the L channel is used to refer to luminance, while the A and B channels represent the colors from green to magenta and blue to yellow, respectively.

NOTE

Just when you've learned the basics about hue, saturation and brightness, someone throws the term *gamma* at you! What is gamma, anyway? Gamma correction is needed because any hardware system used to reproduce colors, particularly color monitors, won't respond to colors in a linear way.

That is, given 256 shades of a particular color, a value of 0 should represent no color, 64 should represent 25 percent intensity, 128 should represent 50 percent intensity, and so forth. However, in real life, this linear scale doesn't apply. You'll quickly find that a value of 64 isn't precisely half of 128; it is some other percentage. The relationship of the actual representation to the ideal is known as a gamma curve.

Scanners do happen to approach the ideal rather closely, but CRTs and printers tend to vary. If you know the gamma curve of a particular device, however, you can correct it. For example, if you know that, with a certain device, a value of 64 produces an intensity that is only 90 percent of what it should be on a linear scale, you can boost that value by an appropriate amount whenever it occurs. This can be done if a gamma correction table has been built in that includes a value for each of the levels used in a system; the correction values can be automatically substituted by your software for the default values, theoretically producing a perfect 45 degree gamma curve. If highly accurate colors are important to you, you'll want to check out third-party calibration and gamma correction routines that let you calibrate your monitor with a great deal of precision.

Understanding Color Correction

Given a calibrated system, you should be able to do a fairly good job of correcting colors in your images using the GIMP. This process is called, logically, color correction. I'll get into the nuts and bolts of color correction in the next chapter. For now, I'll just cover the basics.

Color rendition is the relationship between the colors (usually red, green, and blue) used to produce an image. You need to worry only about three factors. These are the balance between the colors (is the image too red or too cyan, for example), the purity or saturation of the colors, and their relative darkness or lightness.

Color Balance

Color balance is the easiest to understand. If you have too much red, an image will appear too red. If you have too much green, it will look too green. Extra blue gives an image a frigid look. Too much of two of the primary additive colors will produce other kinds of color casts; too much red and green will produce a yellowish bias, combining red and blue tilts things toward magenta, and mixing blue and green creates a cyan cast.

Saturation

The saturation of each color identifies how much of the hue is composed of the pure color itself, and how much is diluted by a neutral color, such as white or black. Think of a can of red paint and white paint. Pure red paint is fully saturated. As you add white paint, the color becomes less saturated, until you reach various shades of pink. You can also desaturate color by adding black paint, making it darker. (The GIMP can help you adjust the saturation of a color by removing these neutral white or black components.)

Brightness and Contrast

Brightness and contrast refer to the relative lightness/darkness of each color and the number of different tones available. If, say, there are only 12 different red tones in an image, ranging from very light to very dark, with only a few tones in between, then the red portion of the image can be said to have a high contrast. The brightness is determined by whether the available tones are clustered at the denser or lighter areas of the image. Pros use something called histograms (which I will discuss in the next chapter) to represent these relationships.

What Causes Bad Color

Why do you even encounter images that need correction in the first place? The major sources of bad color are discussed in the following sections.

Misbalanced Light Sources

Most films are intended for shooting in daylight, and are balanced for the bluish light found outdoors. If you shoot those films under reddish indoor illumination, your pictures may have a red cast. Fluorescent light sources introduce their own color problems, because the light they emit doesn't necessarily have a continuous spectrum. Some types of fluorescents have "gaps" in the kinds of reds they produce, which is why faces look so ghastly under anything other than "daylight" fluorescents. Sometimes, but not always, this kind of bad color can be corrected at the photofinisher.

Mixed Light Sources

A picture taken indoors with illumination from both lamps and windows will have shadows and highlights, with color casts from these mixed light sources. You can get the same effect from a brightly colored wall that reflects tinged light on your subject. This, too, is difficult to compensate for. It's best to avoid such problems at the start.

Bad Photofinishing

Sometimes one can legitimately blame bad color on the photofinisher. Automated photofinishing equipment sometimes fails to differentiate between pictures that are off-color and those that contain a lot of one particular color naturally. When they try to compensate for the latter, bad color results. Really bad finishing can damage your negatives or slides, and produce off-color results.

Mistreated Film

If the last roll you turned in for finishing has pictures of three consecutive Thanksgivings, it's probably outdated, and you'll get prints that are off-color. The same thing can happen if you store a camera in the hot glove compartment or trunk of your car. If your prints have a nasty purple cast, or even some rainbow-hued flares in them, your negatives probably suffered this indignity. Film damaged in this way often cannot be corrected, even by scanning and image-editing.

Faded Colors

Dyes used in color prints and slides will change when exposed to strong light or heat for periods as short as a year, or even when kept in a cool, dark place for longer periods (up to 20 years). You may be able to make a new print from the original negative. The second-best remedy is to try correcting the image in your image editor.

The biggest challenge in correcting color may be in deciding exactly which direction you need to add/subtract color. Magenta may look a lot like red, and it's difficult to tell cyan from green. You may need some correction of both red and magenta, or be working with a slightly cyanish-green.

Color Depth

The final color concept you need to understand is the idea of *color depth*. The term is a way of describing how many different colors are in an image. Computers can't work with a continuous, or analog, range of colors. Like all computer information, colors must be divided into discrete digital values before they can be processed. Obviously, the wider the choice of individual colors your computer has to work with, the more closely the tonal range of your image approximates the original.

In digital fashion, your computer assigns each shade and color a number, based on its density and hue (for example, Red, 128; Blue, 63; Green, 0). The color depth refers to the number of bits used to store this information. A 2-bit image could represent four tones—with values 00, 01, 10, and 11. An 8-bit byte could represent any number from 00000000 to 11111111 (binary), or 0 to 255 (decimal); that's why an image saved with no more than 256 colors is often called an 8-bit image. Grayscale and some color images (called *indexed* color) are 8-bit images.

As you saw in the discussion of channels in the last chapter, a color image is nothing more than three different grayscale images, each one representing the amount of red, green, and blue in the original, as in the earlier R128, B63, G0 example. The three 8-bit red, green, and blue images are combined into one 24-bit file. (You may hear full-color images referred to as "24-bit color"; this identifies the minimum amount of information required about each pixel.) Where 8 bits can be used to represent 256 different colors, three sets of 8 bits can represent 256 x 256 x 256, or nearly 17 million, different colors.

There are other color depths in addition to 8-bit and 24-bit versions. Nearly all video cards today have enough memory to display 24-bit color, but older cards can show only 15- or 16-bit renditions of 24-bit files; these result in 32,767 and 65,535 colors on your screen, respectively. (Keep in mind that the original color image can still be a 24-bit image even if it can't be portrayed as such on the screen; the video card converts it to "high color," as opposed to "true color," to display it.)

Many devices, particularly scanners, now go beyond 24-bit color to capture 30, 36, or 48 bits of information per image. A 30-bit scanner, for example, grabs 10 bits per red, green, or blue color (30 bits total); a 36-bit scanner 12 bits per color, and so forth. Until recently there were few applications that could handle these ultra-color files, so scanners automatically converted them internally to 24-bit versions before they were stored on the computer. (If you end up with a 24-bit image in the end, why grab 30- or 36-bit images in the first place?)

Theoretically, 24-bit color should provide plenty of colors for most images, as the human eye can't differentiate between anything approaching 17 million different shades. In practice, color scanners always lose a little information, because of the inherent noise in any analog electronics system, much like the sound on your car stereo suffers when you roll down the windows—with the wind whistling past your ears, you may have to turn up the volume to compensate. Extra-color scanners work a little like that.

Noise affects a scanned image only from the time of capture until it is converted to digital format. So, instead of 256 colors per channel, you may end up with only 128 different colors per channel. When a system is capable of reproducing 256 different colors, but only 128 are available, it's likely that one of the available colors will have to be substituted for actual colors in an image. That is especially likely to happen when you are scanning transparencies, which have a wider dynamic range—detail all areas from deep shadows to lightest highlights—and may easily contain 256 or more colors in a particular color layer or channel. (CCD scanners are notorious for coming up with suspect values in shadow areas, because they lack sensitivity in dark regions.)

So, many scanners now grab more bits per channel: 30-bit scanners can discern 1024 colors per channel (or nearly 11 billion colors overall), while 36-bit scanners grab 4096 hues per channel (7 trillion colors). With so many extra colors, these scanners can afford to lose a little information to noise, and still retain plenty of data to create an accurate color image. Even grayscale scans can benefit from the extended range of such units. Extra-color scanners often can sense 1024 or more different graytones, and reduce the information to the best 256 shades for your final image.

What's Next

With the color theory under your belt, it's time to move on and begin actually tweaking color images to arrive at the best possible color. You'll learn next how to manipulate colors, adjust brightness and contrast, and apply special color effects.

As the philosopher Kermit The Frog once observed, it's not easy being green. Nor is it easy being orange or purple, but that's what can happen if the color balance of your images is a bit off. In the last chapter you learned how color works and what can cause bad color. In this chapter, you're going to deploy the GIMP to solve some of those problems.

First the bad news. Unlike many of the other GIMP skills you have learned so far, precise color correction is a very complex art and science—one about which volumes have been written. It's unlikely that you want to read volumes right now. On the plus side, it's also very unlikely that you need the kind of precise color correction required for making color separations. Your job is probably to get the color of an image the way you want it, then drop it on a Web page or, perhaps, turn it over to some pre-press geeks who will handle all the pain of getting the image from your electronic file onto the printing press.

That's only part of the good news. The really good news is that basic color correction is something that can be picked up fairly quickly. This chapter will provide a color correction overview, along with an introduction to the basic GIMP color tools and techniques—in other words, a foundation from which you can build your own expertise.

What's Color Modification

I use the term modification rather than correction here because not all changes you make to color are intended to correct some defect. In many cases, you may be looking for some special effect. Perhaps you want to add a warm orange-red glow to an image to simulate a sunset. Or, you may want to shift colors around to provide a retro-psychedelic look. Producing non-realistic color is actually a lot easier than creating corrected color. You can play around with various controls as much as you like; when you get something interesting, just pretend that you meant to do that very thing all along.

However, the techniques used to distort color are the same as those used to correct it, so you'll find both aspects covered in this chapter. Either way, you're simply converting pixels of one color or brightness value to another color or brightness value. Change all the red pixels to cyan, blue pixels to yellow, and green pixels to magenta, and you've created a reversed-color image. Make all the dark pixels light and the light pixels dark in the correct way, and you've generated a negative or inverted image. Add a bit of red and the image becomes warmer looking. The basic concept is quite simple.

One important thing to remember is that the GIMP can only change colors by converting the pixels that are already there. One net result is that colors are lost, making the image less colorful. The colors may look better, but there will be fewer of them in the image. If an image is a little too red, you can make the green and blue pixels brighter so they will stand out more. The overall effect will be a picture that is less reddish, but there will also be a smaller range of green and blue pixels.

However, if virtually all the pixels in a photo are red (as in a picture of a sunset), there are few, if any, green and blue pixels to brighten. Instead, pumping up the green and blue simply darkens the image, because you've added green and blue to the red pixels, and red, green, and blue together make a neutral black or gray tone. And, you've still lost some color.

Analyzing an Image

The instructions in this section will be general enough that you can use any photograph you like. This old photograph (Figure 7-1 and in the color insert of this book) will be your starting point.

If you want to work with the same picture I did, you can download a copy at my Web site, at `www.dbusch.com/gimp`. It will also help you to better see the color problems, as opposed to the black and white image on this page.

Because of the vagaries of the color reproduction process, the image in the color insert probably won't look as bad as that in the original. I'm using a photograph of a woman, because human figures show the effects of bad color more readily than other subjects. We all have a firm picture in our minds of how a person should look. This picture was taken partially in the shade, and was somewhat underexposed. But what else is wrong with it? Everything!

- Overall, the image is too dark.
- There's a magenta color cast to the image. This is most evident in the light areas of the woman's hair, which appear pink, and in the ruddy facial tones.
- With the exception of the burned-out hot spots in the hair, there is little contrast in the photo. It looks muddy.
- There are no true whites and blacks.

Figure 7-1 *Your original photograph*

Before doing any corrections, make a copy of the original image by pressing Ctrl-D. This way, you can experiment with changes, if necessary making a fresh copy off the original to try other changes. As you work, you can constantly compare the modified version with the original. Figure 7-2 shows what the finished image might look like.

Adjusting the Brightness and Contrast

The first step is to correct the image brightness and contrast, which is the same component whether the image is color or grayscale. The GIMP gives you several ways to do this. In ascending order of complexity, these are the Brightness/Contrast sliders, the Levels dialog box, and the Curves dialog box.

Brightness/Contrast Sliders

The GIMP's brightness/contrast sliders are handy, easy-to-understand controls that are a breeze to use. The big problem is that they apply changes to your whole image. You can decrease/increase the contrast of the entire image, or you can make the whole image brighter or darker. In the real world, you'll want to apply changes only to parts of an image. For example, you may want to lighten shadows while keeping the lighter portions of the image just the same. See Figure 7-3.

Figure 7-2 *The modified version of the original*

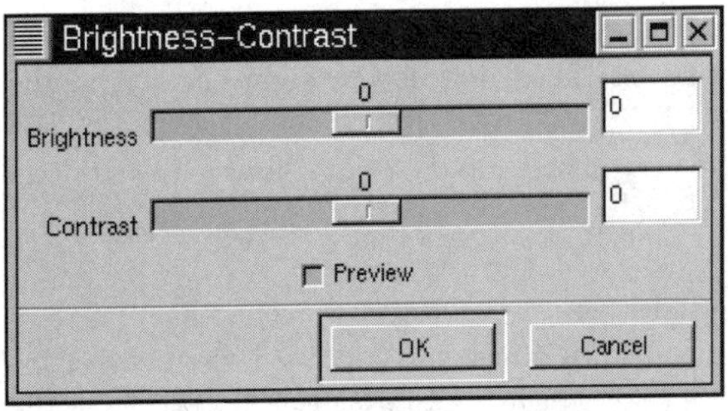

Brightness-Contrast

0

Brightness   0

0

Contrast   0

☐ Preview

[OK]   [Cancel]

Figure 7-3 *The GIMP's brightness/contrast controls*

The sample image has some dark portions. Some of the highlights, though, are already too washed out. Using the brightness/contrast sliders won't do the job, as you can see in Figure 7-4 and in the color insert of this book.

At left is the original image. At right, I've cranked up the brightness control so the shadows (for example, around the face and left shoulder) aren't so dingy, and adjusted the contrast to clear up the muddiness. This is no good. Now the highlights, such as the hair and right shoulder, which were already bright, are completely washed out, and boosting the contrast made the shadows dark again.

Figure 7-4 *The unmodified image (left) and a version with brightness and contrast increased (right)*

In some cases, you might want to play with these controls to help images that need only minor modifications. You can access the dialog box by right-clicking in the image and choosing Image | Colors | Brightness-Contrast. If you click the Preview button, the GIMP will show the changes you make in the original image in real time.

Using Levels

The next step up in fine-tuning an image's brightness and contrast is the Levels control. Right-click in the image, and choose Image | Colors | Levels. You'll see the Levels dialog box shown in Figure 7-5.

The mountain-like graph you see is called a histogram. It consists of 256 vertical lines, each representing the relative number of pixels at each particular gray tone within the image. Pictures with lots of dark shadows will have a clump of tall lines at the left (black) end of the histogram; images with detail in the highlights will have tall lines at the right end of the histogram. Because there are only 256 different tones that can be used to represent a grayscale image (or each red, blue, or green hue of a full-color image), it's important to make sure that none of these tones are wasted. Before I go on and use the Levels control to correct this image, I'm going to stop and explain how this feature works a little more thoroughly.

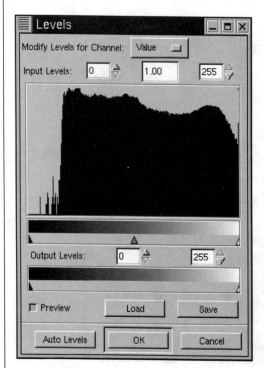

Figure 7-5 *The GIMP's Levels dialog box*

Take a good look at Figure 7-6. I've simplified the Levels dialog box, cropping it down to the histogram and the sliders that control the output levels. Below the dialog, I've placed a sample of the image as it looks before modification. There are four important parts to the dialog box, described in the following sections.

The Histogram Graph

As I mentioned, each of those vertical lines represents a gray tone from pure black (at the left of the scale) to pure white (at the right of the scale). Although there are no numbers, there are 256 different vertical lines, one for each tone from 0 (black) to 255 (white). The height of the line represents the amount of that tone. A very short line means very little of that tone is in the image. A tall line means that a lot of that tone is in the image. With me so far?

Notice that at the far left and far right ends of the graph, the lines are very short. This means that there are very few true black and true white tones. All the tones of the image are compressed into the middle part of the graph.

What does that mean exactly? Because the GIMP has only 256 different tones to represent the image, some of the available tones at each end are going unused. Let's say that the "mountain" represents 200 different lines. A good 56 tones are being wasted.

You can fix that.

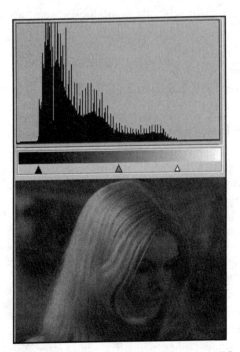

Figure 7-6 *Histogram and image before modification*

The *input level strip* is the grayscale strip underneath the histogram graph. It shows the relative brightness value of the vertical lines above it. You can view this strip and compare it to the histogram to get an idea of what tones are available in your image.

Black Point, White Point, and Midpoint Arrows

Below the histogram in the Levels dialog box, located under the input level strip, are the output sliders. These three arrows indicate the point at which the GIMP will use as the pure black, pure white, and midtone gray of your image. When you first view a histogram, the black arrow is located at the far left, the white arrow at the far right, and the midpoint arrow halfway between them (as you saw in Figure 7-5).

Moving the black triangle to the right reduces the contrast in the shadows, and lightens the image. Moving the right triangle to the left reduces the contrast in the highlights, and darkens the image. (You can get the same effects by typing a number into the left and right option boxes at the top of the dialog box.) To put those wasted tones to better use, you can tell the GIMP to move its black point to the position where the image does include dark tones, and move its white point to the position where white tones actually begin to have some detail; just slide the black arrow and white arrow inward (in this case), so they align with the base of the histogram "mountain" (as shown in Figure 7-6).

When you click OK, the GIMP recalculates the image, applying the new black and white points. Immediately view the histogram again. The image will look somewhat like the sample at the bottom of Figure 7-7.

What's happened here? Notice that the general shape of the "mountain" is roughly the same as it was. However, its base has been expanded to cover the entire brightness spectrum, so the tones are spread out over a full 256 vertical lines. There are now more tones available to represent black, white, and everything in between.

You have a lot of flexibility when using the Levels control. If you feel that some of the black or white tones can be sacrificed, you can move the black or white point arrows even closer towards the center, to provide more of the 256 shades to cover the other tones in the image. Or, you may want to slide the midtone arrow to the right or left to change the relative brightness of the middle shades of an image. The best way to learn to use these tools is to play with them. (When the Preview button is checked, the GIMP will show you the effects you've chosen as you move the sliding arrows.)

The Auto Levels button in the lower-left corner of the Levels dialog box can often speed up making these adjustments. This resets the white point and the black point, and redistributes the gray values of the pixels in between. Afterward, the histogram shows that the pixels fill the complete range from white to black. I usually find, though, that setting the black, white, and midpoint tones manually does a better job.

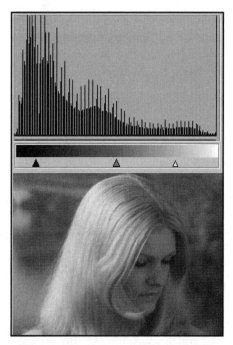

Figure 7·7 *Histogram and image after modification*

Adjusting the Midtones

The center (gray) slider in the Levels histogram is used to adjust the midtones, which are called the *gamma* values. Dragging this arrow to the left lightens the midtones. Dragging it to the right darkens the midtones while leaving the highlights and shadows alone. You can also move the gray slider by entering numbers from 10.00 to 0.00 in the center option box at the top of the dialog box. The default value, 1.00, lies exactly in the middle of the range.

You may find it convenient to save the adjustments you make to an image, especially if you are processing a batch of photographs that were taken under the same conditions, or if you are retouching a series of video frames. Save your settings by clicking Save and saving them as a file. (You will be able to load this file later by clicking Load.)

Controlling Output

The final control of the Levels dialog box is the Output grayscale control. It has black and white point control arrows just like the Input scale. The Output control is used to specify the lightest and darkest pixels that result in your finished image. Move the black triangle to a new value (higher than 0), and the darkest pixels will be no darker than that. Move the white triangle to a value lower than 255, and the lightest pixels will be no brighter than the new value.

One thing you can accomplish using this control is to invert your image in interesting ways. Just swap the positions of the white and black triangles, or move them to any setting in between. You can get some interesting effects that wouldn't be possible using only the Invert command (described below).

Using Curves

Curves is one of the most advanced GIMP tools, offering the user subtle control over the brightness, contrast, and gamma levels in an image, control that is far beyond that offered by the Levels and Brightness/Contrast dialog boxes. The Curves dialog box is truly complex, and probably offers control needed only by very experienced workers and imaging professionals; less advanced users might, though, want to play with Curves to see what special effects they can achieve. I will give you only a brief introduction to its power here.

The Brightness/Contrast dialog box lets you change an image globally, with no difference in application to the highlights, midtones, and shadows. The Levels command adds more control, allowing you to change them separately. The Curves command goes all out, letting you change pixel values at any point along the brightness level continuum, giving you 256 locations at which you can make corrections.

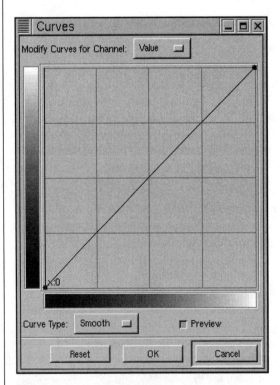

Figure 7-8 *The Curves dialog box*

TEXT EFFECTS

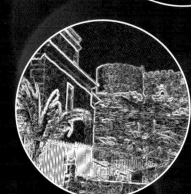

PHOTO RESTORATION

FILTERS AND PLUG-INS

COLOR MODIFICATION

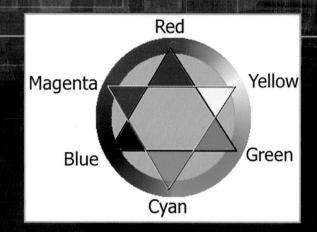

The color wheel,
additive color model, and
subtractive color model.

This image shows the effects of reducing the number of colors in an image, as you'll often do when you create a GIF file. Using Image | Indexed, the colors in the original photo of sheep grazing are reduced to 8 (top) and 32 (bottom).

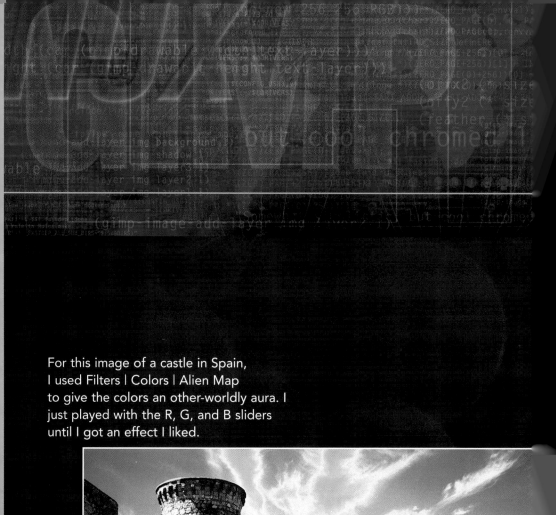

For this image of a castle in Spain,
I used Filters | Colors | Alien Map
to give the colors an other-worldly aura. I
just played with the R, G, and B sliders
until I got an effect I liked.

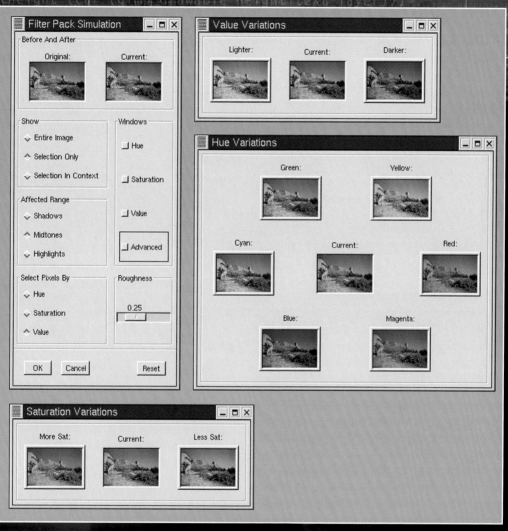

Those looking to correct colors will find the Filter Pack plug-in invaluable. It provides a set of preview images with before and after samples, and dialog boxes for setting hue, saturation, and brightness values.

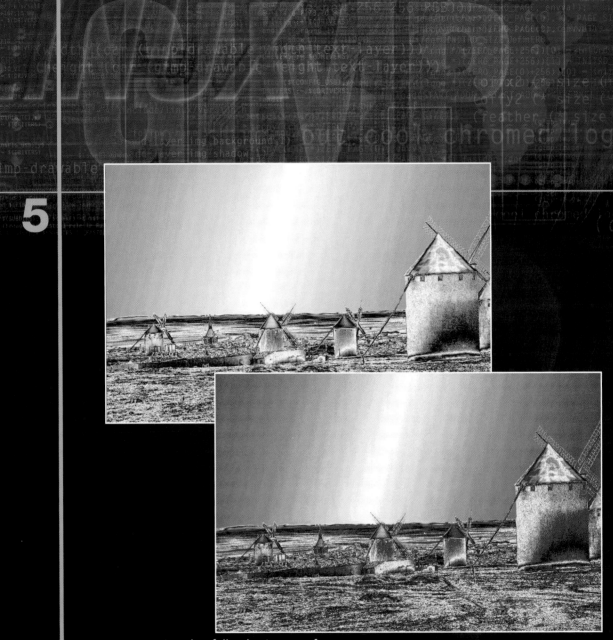

5

I took a full-color image of some windmills and applied Filters | Colors | Gradient Map to it. This produced a metallic gray-toned image, so I adjusted the hues in the RGB image to give it an eye-catching magenta tone.

Each of these three images shows how a multi-colored layer and an image are merged using the various blending modes.

Color 6a:
Left to right, Normal, Dissolve, Multiply, and Screen blending modes.

Color 6b:
Left to right, Overlay, Difference, Darken, Lighten blending modes.

Color 6c:
Left to right, Hue, Saturation, Color, Value blending modes.

Using layers, you can create one image out of four separate images. Above are the four images I composited to create the image at left; clockwise from upper left, a photo of Big Ben in London; some random clouds; a Spanish castle; and the Mediterranean Sea.

Color 8a:
Original image
of the Alcazar in
Segovia, Spain.

Color 8b:
This is the final result,
with the castle transformed
into a mosaic that looks as if
it could have been done by
a skilled artisan.

Color 8c:
I set the tile size,
grout thickness, and
other parameters in
this dialog box.

Use the Cubism filter
if you want to become a
post-modern Picasso.

Color 9a:
To create a cubist image, I
started with this photo of a
well-known clock tower.

Color 9b:
I set the parameters in the filter's dialog
box, choosing slightly larger cubes to
break up the image.

Cubism

Parameter Settings

☐ Use Background Color

Tile Size   10.0

Tile Saturation   2.5

OK   Cancel

Color 9c:
This is the final image
(right) with the original
shown at left.

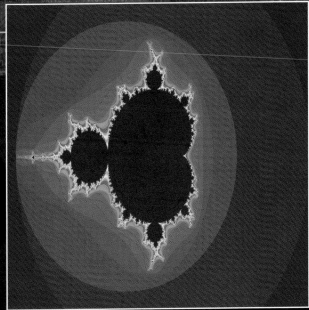

Simple fractal image created with the GIMP's Fractal Explorer.

This was simply a blank image filled with the Filter | Renders | Diffraction Pattern plug-in, which is an excellent foundation for interesting textures and patterns that can be applied to other images.

12

The GIMP's Film filter lets you choose a series of images, which it then deftly uses to re-create a 35mm film strip.

13

Applying Filters | Edge Detect | Edge to this image produced an eerie, night-time scene. Then, I added an "exploding" sun with Filters | Lighting Effects | Gradient Flare.

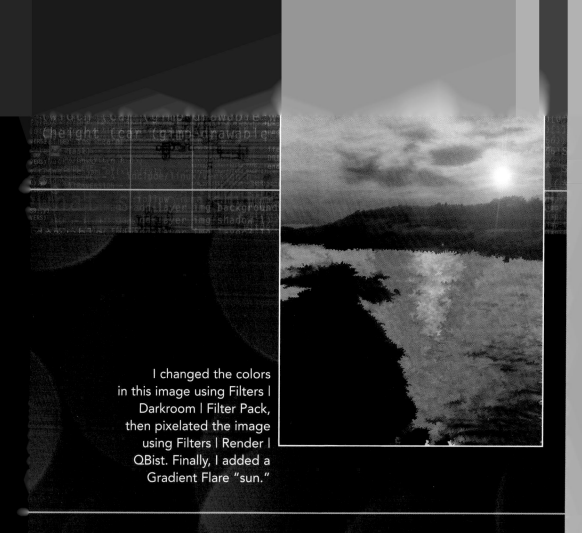

I changed the colors in this image using Filters | Darkroom | Filter Pack, then pixelated the image using Filters | Render | QBist. Finally, I added a Gradient Flare "sun."

The GIMP allows you to retouch defects on your photos. The original photo, at left, is a dark image with lots of

The effects of enhancing an image with the GIMP: At left, the original image, with notable defects; below, the new, improved photograph.

I first converted this black and white original to an RGB image, then colorized it using Filters | Colors | Colorify, then gave it a painterly effect with the Oilify filter.

These are all variations of buttons, produced using the Glass Lens filter and other effects. For example, the grooves in the button at the upper right were drawn manually, while the texture in the button at lower right is just the GIMP's Canvas texture.

19

I produced this Web page logo using the Logulator to generate the raised, 3-D text. Then, I copied the logo onto a new layer, blurred the copy using Gaussian Blur, and filled the glow with green. I put all the layers on a black background and flattened.

20

This one took a lot of steps, but was easy to do. After generating the text using Logulator, I applied a blue-white-gold gradient similar to the one used in the Logulator's Cool Metal effect. I copied the text, blurred it, and filled it with black to produce the drop shadow behind the text. Then I created several more layers, filled them with the same gradient, and created another drop shadow behind the middle layer.

The test photo you've been working with is dark, and its contrast reduced. You can correct it using Curves. You open the Curves dialog box by right-clicking on the image and choosing Image | Colors | Curves. A graph will appear. (See Figure 7-8.)

The horizontal axis of the graph maps the brightness values as they are before image correction. The vertical axis maps the brightness values after correction. Each axis represents a continuum of 256 levels, divided into four parts by gray lines. The lower-left corner represents 0,0 (pure black); the upper-right corner is 255,255 (pure white).

Whenever you open the Curves window, the graph begins as a straight line at a 45-degree angle from lower left to upper right. That's because unless changes are made, the input will be exactly the same as the output—a direct 1:1 correlation that can be represented by the 45-degree line. (I can see the eyes of non-math types glazing over already; don't worry, you can play with Curves even without using math.)

You can see how the graph works by dragging various points of the line. When Smooth is selected as the Curve Type, you can click on the curve to produce a handle that can be dragged to create a smoothly curving line. Try dragging the middle of the curve up, down, and from side to side to see what happens; dragging down makes the image darker, while dragging up makes it lighter. When you choose Free as the Curve Type, you can draw a freehand curve with a pencil tool, producing more abrupt changes. Experiment with Curves often, because you can produce some interesting special effects, and everything you try will teach you more about this tool.

Correcting Color

So far, you've investigated ways to adjust the brightness and contrast of an image, which is, of course, only one component of image correction. Most of the time, you'll also want to tweak the color of an RGB image. The GIMP gives you some great tools to use for this task, as well.

Correcting with Color Balance

Right-click on the image and choose Image | Colors | Color Balance. Notice the three color sliders, which by default rest in the center (neutral) position. If you remember your color theory from the last chapter, the operation of these controls will seem logical to you. (See Figure 7-9.)

The top slider is labeled Cyan at the left side and Red at the right side. Moving the slider to the left adds cyan to the image, while subtracting its complement, red. Moving the slider to the right adds red, while subtracting cyan. The same is true for the magenta/green and yellow/blue controls. Whenever you add one color to an image, you are simultaneously removing its complement or "opposite" color.

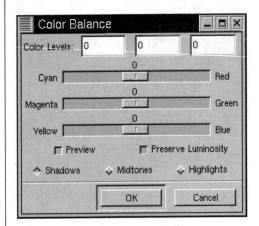

Figure 7-9   *Color Balance dialog box*

The test image (Figure 7-1) is too magenta, so you can correct this by adding green. However, images will rarely have casts that are 100 percent a single color, that is, solely cyan, magenta, yellow, red, green, or blue. You'll often have to use a combination of sliders to make a correction. Exactly which controls to use will depend on the color you want to correct and, to an extent, on your personal preference.

One thing you will generally not want to do is use more than two sliders. Thinking back to the RGB and CMY color models will tell you why very quickly. Look at it this way:

If you add two of the RGB colors together, you are subtracting their two CMY complements, leaving only the third color unchanged. That is, add red and green and you subtract cyan and magenta, leaving yellow. Add red and blue and you subtract cyan and yellow, leaving only magenta. It works in the other direction, too. Add cyan and magenta, and you end up with blue. (Try dragging the controls in the Color Balance dialog box to see what I mean.)

But when you add or subtract all three of one type of primary color, to some extent you're canceling part of the color correction. Add equal amounts of red, green, and blue, or equal amounts of cyan, magenta, and yellow, and the color balance remains the same. For that reason, you'll usually manipulate only one or two sliders at a time, and then only because you need to add or subtract different amounts of a particular color.

You can also make color changes by entering numerical values in the Color Levels option boxes at the top of the dialog box. Each of the boxes represents one of the color scales, with +100 as the right-side color and -100 as the color on the left. For example, to adjust the cyan/red scale toward the red, you would enter a positive number in the first box. To adjust the magenta/green slider toward the magenta, you would enter a negative number in the second box.

The Color Balance dialog box has three buttons you can use to select Shadows, Midtones, or Highlights. You can adjust the color of any one of these one at a time. The Preserve Luminosity button keeps the brightness values of your image the same as you modify the color values.

Correcting with Hue and Saturation

You can also correct color using the Hue/Saturation dialog box. You might remember the brief discussion in Chapter 6 of the HSB (*hue-saturation-brightness*), HLS (*hue-lightness-saturation*), and HSV (*hue-saturation-value*) models.

This is another way of representing color, and the GIMP gives you a way of modifying these attributes directly.

Access the dialog box by right-clicking on the image, and choosing Image | Colors | Hue-Saturation. The dialog has three sliders, representing the Hue, Lightness, and Saturation. There are seven buttons stacked along the left edge, representing the Master channel (all the primary colors), or the Red, Green, Blue, Cyan, Magenta, or Yellow channels alone. Usually, you'll want to work with the Master channel, correcting all the colors of an image at once. (See Figure 7-10.)

The Hue slider represents a trip around the outer edge of the color wheel, up to +180 degrees or -180 degrees. You can view the color wheel by double-clicking one of the color patches in the toolbar and clicking the Triangle tab in the Color Selector dialog box. As you move the Hue slider, you can see the color shift through the spectrum towards blue (which resides at +180 and -180 degrees). The Lightness slider changes the brightness or darkness of the color, while the Saturation slider fades the color or makes it richer. The Hue/Saturation dialog box is especially useful when you want to change the saturation of a color, as it's usually the easiest way to accomplish that change.

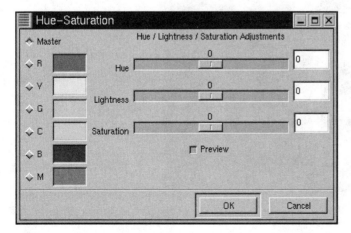

Figure 7-10 *Hue/Saturation dialog box*

Other Correction Tools

The GIMP also includes specialized tools that help correct certain types of image or color defects. You'll find all these by right-clicking on the image and choosing the Colors menu.

Invert

The Invert command turns an image into its negative—black becomes white, white becomes black, and colors are reversed. The process is simple. Pure colors just become their complements on the color wheel; red becomes cyan, blue becomes yellow, and so forth. Grayscale tones for 0 to 255 are tipped end-over-end, too, by changing them to a value of 255 minus their original brightness value. For example, a dark tone with a value of 20 becomes a very light 235 (255-20). A light tone with a brightness of 240 becomes a dark 15. A medium gray at a brightness value of 128 would stay virtually the same. The result: a negative image.

The good news with the Invert command is that no colors are lost. If you change your mind, you can re-invert the image to get back to where you started. (An inverted image is shown in Figure 7-11, alongside its original version.)

Figure 7-11 *Original image (left) and inverted image (right)*

Equalize

Using Equalize balances the brightness and contrast of an image so that the pixels represent the entire range of values, from black to white. It also equalizes colors. When you equalize an image, the GIMP looks at all the pixels; finding the brightest and darkest ones, it converts them to white and black, respectively, and averages out the others to fill the full 256-tone range. This generally improves the contrast in an image, but can lighten or darken a picture too much. However, in some cases, it may lighten the picture too much.

The Equalize command can be applied to a selected area only, or it can be applied to the entire image on the basis of the pixel values in a selected area. If the pixel values in the selected area are very dark, the entire image will be lightened excessively. The Autostretch HSV, Contrast Autostretch, and Normalize commands perform similar functions. You may have to try out all four on an image to see which works best.

Threshold

The Threshold command lets you change images (grayscale or color) into high-contrast black-and-white images, without converting the file mode into a 1-bit image first. Threshold is ideal for making high-contrast images that can be traced in an illustration program. What it does is use a number you specify from 0 to 255, and then change any that are less than that number to black, and any that are above that number to white. For example, a value of 127 would divide the grays of an image in half; everything darker than 128 would become black, and anything 128 or lighter would become white.

The power of the Threshold command is that you can choose the number to best fit the effect you want to get in your image. The Threshold dialog box presents you with a histogram showing the distribution of tones in your image. It helpfully colors those below the threshold black and those above white. You can enter different values, and see how the new image looks via the preview. (See Figure 7-12.)

While the default value for the threshold is 128, that isn't usually the best choice. A setting of 128 will divide an image with gray tones spread over the full 0-255 range into neat halves of black and white. But most images aren't so tidy, as the histogram shows. Try choosing a value that divides the gray tones that do appear in your image in half. If there are very few tones at the left end, increase the value. If you're missing some at the right end of the scale, decrease the value. Or, you can simply play with values until you get something you like. (Figure 7-13 shows an image converted to black and white using two different threshold values.)

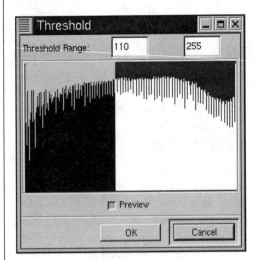

Figure 7-12   *The Threshold dialog box*

Figure 7-13   *Image converted to black and white with Threshold command, using settings of 68 at left and 110 at right*

Posterize

Posterize is like the Threshold command, except that instead of changing all pixels to either black or white, you can select a number of pixels. Then, a grayscale or color photograph is changed so that all pixels are reassigned to a limited number of gray or brightness levels. This results in a posterized effect. The control is a simple dialog box, with space for you to type in the number of levels you want, from 2 to 255. Use small numbers to generate the most poster-like effect. (Figure 7-14 shows an image that has been posterized using two different settings. This image is also in the color insert of this book.)

Desaturate

This command is nothing more than a quick way to switch tones to grayscale, without changing mode. Suppose you wanted to change the tones of an RGB image or a portion of such an image to gray, but then continue to work on the image in RGB mode. You might wish to change a color photo to gray, then add color callouts. The long way to do this would be to change to Grayscale mode, then back to RGB. The Image | Colors | Desaturate command does the same thing in one step, with the added bonus that you can desaturate only one layer or selection at a time, thus converting only portions of an image to grayscale.

Figure 7-14 *Image posterized using settings of 3 levels (top) and 5 levels (bottom)*

Filter Pack Simulation

The GIMP also includes a handy plug-in that provides much the same effect as Photoshop's Variations command. You can locate the Filter Pack Simulation dialog box by choosing Filters | Darkroom | Filter Pack. A dialog box like the one shown at upper left in Figure 7-15 appears (this image also is shown in the color insert of this book). You can also choose Hue, Saturation, and Value dialog boxes from it. This plug-in lets you modify color by comparing images with various effects applied to them, and selecting the one that looks best to you. Although it's not an exact color correction method, Filter Pack Simulation can help you narrow down the possible remedies to your bad color.

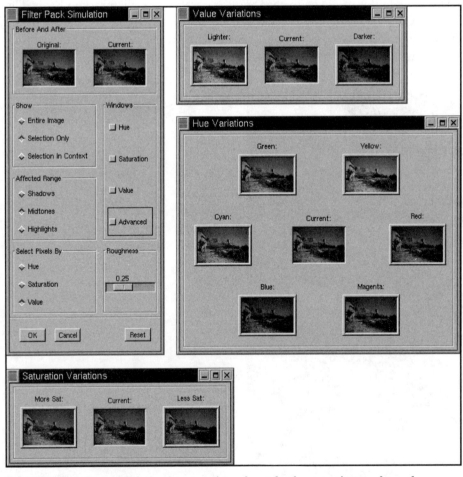

Figure 7-15 *Filter Pack Simulation lets you mix and match color corrections to choose the effect you want visually.*

What's Next

Consider this chapter just an introduction to color correction. This is one task that deserves a lot of practice. The more you experiment, the better you'll get. Plus, along the way, you're likely to discover some very cool special effects. In the next chapter, you'll learn how to create special effects in another way: by flipping, rotating, and twisting your images until they shout.

Chapter 8: Transformations

O f course, every time you change colors or paint something on an image, you are transforming it. But in GIMP-speak, transformations are something you do with one of the transformation tools I described earlier in the book. They're the gadgets that resize, crop, flip, or rotate selections or images. In this chapter I'm going to show you how to use the GIMP's key transformations tools (with the exception of the Magnify and Move tools, which were covered in Chapter 2).

Cropping

Cropping is a handy way of "framing" your image so it includes only the parts you want; because images must be rectangular in shape, you can only crop to a rectangle, but, aside from that constraint, the GIMP gives you lots of options. To use the Crop tool, click its icon in the toolbar. When you move the cursor back into the image, it changes into a double crosshair. The center of the crosshair marks where cropping begins. You can position the cursor accurately by monitoring its location on the rulers at the top and left side of the image window, or by viewing the coordinates (in pixels) as displayed in the status bar in the lower-left corner of the image window.

Click once in the image, and a pair of intersecting guidelines will appear. These will show where the crop will begin. You can move this origin point at any time—even after you've defined a crop area—by moving the cursor to a new location and clicking again. Figure 8-1 illustrates cropping in the GIMP.

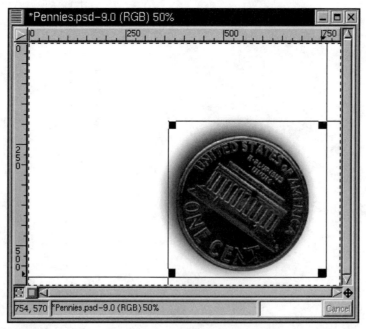

Figure 8-1 *The Crop tool trims an image to a size you specify.*

At the same time, the Crop & Resize Information dialog box appears. You can watch entries in this dialog box as you move the cropping boundaries, to confirm the size of the area you are defining. It shows the X and Y coordinates of the borders, as well as the width and height. The default unit for this information is the pixel, but you can specify another measurement, such as points, inches, millimeters, and so forth. (See Figure 8-2.)

To set the crop borders, hold down the mouse button and drag in any direction. A set of four handles appears at the corners of the cropped area, and the guidelines move to show you where the borders are located. When you've defined your crop area to your satisfaction, click the Crop button on the dialog box, and the image will be trimmed to the new size.

Cropping Precisely

You may often need to crop an area very accurately. For example, in producing the screen shots for this book, I sometimes wanted to extract a single dialog box from a full screen shot. Try this exercise to learn some techniques for doing this quickly.

1. Capture a full screen picture using the GIMP's snapshot feature. Choose File | Acquire | Screen Shot. The Screen Shot dialog box (shown in Figure 8-3) appears.

2. Click the Grab the whole screen box, then click the Grab button. An image of the entire screen appears in a GIMP image window.

3. Zoom in on a window within the screen shot (perhaps using the GIMP toolbar), and make a rough crop border around it with the Crop tool, as shown in Figure 8-4.

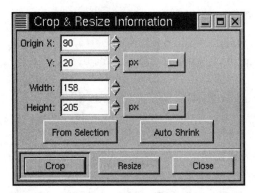

Figure 8-2 *The Crop & Resize Information dialog box*

Figure 8-3 *The GIMP's Screen Shot dialog box*

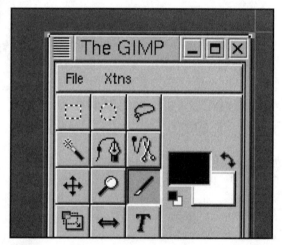

Figure 8-4 *Use the cursor keys to crop tightly around an image.*

4. Move the top crop border down, by pressing the down cursor arrow key on your keyboard. Move it so it is aligned exactly with the top line of the dialog box or window.

5. Press the right cursor arrow key to move the left border towards the right until it is aligned with the left edge of the dialog box or window (as shown in Figure 8-5).

6. Click the Crop button on the Crop & Resize Information dialog box, to trim the image at the top and left.

7. Make another crop border around the dialog box or window; using the up and left cursor arrow keys, align the bottom and right borders with the respective edges of the area you want to crop.

8. Click the Crop button again, and you'll have an image cropped exactly at the edges of the dialog box.

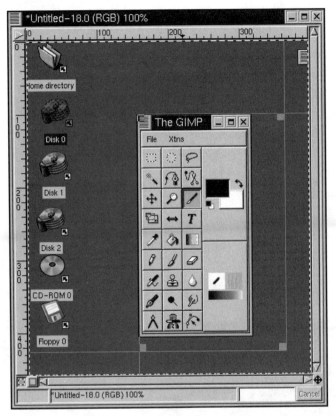

Figure 8-5 *Crop border aligned with left edge of the dialog box*

Here's an alternate method, using a different feature of the GIMP's Crop facility.

1. Repeat Steps 1 and 2 in the previous exercise to get another full-screen shot to crop.
2. Make sure the Snap to Guides feature is turned on. Right-click in the image window, and choose View | Snap to Guides, as shown in Figure 8-6.
3. Put the cursor in the horizontal ruler, hold down the mouse button, and drag a guide line down, positioning it exactly at the top edge of the window you want to crop to.
4. Drag another horizontal guide down, and place it exactly at the bottom edge.
5. Drag two vertical guides from the vertical ruler, and place them at the right and left edges of the window.
6. Use the Crop tool to crop around the window, staying as close as you can to the guides. The crop borders will snap to the guides precisely (as shown in Figure 8-7).
7. Click the Crop button when you're satisfied, to resize the image.

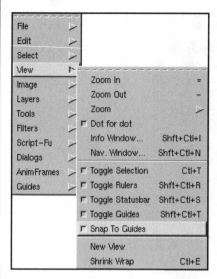

Figure 8-6 *Snap to Guides allows cropping to guidelines you define.*

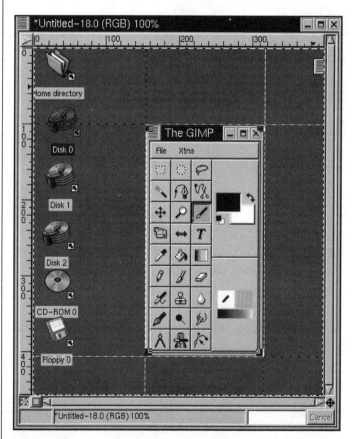

Figure 8-7 *Snap crop borders to guides.*

Here's yet a third way to crop precisely.

1. Grab yourself a full-screen image, as in the previous exercise.

2. Use the Rectangular, Elliptical, or Freehand selection tool to select an area you want to crop.

3. Click anywhere outside the selection with the Crop tool.

4. Click the From Selection button in the dialog box. The crop borders appear at the boundaries of a rectangular selection. If you made an elliptical or freehand selection, the crop borders form the smallest rectangle that encompasses the widest and tallest portions of the selection.

But wait, there's more! If your object is surrounded by a plain background, you can use the Auto Shrink feature to crop it automatically.

1. Create a full-screen shot.

2. Using the Crop tool, draw a rough cropping around the object.

3. Click the Auto Shrink button. The crop borders shrink to encompass the object.

You're not done yet. Check out the Zealous Crop and Auto Crop features.

1. Create a full-screen shot.

2. Right-click in the image, and choose Image | Transforms and then either Zealous Crop or Auto Crop.

Auto Crop removes any solid color borders around an image, so if the window or dialog box you want is on a plain background, the GIMP will automatically crop for it. Zealous Crop removes a highly contrasting color (again, such as a background), performing much the same function.

NOTE

Transform

The general-purpose Transform tool lets you perform a variety of transformations on your image. Its chief drawback is that you must select which of its functions you want to use each time, using the Tool Options dialog box. Double-click the Transform Tool to view the dialog box shown in Figure 8-8.

Figure 8-8 *You can select portions of an image in rectangular, elliptical, or freehand mode.*

The main transform options are rotation, scaling, shearing, and perspective. I'll explain each of them separately. You have several options for all variations of this tool; here are the most important ones:

- The Show grid button turns a reference grid on or off. The grid can help you see the effects of your transformation.

- Enter a Grid density value from 0 to 5 to specify the density of the blocks in the grid, with 0 being coarse and 5 producing a fine grid.

- The Smoothing button anti-aliases the edges of the transformation.

- When the Clip result button is pressed, the transformed selection will be clipped to fit into its original area. When the option is turned off, the transformed selection remains intact. (Figure 8-9 offers an idea of how this works.)

Rotation

When the Rotation tool is active, clicking in the image causes a grid to overlay the picture. You can drag with the mouse to rotate around the center point, represented by a dot in the center of the grid. You can drag the center point to a new location if you'd like to rotate around a different point. (See Figure 8-10.)

While you're using the tool, the Rotation Information dialog box appears, showing the angle of rotation and the coordinates of the center point. If you want a precise amount of rotation (say, 45 degrees), you can type it or dial it into the Angle box. You can also drag the Angle slider to rotate the image. You can move the center point precisely by entering the X and Y coordinates in the boxes in the dialog box. (These controls are all new to the latest version of the GIMP.) When you're satisfied with the amount of rotation, click the Rotate button in the dialog box. (If you hold down the Ctrl key while rotating, the angle is constrained to 15-degree increments.)

Figure 8-9 *Transformation clipped (left) and not clipped (right)*

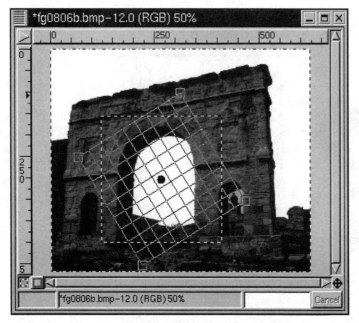

Figure 8-10 *A grid overlays the selection when any transformation tool is active.*

Scaling

When Scaling is activated in the Tool Options dialog box, clicking the Transform tool anywhere inside a selection or image also activates a grid overlay. You can then drag the handles to resize the image or selection in the X or Y directions, or both. Holding down the Ctrl key constrains resizing to the horizontal direction only; holding down the Shift key constrains resizing to the vertical direction. If you hold down both the Ctrl and Shift keys, the image or selection is resized proportionately, that is, by the same amount in both X and Y directions. (See Figure 8-11.)

Using the Scaling tool produces the Scaling Information dialog box. The original width and height, the current width and height as scaled, and the ratio of width to height are shown. You can type or dial in a width or height to resize precisely. When you've resized to your satisfaction, click the Scale button to apply your change. (See Figure 8-12.)

Shearing

Shearing produces a sort of leaning effect. You can lean the image or selection to either side by dragging one of the corner handles of the grid sideways, or lean up or down by dragging one of the corner handles up or down. (See Figure 8-13.)

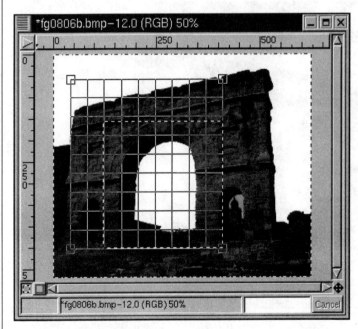

Figure 8-11 *The Scaling Transformation tool*

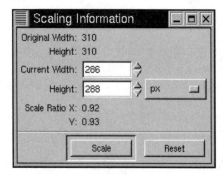

Figure 8-12 *The Scaling Information dialog box*

Figure 8-13 *Shearing effect: vertical (left) and horizontal (right)*

You can't, however, apply both transformations in one step. Once you begin dragging horizontally or vertically, you must continue in that mode. If you'd like to apply the other shearing mode, you must select another tool, and then return to the Transform tool.

During the shear operation, a Shear Information dialog box appears. You can type or dial a magnitude for the shear for either X or Y axes (but not both at once). Click the Shear button to apply your change.

Perspective

The Perspective tool lets you distort an image by dragging each of the four control handles independently. You can use this to produce a perspective-like transformation, as if the image were receding to a vanishing point (as you can see in Figure 8-14).

Flip Tool

The Flip tool creates a mirror image of a selection either horizontally or vertically. You must set whether you want horizontal or vertical flipping in the Tool Options dialog box. Once you've done that, just click in an image or selection, and the picture will be reversed. (See Figure 8-15.)

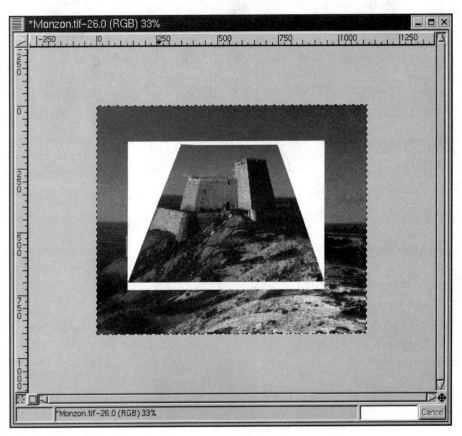

Figure 8-14 *Perspective effect*

Figure 8-15 *An image or selection can be flipped horizontally or vertically.*

What's Next

This concludes your introduction to the GIMP's basic tools. In Part II, starting with the next chapter, I'm going to show you what you can do with these implements. From time to time, I'll also explain new ways to use familiar tools, and introduce a few capabilities (such as that infamous Modes capability I've been threatening you with) as you go.

PART II

Putting the GIMP to Work

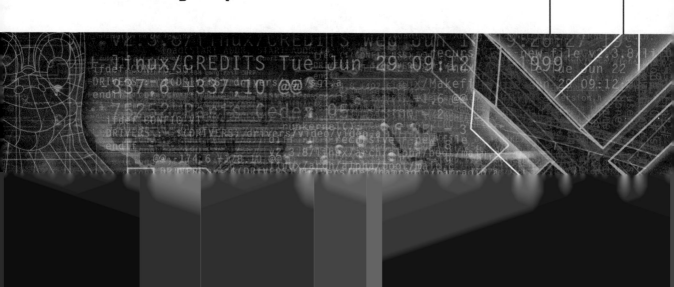

Every picture tells a story, but even the best stories can benefit from a little editing with the GIMP. One of the many differences between very good amateur pictures and most of the professional photographs you see published is that the pro image probably had some retouching done some time during the production process. Subtle tweaking here and there can make dramatic improvements.

This chapter shows you how easy digital manipulation of images can be with the GIMP, and reveals a few simple techniques that you can use to transform sound (though imperfect) images into prize winners. The emphasis is on improving the appearance of color or grayscale images. Unlike previous chapters, which concentrated on introducing and explaining new GIMP features, this one will use everything you've already learned, as well as some new skills, to improve a photograph.

Photocompositing and Retouching Defined

Photocompositing is the art of combining two or more images smoothly enough that the result doesn't look like a third-grader's first attempt at collage. *Retouching* is the even finer art of manipulating images so the subject looks like we think it should, rather than the way it really is. At one time I was a professional photographer, with a studio that was always teeming with glamorous models and truck clutches that needed photographing. After I was seduced by the dark side of technology, most of my photos have been of the snapshot variety, often with digital cameras. Today, the chief difference between a photographic neophyte and me is that when my pictures come out looking ghastly, I can identify in technical detail exactly what I did wrong, and then fix up many of these pictures using the GIMP.

Retouching is one area that has seen the most dramatic changes wrought by computerized image-editing software. The goal of simple retouching is to remove defects from a photograph. Of course, a defect is often in the eye of the beholder (if not in the bags underneath). A high school senior portrait (male or female) showing less than silky-smooth skin is sometimes viewed as a disaster by those who have just traversed the rocky roads of puberty. On the other hand, removing the character lines from the face of a corporate CEO might provoke outrage; emphasizing that steely glint in the eye may be much more important.

In advertising photography, The Product must be presented just so, and if 20 hours of retouching is required to achieve the desired effect, so be it. Since it may be prohibitively expensive to reshoot the entire photo series (thousands of dollars in location shooting, props, models, and stylists may be involved), it may be much cheaper to pour some bucks into retouching an original transparency. The defects removed by retouching may, in fact, be minor. In the old days (less than 20 years ago), nearly all retouching was done using the photographic media—negative, slide or print. Skilled retouchers can use special dyes to smooth out the smiling faces of high school seniors right on the color negative film. Extensive work can be performed on medium- to large-format color transparencies (4 x 5 to 8 x 10 inches, or larger). Frequently, color or black-and-white prints are almost good enough to use, but will have a few white spots caused by dust on the negative; a few minutes with a spotting brush can clean them up nicely. Photocompositing can be another form of retouching, the kind you see (or don't see) in those cover photos in supermarket tabloids (you know, the one with the Iowa farmer wrestling a 60-pound grasshopper to the ground).

Retouching a Portrait

The easiest way to experiment with simple retouching techniques is to fix up an actual photo. You can use your own photo if you like; yours may well have one or more of the defects I've deliberately included in my sample. If you'd rather work with the same image I did, you can download it from my Web site, `www.dbusch.com/gimp`.

For this exercise, you'll work with a portrait, since most people are inherently more fussy about portrayals of human beings, particularly faces. An unfortunate shadow on a picture of a tree may be unnoticed or ignored, but it may convert a serious portrait into an unintended rendition of Pinocchio. You'll find that much of the photo retouching you do will involve making people look more like themselves, or more as they'd like to look. The picture I started with is shown in Figure 9-1; not all the defects in the original will survive the halftoning process as this book is printed, so you'll want to check out the color version of the image in the color insert of this book.

What Went Wrong?

You never really believe that a picture is worth a thousand words until somebody starts critiquing one of your beloved photos. I could easily take a thousand words to describe the minor problems with the original photo—so I'll do so. Maybe you can learn something about the common defects you're likely to find in a photo image. I'll list them in order of frequency and importance.

Dust Spots

The most common defect you'll encounter in an original will be dust spots, especially when the photo was made from a 35 mm negative or slide original. Because 35 mm film must be enlarged at least four times from its tiny 24 x 36 mm size (that's an inch by an inch and a half), any dust present is enlarged, too. It's difficult to keep a negative or slide 100 percent spotless, so your prints (and reprints, especially) are likely to have at least a couple of these little devils.

Dust on color or black-and-white negatives will manifest itself as white spots on the print. Dust that resides on a color slide will appear to be black when the transparency

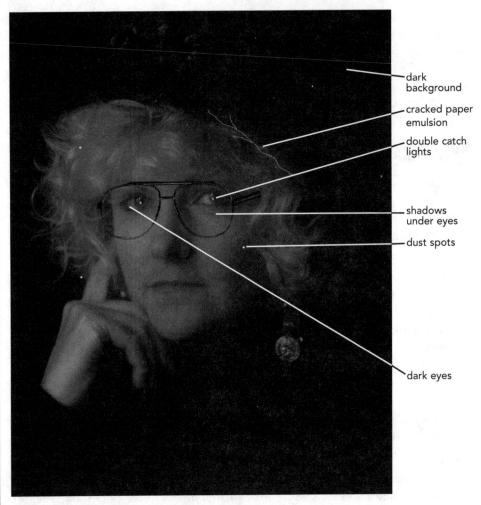

Figure 9-1 *The original image, before retouching*

is viewed or printed. It's well known that there are two colors of dust—white dust, which settles on dark-colored automobiles, and black dust, which is attracted to white or light-colored automobiles.

Actually, both kinds of dust are the same; the material on negatives is reversed from black to white, just like the rest of the image, when the negative is printed. If you happen to notice black specks on a print made from a negative, or white (or, more often, colored) specks on a print made from a transparency, you probably have a defect in one (or more) of the film's emulsion layers, which make up the image.

Luckily, white or black, these specks are easy to fix. The sample portrait is peppered with them, including a couple humongous spots that have germinated on their way to becoming dust bunnies. You'll remove these later.

Scars, Skin Blemishes

A little before most of us are able to sit up unaided, our skin loses its perfect complexion. We're usually able to live with these small defects in real life, but we don't want to be reminded of them in our portraits. Although a few celebrities have converted minor facial characteristics into trademark features, you'll want the option to remove them if you or the subject deems it desirable. You're going to remove a few skin blemishes from the sample portrait.

Technical Stuff

There are several kinds of defects that only photographers know about, but which are important nevertheless (that's why they're pros: they know this secret stuff). For example, whether you're conscious of it or not, you're acutely aware of those little reflections—called *catch lights*—that appear in the eyes of every portrait subject who is looking at the camera. When a catch light is present, the subject's eyes look lively and alert. If no catch light is found, the eyes look dead and dull.

If you don't believe me, open up a copy of Time or People magazine, find a few photos of famous people you hate, and color in all the catch lights with a marking pen. Notice the difference? With a stroke of a pen you can convert a fiery politician into a sedated serial killer. This is much more subtle and devious than blacking out a few teeth or drawing a mustache (plus it works with males and females alike). Figure 9-2 shows how dramatic the change can be.

To produce the desired favorable effect, catch lights must be clean and visible, appropriately positioned (not on opposite sides of the pupil, for example), and not oddly shaped. Since they are often reflections of windows, square or roundish catch lights

Figure 9-2 *Removing catch lights can take all the life out of the eyes.*

are best. Often, you'll see hexagon-shaped catch lights representing the photographer's umbrellas; that's distracting—unless you're doing a photo story about a model or actor.

Double catch lights, which are reflections from two different light sources, are also a no-no. The sample picture, Figure 9-1, suffers from these. The solution will be simply to blacken or remove the extra reflection in each eye.

Dark Shadows

The model in Figure 9-1 didn't really have bags under her eyes, but the way the shadows fell made it appear so; in addition, the lighting darkened the white part of the eye (the sclera) so it appears gray rather than white in the original photo. You can lighten these shadows easily, so the eyes show up better and more attractively in the final version. You can use the same techniques to improve the appearance of subjects who have "sunken" or bloodshot eyes. You'll need to use restraint, however: eyes, nose, and mouth are the features used most to identify other humans. They must be represented accurately or the portrait won't look "right." The simple lighten/darken techniques you'll learn in this chapter can be applied to other image retouching tasks, too.

Starting the Process

You're going to correct the problems identified by the callouts in Figure 9-1—and then some—one at a time. The first step is to adjust the brightness and contrast, because the image is way too murky. Then you'll work on the dust spots and blemishes. You'll finish up by doing a few really drastic things.

From Murky to Bright

1. Make a duplicate of the image by saving under a different name, so you'll have something to backtrack to if you goof up, or exceed the Undo levels you've set for the GIMP.

2. Right-click on the image and choose Image | Colors | Levels to produce the Levels dialog box you used in Chapter 7.

3. Adjust the black-point, midpoint, and white-point arrows until the image looks brighter, using the histogram. You'll probably move the black-point arrow towards the center only a smidgen, and the mid-point arrow another smidgen to the left. (I moved the white-point arrow about 20 percent of the width of the histogram towards the left.)

4. Click OK when finished. (Your image should look like the one shown in Figure 9-3.)

Figure 9-3 *Brightened image*

The image could also use some sharpening, but only in the hair and perhaps the earrings. In most cases, a softer look in the skin is better for a woman's portrait. To sharpen up only a portion of the image, follow these steps.

1. Make that duplicate of the image again. (Nobody's perfect.)

2. Click the Quick Mask button in the lower-left corner of the screen. The entire image will turn red, showing that the full image is masked.

3. Using a large fuzzy eraser, unmask the hair and earrings. (For the illustration shown in Figure 9-4, I've changed the default Quick Mask opacity to 80 percent, so you'll be able to see the contrast between the masked and unmasked areas more clearly.)

4. Use the Convolver tool in the Toolbar, set to Sharpen, and a fuzzy brush to "paint" some sharpness onto the hair. (Note that you shouldn't be able to see the difference through the halftone screen used to produce black-and-white images.)

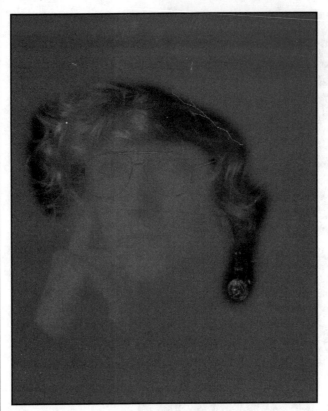

Figure 9-4 *Mask off everything but the hair and earrings.*

Removing Defects with the Clone Tool

As you've learned, the Clone tool, usually represented by a rubber-stamp icon in the Toolbar, duplicates part of an image, pixel by pixel, in a location of your choice; the stamp analogy isn't very good, however, as you're actually drawing with a brush, which you can size and control in other ways. Cloning can be used to copy portions of an image to another location in the same or a different image. If your desert scene is too sparse for you, a single cactus can be multiplied several times, or even copied from a different desert altogether. Or you may add a window to the side of a building by "painting" one from another building. You're going to use the tool to remove some dust spots and a scratch.

1. If you haven't yet goofed badly enough to need your backup copy, make one anyway. There's no point in pushing your luck.
2. Double-click the Clone tool's icon to access the Clone Tool Options dialog box.
3. Choose Image Source as the source, and Aligned as the alignment.

4. Select a small, fuzzy brush as your cloning brush.

5. Zoom in for a close-up look at the area you are repairing.

6. Place the cursor in an area in the photo that has tones that approximate those you'd like to use in "painting over" the dust spot (as shown in Figure 9-5).

7. Hold down the Ctrl key, and click in that location to "pick up" that area onto the cloning brush.

8. Paint over the dust spot. Repeat to eliminate the spots, the scratch, and any blemishes that you find. Remove the extra catch light in each eye. (Your image should look like Figure 9-6.)

Work inward from the edges, changing only a pixel or two at a time. If the area is large (such as the scratch), change the point of origin for the cloning from time to time, to maintain a good match of tones.

TIP

Dodging Shadows

When making color or black-and-white prints by exposing photosensitive paper under an enlarger, the darkroom worker can modify how the image appears; that's done by giving extra exposure to some areas of the print, and holding back other areas so they don't receive too long an exposure. The image is visible in negative form on the paper as the exposure is made, so the process is relatively simple. A shadow that would appear too dark on the finished print can be made lighter, or *dodged*, by inserting an object between the lens and the paper; that portion of the image is then prevented from being exposed for the full length of time.

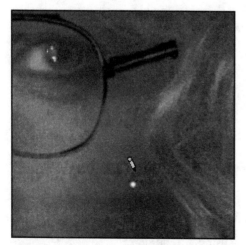

Figure 9-5 *Select an area to clone.*

Figure 9-6 *Dust spots, scratches, and blemishes are eliminated.*

Sometimes the darkroom worker will use a hand to obscure large areas of the image, but more frequently a dodging tool is used. Often handmade from coat-hanger wire and a piece of cardboard, the dodging tool looks something like an all-day sucker (but can actually take any shape). The tool is waved around over the area being dodged, so that the handle doesn't show up and the edges of the dodging effect are feathered.

The opposite procedure, called *burning*, is also used to give additional exposure only to areas of the image that need it, such as highlights that would appear too light or burned out in the final print. The most common tool for this effect is a pair of hands: a roundish opening between them can be varied in size, to burn more or less of the image, as desired. Figure 9-7 shows the difference between dodging and burning.

The portrait needs some judicious dodging to lighten some shadows under and above the eyes of the subject. You can also use dodging to create larger, lighter catch lights in the eyes, and to brighten up the white part of the eye. As you see, dodging is a ver-satile tool, indeed. To dodge your picture, just follow these steps:

1. Make a copy of the image. (Are you sensing a trend here?)

Figure 9-7 *Left to right: Unmodified image; dodged area; burned area.*

2. Double-click the Dodge/Burn tool; in the Tool Options dialog box, set it for Dodge. Click the Shadows button so that your dodging will affect the shadows most.

3. For the first modification, choose the smallest brush size (usually one or two pixels in width), and set Exposure to 50 percent. (The Exposure parameter controls how much the Dodge tool will lighten an area with each application.)

4. Dodge the remaining catch light in each eye. Click on a catch light; then, holding down the mouse button, drag to lighten that area of the pupil. Repeat for the other eye.

5. Select a slightly larger brush size (four to six pixels), one with a feathered edge. (You want to affect a broader portion of the image, to produce a subtler effect.)

6. Reduce the Exposure to 15 percent.

7. Use the Dodge tool to lighten the white part of both eyes, so the blood vessels and dark shadows are no longer visible.

> Try not to remove all the tone and details from those areas. Because the exposure has been reduced, you may have to go over an area two or three times to produce the effect you want.

CAUTION

8. Select an even larger brush size (one about the size of the pupil in the model's eye), and use it to remove the shadows under her eyes and beneath the eyebrows. Don't go overboard: dodge a little at a time, using broad strokes.

9. Stop and look at your results, then apply more lightening until the image looks good (as shown in Figure 9-8).

Figure 9-8 *Shadows under the eyes and sclera of the eyes have been lightened.*

Major Surgery

Many of the photographs you'll need to retouch won't be in as "good" shape as the one you worked on in the first part of this chapter. Frequently, you'll be asked to salvage a real dog of a photo that absolutely must be resurrected from snapshot hell for one reason or another. Perhaps it's the only picture available of someone (or something), or it has some importance for historical reasons. Here are some variations you might encounter.

- Photo restoration. Pictures from 20 to 150 years old may have been damaged by the ravages of time, and you'll need to remove scratches, replace missing sections, and perhaps reconstruct facial features from the fragments that remain.

- Photo travesty. These are snapshots with major digressions from desired content. That is, there's a tree growing from someone's head, an unwanted bystander gawking at the main subject, or other pictorial clutter. Your job will be to remove these elements.

- Major facial surgery. Your subject is wearing glasses in the photo, but switched to contacts years ago. An unfortunate accident of lighting accentuated slightly protuberant ears, transforming them from an interesting characteristic to features that would make Dumbo blush. Bad shadows have given someone a double chin. They don't really look like this photo—can you improve it?

The model in the test photo you've been working on doesn't look her best in those ugly glasses. Let's use the cloning technique to remove them, and then make some other changes. You're going to retouch the picture to replace the glasses with surrounding skin tones.

1. Make a copy of your image. (You're really due for a major gaffe by now.)

2. Duplicate the image layer in your copy. This is a handy trick to help you correct small errors. If you make a mistake, you can erase a portion of the layer you are editing, and reveal the original layer underneath.

3. Using the Clone tool, copy areas of the cheek over the rims of the glasses. Set new origin points constantly, to maintain a good match of skin tones. For example, the rims of the glasses at the left side of the photo can be replaced by the cheek edge immediately below. (In Figure 9-9, I've already replaced part of the lower rim of the glasses at the right side with surrounding cheek tones.)

4. Finish up the cloning. (Your final results should look like the image at right in Figure 9-10; the original image is at left. You also can see Figure 9-10 in the color insert of this book.)

Figure 9-9 *Replacing the glasses with skin tones*

Figure 9-10 *Before (left) and after (right)*

Compositing

If you study magazine ads, you'd think that image editing programs are used primarily to transplant the Eiffel Tower to Sunset Boulevard. Indeed, merging two or more images seamlessly to generate a new one is among the most powerful special effects you can produce with the GIMP. Whether it's rearranging the pyramids of Egypt to produce a better photographic composition (as National Geographic controversially did for one of its covers), or placing Big Ben in the middle of La Mancha, compositing can create new and interesting images from old ones.

In this section, you'll tackle something only slightly more realistic than moving the Eiffel Tower, but still challenging. The goal: combine the best features of four images to produce a postcard-quality photo that doesn't scream FAKE—until you look at it very closely. Let's see what you can do with this collection of off-color, badly composed rejects from a vacation in Europe (as seen in Figure 9-11 and the color insert of this book).

You'll be surprised at how easy it is to fashion a silk purse when you have the right tools. Compositing actually requires some retouching skills, and the ability to cut and paste creatively. That's about all there is to it.

Figure 9-11 *Four shoebox rejects ready for compositing*

How Green Is the Ocean

This is an advanced exercise. I won't give you detailed step-by-step instructions, but rather will tell you what I did in more general terms, so you can try the techniques out on your own. You can download the images I worked with from my Web site at www.dbusch.com/gimp.

1. The first step is to open the file Monzon.jpg, which contains a photo of a castle located somewhere in Spain. Then open the file Sea.jpg, which contains a picture of the Mediterranean.

2. Add some contrast and snap to the water, using the GIMP's Brightness/ Contrast controls; boost those values by around +13 percent for brightness and +30 percent for contrast.

3. Next, make the water even bluer and more saturated with the GIMP's Hue/Saturation control. Finally, switch to the Monzon image; using Quick Mask, paint a "seashore" selection around the lower edge of the image (as shown in Figure 9-12).

Figure 9-12 *Mask everything except a seashore shape.*

4. Then go back to the Sea photo, and copy it. In the Monzon image, paste the sea into the selection. Use the Dodge tool to darken the sea along the shore. (Your image should look like Figure 9-13.)

5. Now remove the sky portion of the image, by selecting it and then pressing Ctrl-X. The sky is homogeneous enough in tone that the magic wand does a good job of grabbing most of it. Set your magic wand to a pixel tolerance of about 32. Add to the selection, to round up any loose pixels. When you've selected the entire sky, load the Clouds.jpg image, copy it, and paste it into the Monzon image in the sky selection. (Your image should now look something like Figure 9-14.)

Some Subtle Touches

Add some subtle touches to make the image look even better.

1. Use the Dodge tool to darken the top third of the sky, giving the picture a more dramatic look.

2. Add a faint "shadow" to the sea by drawing, on a separate layer, a shape that approximates the outline of the castle. Fill it with black, and then blur it so it looks shadow-like. Then invert the shadow, use the Transform tool to add a slant, and change the opacity of the layer to about 30 percent.

Figure 9-13 *Seashore has been inserted*

Figure 9-14 *Adding the sky*

3. Carefully select Big Ben from its image, and paste into the composite. Use the Dodge tool to darken the right half of the tower.

4. Then, flatten the image and make any final changes you want. You can blur the seashore a bit, as if it were being washed by waves. (The final image is shown in Figure 9-15 and in the color insert of this book.)

Advanced Compositing

Once you begin serious compositing and retouching, you'll want to learn more advanced ways of pasting images together. The GIMP includes a facility called Blending Modes, which lets you have a great deal of control over how pixels are merged when you combine layers or paint with a tool. When you're blending pixels, the mode determines whether the pixels you paint or the pixels in the upper layer (if you're blending layers) are opaque, become darker or lighter, or add or subtract the values of the pixels beneath.

If it sounds complicated, it is, at least when it comes to understanding how each mode works from a description alone. This is one feature that you must try out to really grasp. I'll start you out with a few simple modes to help you get the idea. For

Figure 9-15   *The final composited image*

now, assume that the image information in each layer is 100 percent opaque, and that transparent areas in the image are 100 percent transparent. Figure 9-16 shows four images of Big Ben on a transparent layer, with a rainbow gradient in the layer underneath. (You can see this same image in the color insert of this book also.)

At left, I've blended the two using the *Normal* blend mode. In this mode, every non-transparent pixel in the upper layer obscures every pixel of the layer underneath. If there are transparent pixels, they mix according to their respective opacity settings. Nothing difficult to understand here.

In the next image from the left, the mode was set to *Dissolve*, which affects soft or feathered edges, by randomizing which pixels in the edges of objects in the top layer become transparent, allowing the pixels underneath to show through. Notice how the side edges of Big Ben, which are feathered, seem to dissolve, while the base of the tower, which has a hard edge, remains undissolved. This mode requires at least some semitransparent pixels (as found in feathered edges) to operate.

Next is the *Multiply* mode, which is a good tool for making shadows and dark areas even darker. It acts as if both layers were transparencies superimposed on a light table. As you view this "sandwich" of layers, the pixels that are on top of each other become darker, producing an overall denser image.

Figure 9-16 *Left to right: Normal, Dissolve, Multiply, and Screen blending modes*

At far right is *Screen* mode, which operates as if you had a pair of slide projectors and were projecting both transparencies onto the same screen, producing a lighter image where pixels overlap. If you recall the additive color model, this effect will make more sense to you: beams of light when added together produce a lighter color. The effect is similar to what you get with the GIMP's Addition mode, but note that the differences don't show up well on the printed page.

Four more blending modes deserve mention.

In *Overlay* mode, the pixels in the upper layer modify those in the lower layer, multiplying the dark pixels and screening the light pixels, producing an interesting blended effect.

Difference mode (which produces results similar to the GIMP's Subtraction mode) inverts the pixels in the lower layers according to the brightness values of the upper layer; a white pixel in the upper layer inverts the lower pixels completely, a black pixel has no effect, and gray pixels in between have proportionate values.

In *Darken* mode, the colors in the top layer are applied only if they are darker than the pixels below, in effect producing only darker colors and no lighter ones.

Lighten mode is the reverse: the pixels in the top layer are applied only if they are lighter than the pixels underneath. (See Figure 9-17 and the color insert of this book.)

Four last modes let you change one of the hue, saturation, color, or value settings without altering the others.

In *Hue* mode, the hue values from the upper layer are mixed with the saturation and value settings for the layer underneath.

Saturation mode keeps the saturation values from the upper layer, and mixes them with the hue and value settings for the layer underneath.

Color mode combines the hue and saturation modes, keeping both the hue and saturation values of the upper layer, mixing them with the value settings of the layer underneath.

Value mode keeps the lightness values from the upper layer, and mixes them with the hue and saturation settings of the layer underneath. (Merging an image using these modes and converting to grayscale yields less-than-impressive results, as you can see in Figure 9-18; for the real dope, check out the same image in the color insert.)

Figure 9-17 *Left to right: Overlay, Difference, Darken, Lighten blending modes*

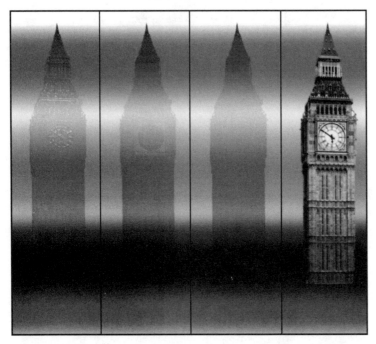

Figure 9-18 *Left to right: Hue, Saturation, Color, Value blending modes*

What's Next

In this chapter, you started using the features you mastered earlier in the book in a useful way, for retouching and compositing images. But the material here was only a starter. To become adept at combining and manipulating images, you need to practice what you've learned. I'll show you some ways to put these skills to work in the next chapter, where you will learn to use the GIMP to create Web graphics.

f ever there were a match made in heaven, it's Linux and the World Wide Web. Both emerged in the early 1990s and became popular because they fostered a totally free flow of information. It's no accident that the Linux-based Apache Web server is in the midst of seizing from UNIX the mantle of favorite Web server platform. Linux and the Web—and hence the GIMP—were made for each other.

Indeed, you'll find more Web-friendly features built into the GIMP than in most other image-editing programs for any operating system. Creating eye-catching buttons, rules, logos, and other artifacts is not only easy, but in some cases completely automated for you. The GIMP also has built-in tools for creating image maps and animated graphics. This chapter will look at some of the things you can do on the Web with the GIMP. Unfortunately, there's not room in this book to teach you everything you need to know about HTML, dynamic HTML, animation, image maps, or other specialized tools; the best that I can do here is provide an overview you can use to launch your own further investigations.

Browsers Retrieve Your Web Graphics

It's easy to forget that as recently as a few years ago, Linux was a command line-heavy clone of UNIX, and the Web consisted mainly of linked text documents. Today, both are brimful of graphics. However, graphics intended for Web pages have some special requirements. You can't take any image you've patched together and embed it in a Web page. It may be too large, too blurry, take too long to download, or have colors that won't show up well in all visitors' browsers.

Sloppy efforts make a Web page look ugly, and can serve more as a distraction than as an attraction; worse, just one pixel-heavy image that takes agonizing minutes to download can send your visitors fleeing faster than you can click a Back button.

Before I jump into the meat of things, let's get a little of the obligatory "history of the World Wide Web" background out of the way. U.S. Department of Defense Advanced Research Projects Agency (ARPANET). Tim Berners-Lee. HTML. Mozilla. Apache. Java. AOL. Microsoft. XML. MP3. DSL. That about covers it. In 20 years, those 11 phrases are all you'll remember about the Web anyway, so why not just memorize them now and move on? I hate rehashing background stuff. Web pages consist of simple ASCII files, which contain text, instructions that tell a browser how to display the text, and information about any accompanying images. When your browser goes out to retrieve something from the Web, it supplies the URL; it receives in turn either the HTML code for the page, or an image, or some other file. As the browser receives these files, text, and instructions, you see a page, view an image, or are offered a file for downloading (or a combination of these occurs). Amidst all the HTML tags for formatting stuff, some instructions point to the URL of your immortal Web graphics.

What the GIMP Can Do

Your favorite Linux image editor can help you create, format, colorize, and squeeze down to palatable size any graphics you want to put in your Web pages. The GIMP is outstandingly flexible when it comes to building Web graphics. You'll use it for any or all of the following functions:

- **File conversion.** Even if you have an image ready to go, you'll still have to convert it to one of the formats supported by Web browsers. If you've already had some experience in Web page design, you know that it is essential to have some way of saving files as conventional, interlaced, or transparent GIF (*Graphics Interchange Format*); you also need to be able to save them as standard or progressive JPEG (*Joint Photographic Experts Group*)—at selected compression/quality ratios. If the PNG (*Portable Network Graphics*) format ever becomes popular, the GIMP will handle that as well.

- **Image enhancement.** Even great images can benefit from cropping, flipping, or rotating, and, if a GIF format is your target, convert 24-bit, 16.7 million-color images to an optimized palette of 256 or fewer hues.

- **Image modification.** Many images may require retouching, the addition of cool textures or special effects, and other modifications.

- **Image creation.** If you're building buttons, designing your own horizontal rules, creating a few arrows, or concocting a logo, you'll want the most flexible set of pixel-bending tools available for working with an empty canvas. Fancy options for creating type and 3-D images that jump off the page are cool, too. You can do all these things with the GIMP; best of all, it also includes automated Script-Fu features to take care of the most tedious tasks for you.

- **Specialized Web tools.** The GIMP has everything built in that you might need to create animations, image maps, and other Web page enhancers.

Image Requirements for the Web

Compromises. We always have to make compromises. You want as much information and detail in your images as possible, but the human life span is limited, and the attention span even more so. It would be nice to show that snazzy picture as a full-sized 1024 x 768 pixel graphic, but many of your visitors would end up viewing only a corner of it at a time. You want a lot of color, but some visitors may be using chromatically challenged monitors. The following sections describe some of the compromises you must make.

File Size

A 1024 x 768 pixel graphic with 16.7 million colors may knock your eyes out on the screen, but unfortunately you're in the 20-plus megabyte neighborhood (uncompressed) here. Tiny files, in the 7K to 50K range, download much faster—and can look good. The GIMP can help you trim those bloated images to manageable size.

Physical Size

The physical size of your image on the screen also is important when you create your Web images, as the amount of real estate that a graphic takes up affects how the browser displays other elements. The available display area on your visitors' monitors will vary widely. Some may have 640 x 480 displays (or smaller, if they're accessing the Web on a PDA or other handheld), while others may be using a 1024 x 678 window. On a 19- to 21-inch monitor, even larger displays are possible. (I just love my 1280 x 1024 image on a 19-inch monitor, but I wouldn't try to create a Web page that big.) Remember too that even with a given display resolution, the user may have resized the browser window to something smaller, in order to fit more applications on the screen.

Color Depth

Some say that the number of colors in an image has become a non-issue. Everybody has true-color, 16.7-million hue displays now. Who needs to reduce images to 256 colors? Nobody? Guess again. You'll use lots of images with 256 or fewer colors, particularly if you're working with GIFs. If you only have eight important colors in an image, why save it as a 256-color image (let alone one with millions of colors) when an eight-color GIF is so much smaller? The GIMP's Indexed Color mode can help you manage color so you won't get out of your depth.

Browser Compatibility and Common Sense

You'd like your graphics to jump and dance around on the screen. Web page multimedia isn't all that hard to achieve these days, but suffers from two drawbacks. First, not all browsers can handle fancy graphics, especially those that require a special plug-in. Second, if the intent of your Web site is to convey information rather than dazzle or entertain visitors, common sense tells you that overblown graphics may just add to download times and disgruntle the more serious types. And we all know what happens in the wake of disgruntlement.

Meeting these Web requirements is easy, and you've already learned most of what you need to know. To reduce image size, crop an image into a rectangular selection that includes only the most essential parts of your image. Or resize the image to fit more image area in the same pixel map. The GIMP has built-in color reduction capabilities that help you choose the best palette for your GIF images. Here are some rules of thumb to follow:

- Set up your pages to accommodate the likely lowest-common-denominator display size: a 640 x 480 monitor, with a browser window that is smaller than that.

- Try to keep each Web graphic well below 50K in size, especially if you plan to include a lot of them on a page. You'll find that 25K is even better, and things like rules and buttons can often be trimmed to 7K or even smaller.

- Add up the sizes of all the images you want to display on a page, and keep the total smaller than 200K—preferably a lot smaller. A page with that much graphics still takes a minute or so to download with a fast connection, but if you sprinkle in enough interesting text and spread the graphics around, visitors will have something to read while your page downloads.

- Confine the heavy-duty graphics images to certain pages, and provide your visitors with a warning, rather than springing them as a vicious surprise. If you have a graphics-intensive site (say, a display of your photographs or artwork), you might want to include only enough graphics on your main page to entice visitors into your gallery. Those who do not want to wait for long image downloads can avoid those pages.

- Small thumbnail images can be placed on a page and used as a preview of a larger graphic image. You can place the full-size image on another page, or have it displayed when the visitor clicks on the thumbnail. That way, a visual cue is provided that helps the user decide whether to proceed with the full download.

Graphics Formats for the Web

When you're actually creating your images, you can work with any format you like. Indeed, you'll want to save works-in-progress in the GIMP's native .XCF format, so you can retain all the layers and other GIMP-specific attributes. When you're ready to export your image to a Web page, your choices break down into two—GIF and JPEG—with a couple variations of each.

Saving Images in a GIFFY

GIF (Graphics Interchange Format) is a 256-color image format originally developed for use on the CompuServe Information Network. It was created so that online denizens would have a common graphics format to exchange images, regardless of whether they were using Macintoshes, PCs, Amigas, or some other platform. GIF quickly became a universal graphics format on the Web, and support for it has been built into all graphics-ready browsers.

GIF was hit with some controversy a while back when Unisys, which owns the copyright rights to some of the algorithms used to compress GIF files, indicated it would expect royalties from vendors of applications with GIF support. For a while it appeared there would be a mass exodus away from GIF to some other format. A number of alternatives, such as the very cool but very unsupported PNG format, were proposed. (In a way, the situation was a lot like the KDE/GNOME situation; KDE was based on a set of commercial libraries, while GNOME was built on a totally Open Source foundation.) Luckily, some of the major vendors got in line and signed arrangements with Unisys, and there have been no problems since, so GIF appears to be viable online for a while yet.

GIF supports only up to 256 colors. On the plus side, working with 256 or fewer colors means that the resulting images can potentially be viewed on any display screen offering 256 or more colors. Of course, with today's video displays there is less need to comply with the 256-color limitation. (Actually, a safe Web palette consists of only 216 colors, as a group of colors are reserved for some operating systems' use.)

GIF doesn't require a specific number of colors, as long as you use 256 or fewer. If your image contains or looks good with only 87 colors, or 31, or 11, you can reduce the image to that number of hues. The benefits? Your reduced color image will be easier to display on the screen, and the file size will drop dramatically, especially with GIF's compression routines applied.

Because GIF is limited to 256 colors, some types of images, particularly photographs with many different colors, just can't be represented accurately in that mode. Images with subtle gradations from hue to hue don't adapt well to GIF, because the GIMP must clump groups of similar colors together and represent them with a single hue. That produces a banding effect, rather than a smooth transition, noticeable in sky areas of images, and in other portions with gradations. (See Figure 10-1.)

Traditionally, GIF has been only barely acceptable for many kinds of photographs. Its strength lies in handling images with fewer colors, especially images in which lines and sharpness are important. That's because GIF's file compression scheme is lossless: no image information (other than the extra colors you discard) is lost during the conversion to GIF. If an image was sharp before GIF compression, it will be just as sharp when decompressed and displayed on the screen.

Text and lines show up especially well in GIF files. If you want to add some fancy text to a Web page, GIF is often your best choice. There's a special reason for that, in addition to GIF's inherent lossless compression: GIFs can be made transparent.

Well, not really. Transparent GIFs aren't actually translucent. Instead, you can select one color (and only one) that will be ignored by the browser as if it weren't there. The background color will show through instead. So, if you create text on a background and then make that background transparent, the browser will merge the text itself smoothly with its own background. The text will appear to be embedded right in the

Figure 10-1 *Left, an original image; right, reduced to 256 colors*

background page itself, instead of showing within a rectangular image (which is the case with non-transparent Web images). Figure 10-2 shows a transparent GIF image on a Web page.

GIF can be interleaved; that is, alternating lines of the image can be downloaded from your page first, giving the browser a coarse preview of the final image, which then gradually becomes sharper and more detailed as the rest of the GIF data is received. Interleaved GIF images can grab a visitor's eye long enough to lure them further into your page. Of course, the interleaved images are a virtual necessity: GIF files often are relatively large, and therefore take a while to download.

GIFs can also be animated. It's possible to incorporate several images within a GIF file. Most browsers will display each of these images in turn, producing alternating images; if you've made animation-like changes just to small portions of the images, they will create an animated effect. Animated GIFs provide a good way to add movement to your Web page without using Java, XML, DHTML, or complex programming.

Figure 10-2 *A transparent GIF*

More Colors with JPEG

JPEG (Joint Photographic Experts Group) is a flexible format that supports nearly 17 million colors, making it suitable for photographs. Unlike GIF, it has a dial-a-quality mode. This allows you to choose between high-quality, virtually lossless compression (and larger file sizes) or lower-quality, lossy compression (which produces remarkably small image files, at the expense of discarding image information).

JPEG supports very high compression rates, which speed up downloads dramatically. Some image quality may be lost, but the amount of compression and degradation are selectable, so the Web builder gets to decide how much sharpness to compromise in the name of speed and viewer-friendliness.

Because JPEG handles millions of colors, full-color images are reproduced well. The GIMP provides a sliding control that allows choosing between smallest file size/lowest image quality and largest file size/highest image quality. (See Figure 10-3.)

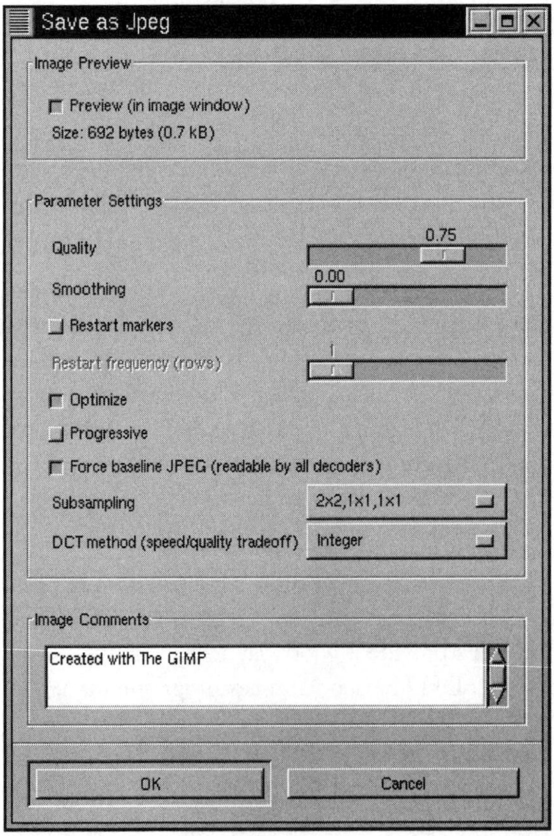

Figure 10-3 *JPEG options dialog box*

The downside is that not all browsers support progressive or transparent JPEG formats.

The smaller file sizes make it possible for a JPEG to download very quickly, making it easier for a Web page to bristle with good-looking images. The lossy compression scheme of JPEG, though, robs many images of needed sharpness; JPEG, with the format's high-color rendition, may be a poor choice for finely detailed artwork.

Those one or two users out there who still have 256-color displays may not be able to view JPEG images as you intend them to be seen.

Saving a File as a GIF

Although a Perl-based filter called Prepare for GIF is in development, you can do a good job just using the GIMP's basic tools. You must first reduce a 24-bit color image to an 8-bit, 256-color image before you can save it as a GIF. Right-click in the image, and choose Image | Indexed; you have quite a few options, beginning with the choices in the General Palette Options area of the Indexed Color Conversion dialog box, which then appears. (See Figure 10-4.)

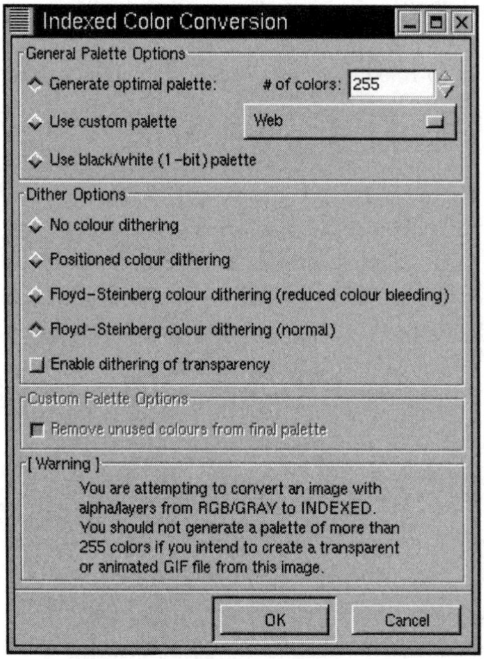

Figure 10-4 *Convert to an indexed image.*

The Generate Optimal Palette Option

The General Optimal palette option will examine all the colors in your image, selecting a palette of colors with a number that you specify, that can best represent the colors in the image. Similar colors will be assigned the same value to reduce the hues in the image down to the required number. Obviously, quite a few colors are lost in the process, but the situation is seldom as bad as you might think; in real life, an image may contain only a few thousand colors, and 256 variations can do a pretty good job, except in the case of images with very fine gradations of color, such as gradients or an expanse of sky.

NOTE

Theoretically, reducing 16.7 million colors to 256 colors would require assigning a single hue to each of around 65,000 pixels. Luckily, no RGB image really has 16.7 million different colors. A rather large Web graphic measuring 320 x 200 pixels would contain a total of 64,000 different picture elements. Even if every single pixel were a different color (an unlikely happenstance), the most colors you would have in the image would be 64,000. That means "only" 250 different hues would have to be represented by a particular color in the worst case.

An optimized palette allocates colors intelligently, on the basis of the content of the image. A portrait of someone wearing a blue sweater would require a lot of subtle shades of blue, and many browns or pinks to make up flesh tones. You might need very few greens or deep reds. So an optimized palette can do an even better job of representing an image with 256 colors.

Some images don't even require that many hues. You may have created a logo that uses only seven or eight colors. The Indexed Color Conversion dialog box lets you dial in the number of colors you need, producing a smaller GIF that downloads faster. If you tell the GIMP to remove any colors not required for the image (in the Use Custom Palette options area of the dialog box), you may end up with an indexed image with fewer than the number of colors you specified (and therefore with a smaller file size).

The Use Custom Palette Option

Sometimes you may not want the colors in an image to represent real life, preferring to reduce the image to a palette of colors that work well with each other; the Use Custom Palette option lets you choose from any of the default color palettes available with the GIMP, plus any you may have created yourself (choose File | Dialogs | Palette or press Ctrl-P to define your own palettes, as described earlier in this book).

The Use WWW-Optimised Palette Option

The Use WWW-Optimised Palette option limits your image's color palette to the 216 "browser" safe colors, leaving the other 40 colors reserved for your operating system for use in displaying its windows and other objects.

The Use Black/White (1-bit) Palette Option

Finally, the Use Black/White (1-bit) Palette option converts your image to a black-and-white image with no colors or grays at all; this can be an interesting effect, as shown in Figure 10-5.

Dithering

Dithering is a way of simulating colors by placing available colors together, so that the eye blends them together to produce a new color. This is much the way the cyan, magenta, yellow, and black halftone dots on a printed page are combined by the eye to produce a full-color picture. The GIMP has several dithering options, including *No colour dithering* (which provides a sharper image, but only with the colors in your palette). The other dithering options provide various color effects, which can vary significantly from image to image. The easiest thing to do is to try them on your image until you find a dithering scheme that works best for you.

Figure 10-5 *A black-and-white bi-level image*

Saving the GIF

Once you have reduced an RGB image to 256 or fewer colors, you can save it as a GIF file. Right-click on the image, choose File | Save As, and select the GIF option. The Save as GIF dialog box, which is divided into sections called GIF Options and Animated GIF Options, will appear. (See Figure 10-6.)

There are two checkboxes in the GIF Options section. When the Interlace box is checked, a flattened image (one without layers) can be stored as layers of odd- and even-numbered lines; a browser can display these alternating lines (first one set, then the other) as a way of providing a coarse view of an image first, before a download is finished. (If you're saving an image for the Web, you'll usually want to have it interlaced.) By checking the GIF Comment box, you can place a line of text within your GIF file (such as the name of the creator, or your Web page's URL); the comment can be viewed when the GIF file is loaded.

Animating GIFs

If your GIF has several frames, you can build them into an animation. Create at least one layer for each frame.

- To produce movement, blinking, or another animated effect, you can either use somewhat different images in consecutive layers, or vary layers slightly with images that don't change much between frames.

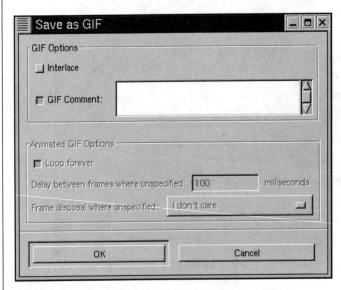

Figure 10-6 *The Save as GIF dialog box*

- Specify the amount of delay between frames if you don't want to use a uniform amount. (You can skip this step if you want, say, to have the same 100 ms delay between frames; that value can be entered when you save the file.) To specify the delay, double-click each frame and give it a name (frame numbers are best, such as **Frame 1** or **Frame 2**), and then place the amount of delay in parentheses after the name. To specify a delay of 200 ms after Frame 1, you'd name it **Frame 1 (200ms)**.

- If you want the frames to combine as they are displayed (that is, the image in the previous layer is visible as the next is displayed), say, for progressively revealed "bullet points," append **(combine)** to the layer's name.

- If you'd rather replace each frame with the next one (as you would do in a movie or cartoon), add **(replace)** instead.

Right-click in the image, and choose Save As. Select the GIF option. The Export File dialog box, shown in Figure 10-7, will appear.

The Export File dialog box advises you that the GIF must be exported to be saved as an animated GIF; the original file and its layers will not be changed by this exporting step. Export the file as appropriate. The Save as GIF dialog box appears again; you can choose to loop the GIF forever (it will play over and over), and you can now specify a default delay between frames for those frames for which you did not explicitly enter a delay period.

Saving as JPEG

To save a file as a JPEG, right-click and choose File | Save As; then choose the .jpg extension. If your image is indexed (say, you had previously converted it to a GIF), the Export File dialog box appears. You can choose to convert the image to RGB or grayscale; clicking Export will also flatten an exported image, if it contains layers. (The Export process creates a new, flattened, .jpg file, and does not modify your original image.) You can select from the following options:

Figure 10-7 *Exporting a GIF file*

- Preview. Creates a preview image that can be displayed by image editors like the GIMP and Photoshop before you load the image.
- Quality. Specifies the trade-off between quality and compression, 0.00 representing the highest compression and 1.00 representing the highest quality.
- Smoothing. Determines how much anti-aliasing will be used to reduce jaggies in your image. (You'll get blurry edges, but the overall effect can be better.)
- Image comments. Adds text that will be saved with the image.

The latest version of the GIMP has several additional technical options, which will be of less use to most workers. For example, you can create a progressive (interlaced) version if you have reason to believe a browser that supports this mode will be used. You can also force a "baseline JPEG," which is the simplest type and can be read by virtually any program that supports JPEG. DCT method lets you set the *Discrete Cosine Transfer* algorithm (you don't want to know what that is) to optimize speed of translation versus quality; either the default Integer setting or the Fast Integer setting will provide the fastest processing times, whereas the Floating Point setting gives the best quality.

Image Maps

An image map is a "clickable" graphic on your Web page. It's a single image with *hotspots*, or regions that are linked to a particular URL or other hypertext link. Instead of embedding a whole collection of images on your page—one for each link—you can combine bunches of links into one or more clickable image maps.

This tool often is not used in quite the way that it used to be for grouping links today; it's usually easier to slice an image up into pieces and to deposit each piece into a separate cell of a table, and many sites have switched to that method.

The cells themselves are linked to the URLs. A sliced image can be faster to load, and you can optimize each slice so it looks its best. An image map can take a long time to load, and as a single image, it must have uniform color depth and other attributes.

However, the GIMP has a good image map tool included, so I'll describe the technique briefly. In an image map, the regions within an image are defined by their coordinates. For example, a region measuring 100 x 100 pixels, starting at the upper-left corner of the image, could be defined by a set of four numbers, representing the ranges of the x and y coordinates within the image—0,0; 0,100; 100,100; 100,0. (That would set the four corners of the region, clockwise from the lower left.) Tell the browser to load a specific URL whenever a visitor's mouse clicks within that area, and you're all set.

Of course, things get slightly more complicated if you want to use a region that's not a rectangle, but the concept is the same, and just as easy to understand. Define a circle by specifying the x and y coordinates of its center, plus the number of pixels in its radius. Or define an irregular polygon by listing the coordinates of its connecting points.

Image maps are divided up into server-side and client-side varieties. With a server-side map, the Web server takes care of all the work. The only thing your browser has to supply the server with is the coordinates of the mouse when you click on one of the labeled areas. The coordinates defining a hotspot are stored on the server, along with the URL to be accessed when a region is clicked, and handled by a CGI script. (One downside is that an overloaded server can slow down image map processing considerably.)

The advent of client-side image maps solved some of the problems found in the original implementation of clickable images on Web pages. To use a client-side image map, a browser must support certain HTML extensions; these are tags that define the image being used as a map (much as the <IMG SRC> tag associates a graphic with a URL), and that define what areas are matched with each hyperlink you want to use. You don't need any CGI capabilities: all the work is handled by the browser, which determines which URL you have requested, and passes your request on to the Web server.

The other advantages of client-side maps are clear. The biggest one is that you can test your image maps locally on your computer, using just your Web browser. With server-side image maps, you must upload the map and revised page, and test it while online. Client-side maps are more portable, as they work on any server, with any browser that supports them.

To create a map for your image, right-click in the image, and choose Filters | Misc | Image Map. A mini-program appears. (See Figure 10-8.)

You'll see a version of your image, along with a set of toolbars, menus, and buttons. The functions of most of these are obvious. The menu options, several of whose functions are duplicated in the toolbar icons and buttons, are in the following categories.

- File: To open and save images and their map files
- Edit: To cut, copy, paste, and select portions of an image
- View: To zoom in and out in the image, and to view information, including the HTML source code being generated by the mini-application
- Mapping: To choose the shape of the region (circle, rectangle, polygon, and so on)
- Goodies: To set up and use grids and guides

To define an image map, just create the regions you want within your image by dragging with the mouse. When you've defined a region, a dialog box pops up. (See Figure 10-9.)

Figure 10-8 *Image Map application*

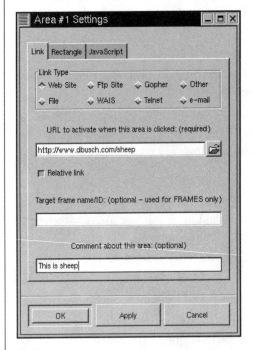

Figure 10-9 *Defining a region*

You can use the *Link* tab of the dialog box to define the kind of URL link (Web, FTP, mailto, and so on), the URL itself, a target (for use with frames), and a comment. The *Rectangle* tab allows you to type in the coordinates for rectangular regions manually. The *JavaScript* tab simplifies entering JavaScript behaviors associated with various actions, such as moving a mouse into or out of a region.

When you click OK, the HTML code needed to create that region is created (you can view it by choosing View | Source). After you've defined your regions, you can save the map file and set it up on your server, as required for the kind of image map you're working with. This certainly beats defining image maps manually!

Creating Rules, Buttons, and Other Artifacts

All the techniques you've learned so far can be applied to creating rules and buttons for Web pages with the GIMP. But here are a few more tools you can use. You'll find some handy Web-oriented extensions in the Xtns menu. Choose Xtns | Script-Fu | Web page themes, and select from among *Alien Glow* (four varieties, including horizontal rule, bullet, and button), *Beveled Pattern* (which lets you create rules, buttons, and headings using text you type in), and *Gimp Org.* (which makes it easy to duplicate some of the effects found on the GIMP Web site). These scripts provide dialog boxes (like the one shown in Figure 10-10) in which you can just enter the parameters you want, such as text and font; the script creates the object for you.

Other Script-Fu scripts can create logos and buttons. Figure 10-11 shows some of the effects you can get.

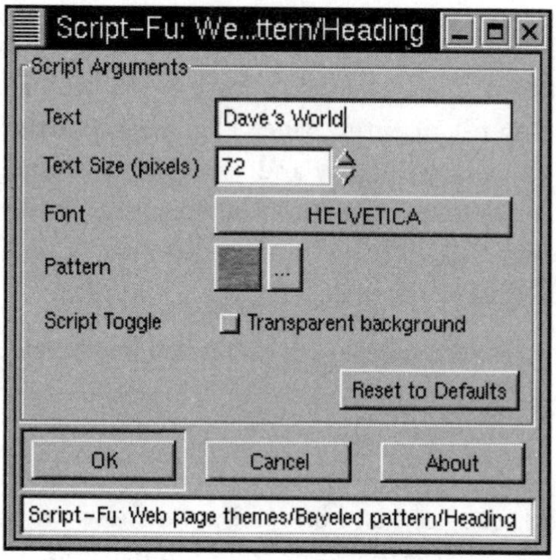

Figure 10-10 *Just add text to create a logo.*

Figure 10-11 *Script-Fu logos and buttons*

The GIMP's filters also can be used to create great-looking effects. (I'll show you how to get some interesting Web graphics using them in the next chapter, which deals with text effects, and the one after that, which offers advice on using the best filters.)

Creating Backgrounds

A good background adds a mood to a Web site, and gives a visitor something to look at while the rest of your graphics and text load. Backgrounds are easy to create, and don't need to be very large, even though they fill an entire page. That's because the browser takes a small image (say, 32 x 32 or 64 x 64 pixels) and repeats it over and over in the form of tiles, covering the whole window. Of course, the edges of the tile have to meld seamlessly with the surrounding tiles, but the GIMP takes care of that for you. To create a simple background, just follow these steps:

1. Create a small file that's the same width as it is high (such as 100 x 100 pixels).
2. Fill the window with a pattern of your choosing.

Two examples of backgrounds I prepared, one light and one dark, are shown in Figure 10-12; you can also select one of the GIMP's patterns from the Patterns palette.

Figure 10-12 *In each case, the tile shown at the left produced the background shown at right.*

3. If you like, add some texture, as I did in Figure 10-13.

4. Adjust the brightness and contrast if necessary. (If the text on your Web page is going to be presented in a dark color, a very light or low-contrast background will look best; that will cause the background to look faded behind the text, making it unobtrusive.)

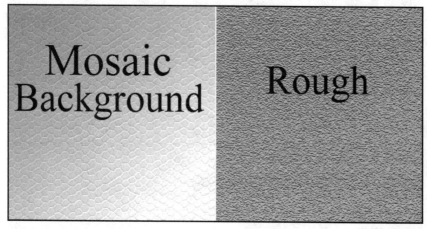

Figure 10-13 *Adding texture*

5. Right-click in the image, and choose Filter | Map | Make Seamless. The GIMP's tiling filter will adjust the borders of the image, so it will tile smoothly with itself.

If you want a background that is plain-colored, but includes one or more vertical bars, the technique is a bit different. In that case, create a very thin, wide image (say 10 pixels high by 1280 pixels wide), and fill it with the color you want for a background. Then draw the vertical bars using the spacing you want. When you define this image as the background, the browser will use it repeatedly, producing an image like the one in Figure 10-14.

Rules and Buttons

You'll find that rules and buttons are basically very similar. The chief difference is that rules are thin and wide, while buttons are most often rectangular or circular. Here are some quick tips for creating simple buttons and rules.

For some instant rules, make a long, thin selection. Choose some contrasting colors for the foreground and background. Apply Shapeburst gradients: the Angled, Spherical, and Dimpled options all produce rather stark effects, while a linear gradient can produce a more shadowed effect. (See Figure 10-15.)

For round 3-D buttons, make a circular selection, and fill with a radial gradient. Apply a texture. Then apply the Filters | Glass Lens effect to make the button shiny. (Check out Filters | Render for some interesting lens flare and glare effects, as shown in Figure 10-16 and in the color insert of this book.)

Figure 10-14 *A background with vertical bars*

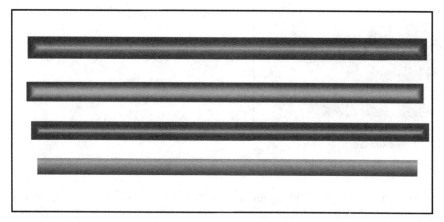

Figure 10-15 *Rules created with Shapeburst (top to bottom): Angled, Spherical, Dimpled, linear gradient*

Place your rules and buttons on a background that matches the background of your Web page, and you can include drop shadows. (There are several filters and plug-ins that produce drop shadows automatically, but you will probably prefer to create custom ones.) Just duplicate an image onto a new layer underneath the original layer, fill its shape with a dark color, and then blur it with Filters | Blur | Gaussian Blur. Offset the shadow slightly. If you like, you can decrease its opacity so it will appear lighter. (Figure 10-17 shows an example of what you can do.)

Figure 10-16 *More 3-D effects*

Figure 10-17 *A drop shadow*

Create a round or rectangular selection; fill it with a linear gradient, starting at the upper-left corner, down to the lower right. Then create a border selection of the same shape, and fill it with the same gradient, but starting in the opposite corner. You'll end up with a raised or depressed 3-D button (like those shown in Figure 10-18).

What's Next

This introduction to Web graphics barely scratches the surface of what you can do for your Web pages with the GIMP. In the next chapter, on text effects, you're going to scratch a little deeper.

Figure 10-18 *Depressed and raised buttons*

Chapter 11: Great Text Effects

The god of Typography must surely have loved fonts, because she made so very many of them. The huge variety of text styles has a purpose; text does so much more than convey words. The shape, size, and arrangement of text in an image can set a mood, affect readability, conjure up a mental image, or offer a subtext that conveys an unspoken message.

If you think that all this sounds a bit heavy for simple GIMP users like you and me, you're probably right. So, in this chapter you won't find lengthy descriptions of how Futura Bold commands authority, or how Souvenir has a friendly, casual aura. Nor will I haughtily condemn this or that font as hopelessly trite.

I won't compare one typeface to another and tell you that one version is a nice cutting—while the same face from a different vendor isn't drawn well. It's not my intent to lecture you at length on how to choose type. The goal here is to make your images look good.

If you mark the sentences in the preceding paragraphs with a yellow highlighter and memorize them, you can drop a few bons mots into your next conversation with typographers. Or you can show them some of your work with the GIMP, and reduce the discussion to comments like "Wow!" and "How did you do that?" Anyway, for most of us, the goal is to use a font as a starting point, letting the GIMP transfer the simplest type into something startling and original.

What Are Fonts, and How Do I Get the GIMP to Use Them?

The font-manipulation facilities built into the GIMP are largely dedicated to doing interesting things with text after you type it into an image. The fonts themselves originate externally to the GIMP, and are supplied by the X Windows font server. That means you don't need to make any special provisions to convince the GIMP to use them. You must only go through hell itself to get X Windows to recognize your fonts. Well, maybe it's not that hard. To get and use fonts, you need understand only two things: what kinds of font-rendering systems there are, and what the techniques are for making fonts available to X Windows.

Font-Rendering Systems

Today there are basically four ways of displaying fonts of importance to Linux users: unscaled, Adobe Type 1, Bitstream Speedo, and Microsoft TrueType. While the Adobe, Bitstream, and Microsoft offerings are not intended specifically for Linux, all three can work well. However, Linux's X Windows font server (usually *Xfree86* for most non-commercial distributions of Linux) has built-in support only for unscaled, Type 1, and Speedo fonts; TrueType support must be added.

Unscaled fonts are nothing more than pixel-pictures of each alphanumeric character in a particular font and size. These fonts can be crafted to look pretty good at their native size, but once you enlarge or reduce them, the dreaded jaggy effects of staircasing appear. Even the best anti-aliasing efforts aren't enough to make an unscaled font look acceptable when enlarged or reduced significantly, as you can see in Figure 11-1.

For that reason, unscaled fonts are often provided in multiple sets. Each set is optimized for a particular size and resolution. Choosing and using the right unscaled font can be tricky.

Other font systems are scalable; that is, the pixels are individually recalculated for each new size, using special algorithms built into the font-rendering technology. Rules called *hints* are embedded in a font's information, to change the way a font is displayed at, say, smaller sizes where individual strokes must be especially legible. Adobe Type 1, Speedo, and TrueType fonts are all scalable. You don't have to perform any extra steps to provide support for Type 1 and Speedo fonts.

Adding TrueType Support

If you want to have access to the broadest range of free and low-cost fonts, you might want to add support for TrueType fonts in the form of a TrueType font server. One such server, called *xfs*, is included with Red Hat Linux distributions, and includes instructions for installation. However, anyone can use another free TrueType server, called *Xfstt*, which you can download from `http://metalab.unc.edu/pub/Linux/X11/Xfstt-x.x.x.tgz` (x.x.x representing the latest version number). Once you've downloaded the archive, copy the TrueType fonts you want to use to a directory, such as the default `/user/ttfonts`. Then extract the *Xfstt* files, and install them in a terminal window using the following commands:

```
make
make install
xset +fp unix/:7100
```

Figure 11-1 *An unscaled font suffers in appearance when enlarged or reduced.*

You can synchronize *Xfstt* to any fonts you add at any time by typing the following:

```
Xfstt -sync
```

Activate the font server by typing the following:

```
Xfstt &
```

Once you've installed support for TrueType fonts, you'll see them in the font list that pops up when you use the Text Tool. There are three tabs. By clicking the middle one of the three, the Font Information tab (shown in Figure 11-2), you can retrieve basic data about any installed font.

Installing Type 1 Fonts

To install Type 1 fonts, the first thing you need to do is log on as root and copy the font files to a directory included in your fontpath (type **xset –q** at a terminal window to view your current fontpath), or create a new directory and add it to the fontpath by typing:

```
xset +fp [path]
```

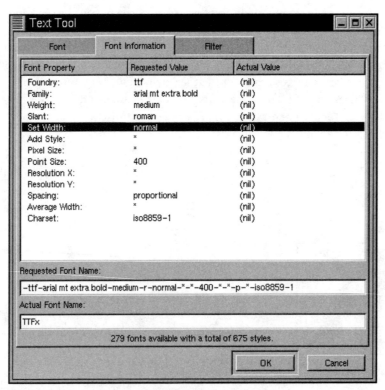

Figure 11-2 *Installed TrueType fonts will appear in the Text Tool dialog box.*

The font server looks for fonts to use in the order they are listed in the fontpath, using the first font that meets the criteria called for by the application. If you want the font server to use fonts in a particular order, you can edit the X86Config file, usually found in `/etc/X11` or `/usr/X11/lib/X11` directories.

Information about the available fonts must be included in a file called fonts.dir residing in each directory in your font path that contains Type 1 fonts. A fonts.dir file must be rebuilt with updated information about the new font names and their characteristics each time you add them.

Although you can edit fonts.dir manually, the easiest way to update these files is with a program called `type1inst-x.x.tar.gz` (where x.x represents the latest version number). The *type1inst* utility reads all the fonts in a directory, and then it creates a new, updated fonts.dir file in that directory. (In case you can't find the utility included with your Linux distribution, you can obtain it from `ftp://metalab.unc.edu/pub/Linux/X11/xutils`.)

Font Styles

You don't really need to know much about font styles to use them: you can simply choose whichever fonts look good to you. However, you'll frequently encounter references to different font styles (for example, "Can you change the headline font to a sans serif style?"), and you should learn a few basics. Here are the main kinds of fonts:

- **Serif.** Serif typefaces include type whose characters contain small strokes, such as the body text in most books. Many studies show that serif fonts are the easiest to read for long blocks of text (the small strokes at the ends of the letters lead the eyes from one character to the next), so in the United States, you will usually find them used for the main text in newspapers, magazines, and books.

- **Sans serif.** Sans serif typefaces, as their name suggests, include type whose characters are without the strokes of serif typefaces. Traditionally, in the United States, sans serif fonts have been used mostly for headlines in the print media. However, in parts of Europe where sans serif typefaces are commonly used for body text, residents of those countries find such fonts much easier to read than serif typefaces.

- **Script.** Script typefaces include type that looks like cursive handwriting. (They in fact are sometimes referred to as cursive typefaces.) Script faces rarely work well as body text. (An image intended to invoke the look and feel of, say, a wedding invitation might be a notable exception.) Script faces are best used as accents in an image, or in some cases for headlines, provided that those headlines are short.

- **Decorative.** Decorative typefaces comprise a catch-all category that doesn't fit in any of the other categories. Generally they are, as their name suggests, decorative, unusual, frilly, or—well, you get the idea. Their purpose in life almost always is to embellish printed matter (or a Web site) with sprinklings here and there for special effect. You should use decorative type judiciously.

- **Monospace.** Almost all typefaces these days are proportionally spaced. That is, each of its characters occupies its own, appropriate width. A capital M requires much more space—often five to seven times the space—than a lowercase i. Monospace typefaces, by contrast, allow the same width for each of their characters. Typewriters of yesteryear (have you been to a museum lately?) generally were monospaced. Monospace type may or may not have serif strokes. Monospace type is good to use when you want all the characters in consecutive lines to line up underneath each other, as each character fits neatly into its own "column."

SideBar

What's a Font?

In typography lingo, a font is a specific typeface in a specific size with a specific weight and style. For example, 10-point Times Roman Medium Italic is a font. Its size is 10 points (roughly 10/72 of an inch), its typeface is Times Roman, its weight is medium, and its style is italic.

The font terminology derived from the simple fact that when movable type was used, each set of type in a certain typeface and size was, indeed, a separate set of characters, kept in their own drawer. Before scalable type (type which can be represented in any desired size without losing sharpness) was introduced to the world of desktop publishing, electronic fonts were often sold by size, typeface, and weight; a particular set for a typeface came in multiple sizes and letter thicknesses.

Now that type has gone completely digital, the term font is often used to mean typeface, which is a particular design and style of type. A typeface family includes all the related typefaces that use similar designs, but may vary by attributes such as stroke thickness. Arial Regular, Arial Italic, Arial Bold, and Arial Bold Italic make up a typical family. Typefaces can also be categorized in even broader families. Arial, Arial Narrow, and Arial Black, for example, are all members of the generic Arial typeface family.

Using the GIMP's Text Tool

Earlier versions of the GIMP had a very simple Text Tool that did little more than let you enter bitmapped alphanumeric characters. The characters couldn't be edited once you'd placed them in an image, even to fix the tiniest typo. Your only recourse was to delete the layer and type in a replacement. The latest version of the GIMP has folded in a much more flexible Dynamic Text plug-in that allows changing the text at any time until the image is flattened. I'll describe both modes.

Working in Standard Mode

To work with the standard mode Text Tool, double-click in the Text Tool on the toolbar. When the Text Tool Options dialog box, shown in Figure 11-3, appears, make sure that the Use Dynamic Text box is unchecked.

If you want to soften the edges of the text to produce smoother lines, click the Antialiasing button. Select the foreground color you want your text to have. Click in the image in the position where you want to insert text. The Text Tool dialog box pops up. The Font tab on the left (shown in Figure 11-4) provides a list of each of the fonts available on your system, in a scroll box at the left side of the tab.

The scroll box in the center shows the font weights and styles (such as light, medium, bold, or italic) available for the highlighted font. The scroll box at right shows the available font sizes, in either points or pixels (depending on whether you have the points or pixels box checked in the Metric area, at lower right). You can also type in a font size if the one you want to use is not listed.

Type the text you want to enter in the Preview window at the bottom of the dialog box; click OK when you're finished, to insert the text in your image. The text appears as a floating selection that behaves more or less like any other floating selection in the GIMP. You can move the text from place to place on your image, by pausing the cursor above it until the Move icon appears (it's not necessary to switch to the Move tool). You can "paste" it down into an active layer by anchoring it (click the Anchor

Figure 11-3 *To work in standard mode, make sure that Use Dynamic Text is switched off in the Text Tool Options dialog box.*

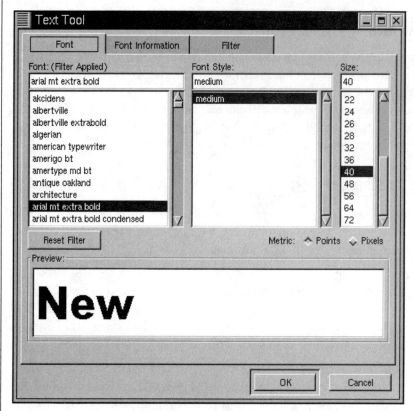

Figure 11-4   *The Font tab shows a list of each of the fonts available on your system.*

button in the Layers & Channels dialog box). Or you can place it in a new layer of its own, either by double-clicking the Floating Selection layer in the Layers & Channels dialog box, or by clicking the New Layer button.

Once the text has been converted from a floating selection, you can no longer edit it, so make sure that you have set the size correctly (and that there are no typos). Although you can resize the text as you can for any bitmapped image, the quality will suffer, so it's best to arrive at a final size before pasting the text down.

If you've placed the text into its own layer, you can change its color. With the text layer active, press Ctrl-A to select everything in the layer. Make sure the Keep Trans. (keep transparent) button is checked in the Layers & Channels dialog box. Then choose a new foreground color, and fill the entire layer with the Bucket Fill tool. Only the non-transparent area of the layer (the text) will be filled with the new color.

Have too many fonts? You can filter the dialog box so that only the fonts meeting parameters you set are displayed. Click the Filter tab (shown in Figure 11-5) in the Text Tool dialog box.

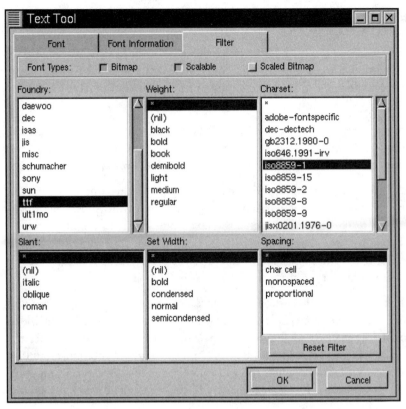

Figure 11-5 *View only the fonts you want to see, using the Filter tab.*

Choose from among font types (bitmap, scalable, or scaled bitmap), type foundry (Adobe, Bitstream, or TTF, for example), font weight, or character set. You'll use the latter option when you want to use a special character set and wish to see only those fonts that supply those characters. You can also specify a slant—italic, oblique, or Roman (upright)—plus width (bold, condensed, and so forth) and spacing, such as character cell, monospaced (both roughly the same), or proportional. For any of these categories, selecting the asterisk makes all fonts in that category visible. Click OK when you've set your filter, to return to the Font tab.

Once you have pasted, you can select letters and kern by hand, to make letter pairs such as WA spaced more closely together. As you know, the GIMP tries to make a new layer as small as possible to conserve space. If you know you'll be moving the contents of a layer around in an area larger than the layer itself (as when kerning), you might want to place some pixels around all sides of the text, using the Border box in the Text Tool Options dialog box.

Working with Dynamic Text

Dynamic Text, available as a plug-in for earlier versions of the GIMP, has been integrated more tightly with the application. This feature lets you format text in more flexible ways, plus the text can be edited at any time. You don't even have to type the text in the GIMP; you can import a text file and insert that in your image.

To use Dynamic Text, double-click the Text Tool in the toolbar, and make sure the Use Dynamic Text button is checked. Then position the cursor in the image, and click. The Dynamic Text dialog box, shown in Figure 11-6, appears.

In the large, scrolling text window, the text that you type or have imported appears. You may type your text into the window as you would in a word processing document. When you reach the end of a line, the text wraps down to the next line. As with a word processor, the line break is soft, and can change depending on how the window containing the text is resized. (Soft returns are indicated with an arrow icon.) If you really want a line break, press the Enter button.

Above the text window are four drop-down lists, which let you choose a font and weight, a size, and the metric (pixels or points) in which the size is represented. In the upper-right corner of the dialog box is a pair of boxes you can use to enter the line spacing of your text (from 0 to 1000 lines), and the angle of rotation, from 0 to 360 degrees. Yes! With dynamic text you can rotate the text automatically, precisely and repeatably. If you want all your text set at a 45-degree angle, this feature simplifies the job considerably.

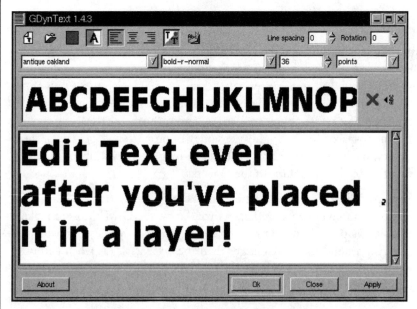

Figure 11-6 *The Dynamic Text dialog box includes many options for formatting text.*

Finally, the button bar contains nine icons representing different features of Dynamic Text. Here are their names and what they do:

- Layer: Click this button to create a new layer for your text.
- Load: Click to load a text file into the text window.
- Color: Click to produce the font color selector dialog box (shown in Figure 11-7).
- Antialias: Click this button to toggle anti-aliasing on or off.
- Format Left/Center/Right: These three buttons make your text flush left, centered, or flush right.
- Preview: This button toggles the font preview mode, which is helpful if you want to see what a font may look like before finishing the layer.
- Special Character: Click to produce the CharMap (shown in Figure 11-8), which displays any special characters (such as ©) available in the selected font, then click Insert to put the selected character in your text window.

If you didn't click in a Dynamic Text layer, the plug-in creates one for you automatically. You can edit the text at any time by making the layer active and clicking in the image. The Dynamic Text dialog box appears again, and you may make any changes. If you want to insert the modified text into a new layer, keeping the original one intact, click the Layer button in the Dynamic Text button bar. Click OK when you're done making changes.

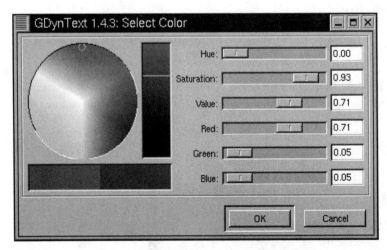

Figure 11-7 *Select a color for your font.*

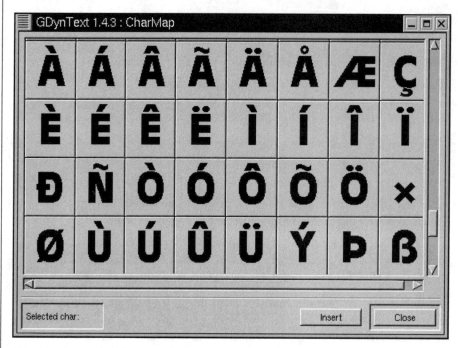

Figure 11-8   *Choose special characters from the Character Map.*

Manipulating Text

There are many things you can do with your text once it's been inserted into an image. Try some of these, using the techniques you've already learned in this book:

- Fill text with a gradient. Text placed in a transparent layer can be filled with a gradient. Put the text on an opposite gradient background for an interesting effect. (See Figure 11-9.)

Figure 11-9   *Gradients can add an interesting look to text.*

- Make drop shadows by hand. Although the GIMP includes automatic drop shadow features, you can create even more impressive effects, like the ones shown in Figure 11-10, by duplicating a text layer, blurring and filling it, then distorting it to produce the shadow shape you want.

- Wrap text around an object, using the GIMP's Filters | Map | Map Object capability (discussed in the next chapter). You can get effects like the one shown in Figure 11-11.

- Apply Filters. Any of the filters I show you in Chapter 12 can be applied in interesting ways to text. Figure 11-12 shows you an example.

- Use text as a "stencil" to cut from a background of your choice. Figure 11-13 shows what you can do with this technique.

Figure 11-10 *Create your own customized drop shadows.*

Figure 11-11 *Map text to an object.*

Figure 11-12 *Filters can give your text a special look.*

Figure 11-13 *Use text as a "stencil."*

What's Next

For even more great text effects, read up on what you can do with filters and plug-ins in the next chapter. Some of these have their own text-generating tools, while others can be applied to text you create using the Text Tool. Eye-catching text can make your image or Web site a real winner.

Chapter 12: Filter, Plug-In, and Extension Arsenal

The GIMP's tools are like a carpenter's tools. You have a toolkit filled with a basic, but comprehensive, set of implements that you can use to hammer, saw, or drill your image into a hand-finished piece of art. Filters and plug-ins, on the other hand, are power tools that spin out completed special effects faster than you can turn a lathe.

Plug-ins, scripts, and filters all perform similar sets of functions, and henceforth in this chapter I'll just call them filters for simplicity's sake. After all, you don't need to know whether a component is, say, a Script-Fu script unless you need to debug or modify it. Filters in the GIMP can perform a variety of tasks for you. Some automate tasks that would be tedious or impossible to carry out manually, such as performing some sort of image processing on each and every pixel in an image or selection. Imagine trying to do that manually!

This chapter will serve as your introduction to the 150-plus filters installed by default along with the GIMP. If you find that you need something different, you can download new components, or even write your own (see Chapter 14 for information on the GIMP's Script-Fu capabilities). The best thing about GIMP filters is that they aren't part of the GIMP itself; they're add-ons that you can plug in, take out, replace, or enhance any time you want. Instead of embedding these tools deep in the bowels of the image-editing application, the GIMP programmers designed an interface between the editor and its extensions. As a result, it's not necessary to rewrite the GIMP to include an improved or totally new plug-in; anyone who cares to can prepare a plug-in, not only giving the GIMP a new degree of flexibility but contributing to the healthy competition among Open Source programmers to outdo one another.

How Filters Work

Filters function much like their counterparts in the real world. An air filter in your air conditioner and the oil filter in your car are designed as barriers that let desirable elements—air or lubricating oil—pass through unimpeded, while things you want to keep out, such as dirt particles, are left behind. Filtering is a conversion process, converting dirty air or oil, say, into clean air or oil.

Plug-ins filter too, either by removing unwanted pixels and adding new ones, or by changing them in density or position. That's virtually everything that any filter does: deleting pixels, adding them, changing their darkness/lightness and color, or moving them around. Each filter consists of a list of rules. In an image-processing filter, the rules, frequently in the form of a matrix, tell the application how to modify a pixel based on the state of those surrounding it. Because filters affect pixels dynamically (the way one pixel has been changed can affect others when it's their turn to be processed), the process is often called *convolution* ("rolling together"). A typical filter matrix is shown in Figure 12-1; the values in the matrix indicate how the pixels surrounding the one in the center are to be modified, either lightened or darkened.

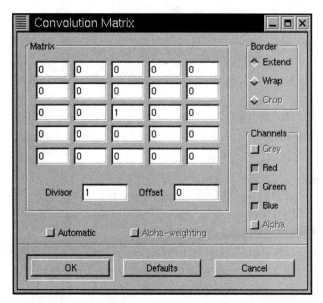

Figure 12-1 *A convolution matrix*

Although you won't find it in the GIMP's Filters menu, the Invert function is actually the simplest kind of filter (to access Invert, right-click in the image, and then choose Image | Color | Invert). Invert looks at each pixel in turn and simply "flips" it to the exact opposite value. In grayscale, a pure white or light gray pixel will be changed to pure black or dark gray. The color value of the pixel will be changed to the color opposite on the current Color Picker's color wheel; a dark blue pixel will become light yellow, and so forth. This is the simplest kind of filtering possible because the values being modified can be processed as a single step; with pixel values stored as numbers, from 0 to 255 for each of the three color channels, plus the lightness/darkness, or gray value, (assuming an RGB color gamut), a single mathematical algorithm can be applied to each pixel to produce the filtered image.

Other filters may remove pixels entirely, or shift them around in an image in relation to others that remain in place. The programs that make up filters can be very simple (so-called "one-step" filters like Sharpen or Blur), or extremely complex, bristling with dialog boxes, slider controls, buttons, preview windows, and other features.

Image processing filters resemble photographic filters in some ways, too; you can buy special effects filters to screw onto the front of a lens to provide wild diffraction, break an image into dozens of "bug's eye-view" elements, and even blur an image across the board—or only selectively at the edges.

While some components are part of the GIMP itself and are considered native features, filters are mini-programs with a life of their own. Upgrading, adding, or removing a filter is as easy as deleting the old filter file, or dragging a new one into the proper GIMP folder. The next time you start the GIMP, the application "builds" itself by looking for available modules, such as filters. Any suitable plug-ins are added to the menus they are destined for automatically.

Using Filters

Here are some general tips that pertain to nearly all filters that you'll be working with. In applying filters, keep these tips in mind:

- To apply a filter repeatedly, press Alt-F. The GIMP will use the most recent filter with the same settings you specified the last time it was invoked. To apply a filter again, but with new settings, press Shift-Alt-F; that filter's dialog box will appear.

- Make sure the layer where you want to apply the filter is visible and active. A common mistake is to have a layer visible on the screen, but another layer is chosen as the active, editable layer. The filter you're applying will process the active layer, which may not be the one you want.

- Many filters won't work on selections or layers that are totally transparent. You may need to fill a selection with random noise, a fill, or something else. The filter will then have something to operate on, even if the contents of the selection will be totally obliterated by the filter itself.

- If you don't select a portion of an image, the filter will be applied to the entire image; since it can take anywhere from a few seconds to several minutes to apply a filter, you may want to work with a representative section of the image first, before applying the filter to the whole thing.

- Choose the portion of the image that the filter will be applied to, using any of the selection tools, such as the marquee, lasso, and magic wand. (Some techniques can be applied only to selections, usually because their effects extend beyond the original selection.)

- It's often smart to copy the entire image to a duplicate layer, and make your selection on a copy; you can play around with different filter effects without modifying your original image.

- Many filters include a Preview window you can use to get an idea of what your filter will do when applied to a selected portion of an image. You'll find this useful to make broad changes in parameters. (I think it's still a good idea to select a somewhat larger area of an image, and apply the filter to that on a duplicate layer.)

- If you have a large selection, a complex filter, and a slow computer, find something to do while the filter applies—but make it something simple and not too CPU-intensive (such as playing Same GNOME). Even filters that work their magic in a minute or less seem terribly slow when you're sitting there staring at the screen. Filter experimentation may be all the impetus you need to upgrade to a faster computer.

- When the filter is finished, be careful not to do anything else (such as, move the selection) until you've decided whether the effect is the one you want, especially if the number of Undos you've set is fairly low.

- When you're really, really certain that the effect is what you want, save the file under another name (use either File | Save As... or File | Save A Copy); use the GIMP's XCF format to preserve the layers and selections. Then, and only then, flatten the layers to merge the effect with your main image. (Some day, you'll be glad you did save a copy of the file when you change your mind about being really, really certain.)

Kinds of Filters

You'll explore individual filters later in this chapter. First, though, you might find it useful to have the different kinds of plug-ins placed in broad categories. Once I've lumped the GIMP's filters into these general categories, you'll look at how the plug-ins are allocated in the Filters menu.

Acquire Modules

These add-ons have one thing in common—they help you load or acquire images for the GIMP to work on. Because they are plug-ins, these modules can be enhanced, and then integrated smoothly with the image editor using the plug-in architecture. The Screen Shot plug-in found in the File menu of the toolbox is one kind of acquire module.

The SANE scanner module, which interfaces with many popular scanners, is also an example of this kind of add-on. In olden times, a separate program was required to capture images from a scanner. These utilities were often separate image-editing programs, with support for specific scanners hard-wired into them, or modules that plugged into the operating system itself.

Today, SANE provides an intermediate level of software (as do other TWAIN-like components); hardware like scanners and digital cameras can "talk" to it in an accepted way, passing along information like "Hi, I'm ready to roll" or "Here's a 24-bit image for you." An application like the GIMP, in turn, can address the hardware through the add-on, issuing commands like "Go ahead and download the image" or "Send image number two from the camera's memory." With the API as an intermediary, the GIMP doesn't need to know anything about how the hardware works or what sort of commands it likes to receive; nor does the hardware need to know how the GIMP operates. (It's a bit like any situation in which someone who speaks, say, both Spanish and English must act as a translator between a Spanish-speaker and English-speaker who know nothing of the other's language.)

Image Enhancement Filters

This broad group of plug-ins improves the appearance of images—sometimes dramatically—while not making major changes to their content. Sharpen, Blur, Unsharp Mask, Despeckle, and similar filters are all image-enhancement plug-ins. Many of these filters operate by changing the contrast between adjacent pixels, often producing a sharpening or blurring effect. (For that reason, blur filters actually do enhance images; there are many images that you can improve by disguising defects such as dust or scratches with some blurring.) This kind of filter can be applied to an entire image or to just a portion that you have selected. Figure 12-2 shows a typical image enhancement filter at work.

Attenuating Filters

Photographers use the word *attenuating* to refer to things that alter a light source, for example "cookies" or "gobos" used to cast strategic shadows. Within the GIMP, filters of this kind may act like a piece of frosted glass, a translucent scrap of canvas fabric, or a grainy sheet of photographic film that adds texture to an image. They include the texture-oriented effects possible with GIMPressionist, any of the GIMP's Noise filter varieties, and the Logulator. Figure 12-3 shows an attenuating filter at work.

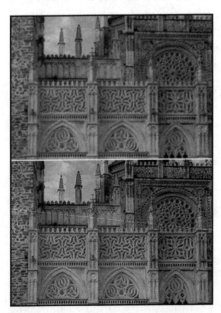

Figure 12-2 *Unsharp Mask is an enhancement filter that can turn a blurry image into a sharp one.*

Figure 12-3 *The Noise filter can attenuate an image to provide a soft texture.*

Distortion Filters

The most notable thing about distortion filters is that they move pixels from one place in an image to another, providing mild to severe distortion. These filters can map your image to a sphere, immerse it in a whirlpool, pinch, ripple, twirl, or shear bits here and there. The effect will be distortion of some or all of the image. (Most of them are easily located in the Distorts submenu.) The Pagecurl filter, shown in Figure 12-4, is one of the most striking (and perhaps over-used) filters in this group.

Figure 12-4 *Coming up with a new way to use Pagecurl is the most difficult thing about this filter.*

Rendering Filters

Rendering filters create something out of nothing. These filters may or may not use part of the underlying image in working their magic, providing jigsaw puzzle, plasma, and sphere effects. The Fractal Explorer rendering filter is illustrated in Figure 12-5.

Contrast-Enhancing Filters

Many filters operate on the differences in contrast that exist at the boundary of two colors in an image. By increasing the brightness of the lighter color and decreasing the brightness of the darker color, you enhance the contrast. Since these boundaries mark some sort of edge in the image, contrast-enhancing filters tend to make edges sharper. (The effect is different from pure sharpening filters, which also use contrast enhancement.) Filters in this category include Edge-Detect and Emboss. A sample contrast-enhancing effect is shown in Figure 12-6.

Other Filters

You'll find many more add-ons that don't fit exactly into one of the preceding categories, or that overlap several of them. Alchemy, for example, is a kind of pixelation filter. (Actually, with so many options for using varieties of brush strokes, it almost deserves a category of its own.)

Figure 12-5 *The Fractal Explorer filter produces mind-boggling fractal effects.*

Figure 12-6 *Edge-Detect produces some startling effects.*

The GIMP's Filter Menu

The GIMP uses its own classifications for plug-ins. There are about a zillion different filters, so I won't be able to explain all of them in great detail, but this overview will help you know what's what and where's where. The Filter menu, shown in Figure 12-7, has 19 different submenus (at least in the version of the GIMP I worked with).

> Your edition of the GIMP may have more or less than 19 submenus, including for example the Crypt entry (for encrypting and decrypting images), which is not part of the basic GIMP distribution.

Animation

The Animation menu has six entries which help you prepare animations, optimize them, and play them back. Animation Playback, for example, can display each of the layers of a multilayer image (including animated GIFs) in turn, as if it were an animation. The Animation Optimize filter analyzes the information in animated GIFs, and discards information that repeats between frames; the result is a smaller,

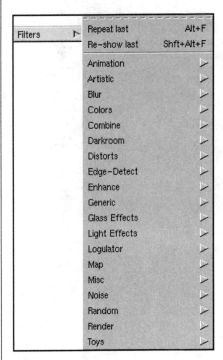

Figure 12-7   *The GIMP's Filter menu*

faster-downloading GIF. Animation Unoptimize performs the reverse function, turning an optimized animated GIF into distinct layers you can edit. You can select portions of an image in rectangular, elliptical, or free-hand mode. (See Figure 12-8.)

Artistic

The Artistic menu has seven entries that you'll find useful for applying painterly effects to an image for those times when you need to take a shoebox reject and turn it into a triumphant prizewinner. (See Figure 12-9.)

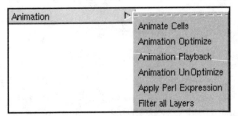

Figure 12-8   *The GIMP's Animation menu has filters that help you prepare and view animations.*

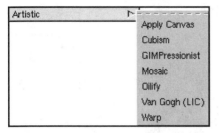

Figure 12-9 *The Artistic menu has filters for producing painterly effects.*

Apply Canvas

If you need a rough, fabric surface for an image, the Apply Canvas filter can give that to you. This is an excellent filter for covering up defects in an image—it might just have some spots or scratches. The filter's Depth slider controls how rough the texture is. An example photo with the Apply Canvas filter applied is shown in Figure 12-10.

Cubism

Use the Cubism filter if you want to become a post-modern Picasso. This filter divides your image into a series of square shapes. The filter has three key options, letting you choose the color between the tiles (either the background color or black), the size of the individual tiles, and how saturated the tiles will be. (See Figure 12-11.)

Figure 12-10 *Apply Canvas provides a rough, clothlike texture to your image.*

Figure 12-11 *The Cubism filter produces great abstract effects.*

GIMPressionist

The GIMPressionist filter is a mini-program that gives you an enormous amount of flexibility in choosing Impressionist effects for your images. The filter's dialog box, shown in Figure 12-12, has six tabs and multiple preview windows, so you can view both the effects as they will appear on your image, and various textures before you apply them. You can control the following parameters:

- Paper: Here you can choose the substrate for your image, with various options such as bricks, marble, or stone available. You can set the scale (how large the texture is in relation to the image) and relief (the extent of the 3-D effect.)

- Brush: Select the size of the brush (in pixels), its width versus depth (in a ratio), relief (in this case, the thickness of the paint), and other factors.

- Orientation: Determine the direction of the brush strokes, and the style (from choices such as flowing, random, or radial. You can even edit your own styles.

- Placement: Adjust the density of the strokes, applying them evenly, randomly, or centered around the middle of the image to create different effects.

- General: Change factors such as how dark the edge of the brush is in comparison to the rest of the stroke; whether the background should represent the paper texture you're adding or the original background; and whether you want the image to be turned into a seamless tile (say, for a Web page.)

- Presets: Contains settings for built-in or custom parameters that produce a specific kind of brush-stroke texture.

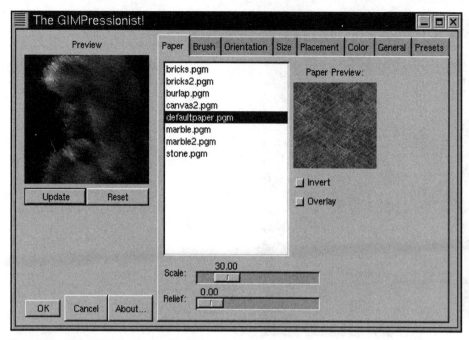

Figure 12-12   *The GIMPressionist filter has a large number of options, so you can create your own painterly effects.*

Others

The Artistic menu includes some other great filters. These include Oilify (which generates an oil-painting look), Van Gogh (I was all ears when I first heard about this one), and Mosaic (which produces great-looking effects). See Figure 12-13 for an example of Mosaic. You can also see this image in the color insert of this book.

Blur

The Blur menu, shown in Figure 12-14, offers seven filters for softening a portion of an image, whether the defects are crow's feet in the corners of the CEO's eyes, or pesky dust spots on an old photo. The choices range from straight blurring, to special kinds of blur, such as motion blur and the zoom lens–style blurs used to create special effects. Figure 12-15 shows you one way that blurs can be used.

Colors

The Colors menu, shown in Figure 12-16, has 16 variations to help you play with the color values of an image. Gradient Map, illustrated in Figure 12-17, creates an eerie effect. You can also see this figure in the color insert of this book.

Figure 12-13 *The Mosaic filter generates great tiled images like this one.*

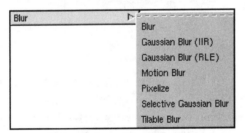

Figure 12-14 *Choose from among seven different blurring effects.*

Figure 12-15 *Radial blur can add a feeling of motion to spinning objects.*

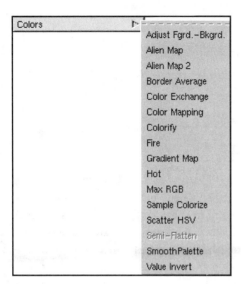

Figure 12-16 *The Colors menu includes choices like Alien Map, Gradient Map, and Colorify filters.*

Figure 12-17 *Gradient Map creates an eerie effect.*

Combine

The Combine menu, shown in Figure 12-18, has just two entries, but offers a wide variety of ways to join images together. My favorite is the Film filter, which creates the illusion of a 35mm filmstrip. You can see an example of this effect in the color insert.

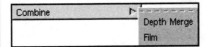

Figure 12-18 *The Combine menu includes the Film filter, for creating the effect of a 35mm filmstrip.*

Darkroom

The Darkroom menu (shown in Figure 12-19) has two entries. Colormap Rotation makes it possible to shift colors around the color wheel, moving all the hues in an image in one direction or another. Those looking to correct colors will find the Filter Pack plug-in invaluable; it provides a set of preview images with Before and After samples, and dialog boxes (shown in Figure 12-20) for setting hue, saturation, and brightness values. You can view Figure 12-20 in the color insert also.

Figure 12-19 *The Darkroom menu includes the Filter Pack color correction tool.*

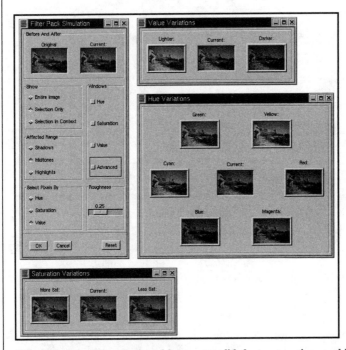

Figure 12-20 *The Filter Pack tool lets you modify hue, saturation, and brightness values using Before and After previews.*

Distorts

The Distorts menu, shown in Figure 12-21, has 17 cool entries for adding mirrored, rippling, and wavy effects to images. The Emboss filter is one of the most popular, providing an elegant, engraved effect when applied to an appropriate RGB image, such as the one shown in Figure 12-22. The Engrave filter provides a similar effect without as much 3-D distortion. You can also create images bent along a curve, Venetian blind effects, and incredible distortions like the one shown in Figure 12-23, using Iwarp (don't let your victims see the result of this filter if you value your health!); the coolest part about this filter is that you can even animate your image, so the distortion will play back in real time.

Edge-Detect

The Edge-Detect menu, shown in Figure 12-24, has three entries, which all do amazing things with the edges of images, turning contours into strong lines. (You can see the dramatic effects of the Edge filter in Figure 12-6, earlier in this chapter, and in the color insert.) The LaPlace version, one of the three entries, creates one-pixel edge lines that you might like for delicate effects.

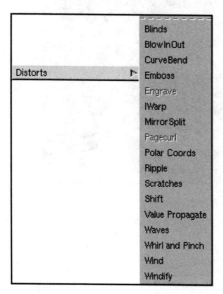

Figure 12-21 *You can spend weeks playing with the effects in the Distorts menu.*

Figure 12-22 *Emboss produces an engraved image, before on the left, after on the right.*

Figure 12-23 *Iwarp lets you apply weird distortions, before on the left, after on the right.*

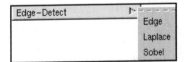

Figure 12-24 *The Edge–Detect menu has three choices for producing different kinds of edge-enhancing looks.*

Enhance

The Enhance menu has six choices, including the all-important Unsharp Mask filter, which (despite what you might think from its name) lets you sharpen up images. Unsharp Mask works better than a plain-vanilla Sharpen filter be„ause it emphasizes sharp edges instead of applying equal sharpening to the entire image (which can cause an artificial appearance). In this menu you'll also find Deinterlace (which removes odd- or even-numbered lines from an image, and can help clean up video captures) and Despeckle, which you can use for removing spots from an image. (See Figure 12-25.)

Generic

The Generic menu may have as few as one entry, or more, depending on how many filters you've added. They're all, like the Convolution Matrix filter (illustrated earlier in this chapter), intended for advanced users who know how to manipulate pixels mathematically. If you like, you can play with this filter even if you don't know quite what you're doing. It's possible to create some interesting effects by accident; just remember to tell everyone, "I meant to do that!"

Glass Effects

The Glass Effects menu (shown in Figure 12-26) has two entries, which create curved glass effects. (Figure 12-27 provides an example of what you can expect.)

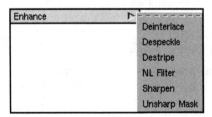

Figure 12-25   *The Enhance menu includes Unsharp Mask.*

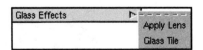

Figure 12-26   *The Glass Effects menu has filters for giving images a curved look.*

Figure 12-27 *Curved looks using the Glass Effects filter: at left, the unaltered image; at right, a lens effect*

Light Effects

The Light Effects menu has five entries that add sparkles, stars, and other light transformations to your images. You can put a blazing supernova in the sky of a bland image, or create more sedate starry or sunlit scenes. FlareFX offers simple lens flare effects, like you get from the reflection off the inner surface of a camera lens pointed at the sun or another bright light source. The Lighting Effects filter gives you your own photostudio, where you can select directional or spot lights, light color, and other details. (See Figure 12-28.) When you use these filters, just move the lights around in the preview until you get an effect you want.

GFlare creates sophisticated graduated flares. It includes an editor you can use to modify the glow settings, gradients, and other parameters. (See Figure 12-29.)

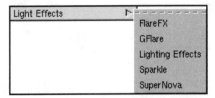

Figure 12-28 *The Light Effects menu helps you bring some flair to your images.*

Figure 12-29 *The GFlare filter is great for adding sunlight effects to an image.*

Logulator

You'll find a whopping 26 entries in the Logulator menu, shown in Figure 12-30, essentially duplicating the Xtns | Script-Fu | Logos scripts. If you're looking for a particular look for your logo, you'll want to experiment with all of these. The effect produced by the Cool Metal logulator is shown in Figure 12-31 and in the color insert; other examples are shown in Figures 12-32 and 12-33.

Map

The Map menu, with 12 menu entries, is your one-stop shopping place for applying bump maps and other displacement effects to the pixels of an image. It is shown in Figure 12-34.

You can use these filters to create 3-D textures that can be "mapped" onto other images, create seamless edges, and even wrap images around shapes. The latter capability produces some fascinating effects. You can wrap images onto planes, spheres, cylinders, or boxes, and change the orientation. (See Figure 12-35.)

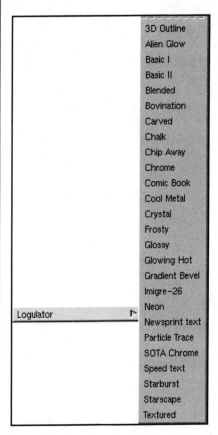

	3D Outline
	Alien Glow
	Basic I
	Basic II
	Blended
	Bovination
	Carved
	Chalk
	Chip Away
	Chrome
	Comic Book
	Cool Metal
	Crystal
	Frosty
	Glossy
	Glowing Hot
	Gradient Bevel
	Imigre–26
Logulator ►	Neon
	Newsprint text
	Particle Trace
	SOTA Chrome
	Speed text
	Starburst
	Starscape
	Textured

Figure 12-30 *Logulator includes a plethora (and then some) of choices for making cool-looking logos.*

Figure 12-31 *The Cool Metal filter proves its mettle with this cool effect.*

Figure 12-32 *The 3-D Outline filter applies patterns and bump maps to your logo.*

Figure 12-33 *Beveled edges are easy with Logulator.*

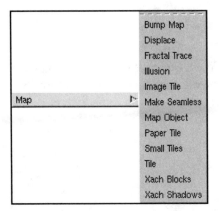

Figure 12-34 *The Map menu has filters for creating a variety of 3-D effects.*

Figure 12-35 *Wrap images around a shape with the Map Object filter.*

Misc

The Misc menu has five filters (or more) that don't fit in with any of the other categories. These include several Web-oriented filters, including the Image Map capability you looked at in Chapter 10, and Prepare for GIF, which optimizes images for the GIF format. (See Figure 12-36.)

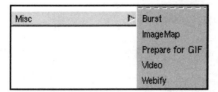

Figure 12-36 *You'll find a variety of filters in the Misc menu.*

Noise

The Noise menu has five kinds of noise filters. You'll find that noise can add a grainy effect to an image, or randomize gradients so they'll reproduce more smoothly. (See Figure 12-37.) You can create great pointillistic effects (as you can see in Figure 12-38).

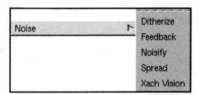

Figure 12-37 *Noise filters add random pixels to images.*

Figure 12-38 *Noise can add an attractive grainy effect to an image.*

Random

The Random menu has three entries. They will randomly displace pixels, using hurling (changes a pixel to a random color), picking (applies values from three random adjacent pixels), or slurring (moves the pixel downward). The differences between the effects are a bit too subtle to show up on the printed page, so I'm not providing an example here. Try out these filters for yourself to see how they work. (See Figure 12-39.)

Render

The Render menu is another heavyweight. It has 24 different effects to create an amazing selection of objects and shapes. (See Figure 12-40.)

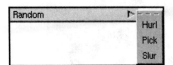

Figure 12-39 *Randomize images to create an interesting fuzzy effect.*

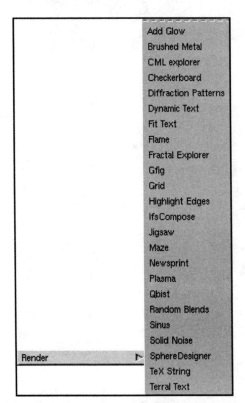

Figure 12-40 *The Render menu has a huge number of interesting filters.*

You can explore the world of fractal images, create jigsaws and mazes, develop random blends, create very unusual textures, boggle the mind with op-art images, envelop an image in flames, and do much, much more. Figures 12-41 to 12-43 show some examples of what you can do.

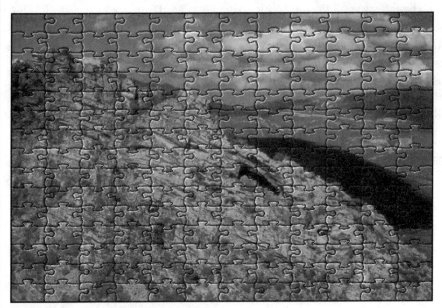

Figure 12-41   *Create a jigsaw puzzle effect.*

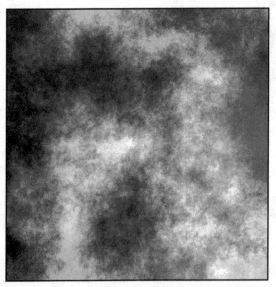

Figure 12-42   *Create cloud-like effects with the Plasma filter.*

Figure 12-43 *Flame effects are available, too.*

Figure 12-44 *The Egg thanks you for using the GIMP.*

Toys

The Toys menu, shown in Figure 12-44, has just one entry, The Egg, which does absolutely nothing but thank you for using the GIMP! I thank you, as well.

What's Next

Scanned images can be one of your best sources for GIMP graphics. In the next chapter, you'll see how to put some great scanners to work.

Chapter 13: Scanning and the GIMP

One challenge facing any GIMP guerrilla is where to get suitable fodder for image manipulation. Certainly, you can download stock photos from the Internet, snag a picture with a digital camera, or even have your conventional snapshots converted to digital form using Kodak's PhotoCD or "You've Got Pictures" services. But pound for pound, pixel for pixel, photon for photon, the best deal right now is in the wonderful world of desktop scanners. With decent scanners available for less than $100, and great scanners topping out in the $300 price range, all image workers worth their NaCl should be able to justify adding a scanner to their GIMP field kit. This chapter will discuss some of the key issues of interest to GIMPcentric scanner users, including software and hardware concerns, scanner nuts and bolts, and tips for getting better scans.

Why You May Need a Scanner

- Jazz up your StarImpress presentations with images.
- Create graphics-spiced Web pages that are more of an attraction than a distraction.
- Snag line art such as logos, drop caps, cartoons, or charts for publications.
- Capture low-resolution images for screen or FPO (for position only) display in publications.
- Grab images for use as drawing templates in StarDraw or a similar program.
- Create a computerized database for your real estate firm, family tree, or online catalog.
- Capture text in OCR (optical character recognition) applications, which should be the next big killer app area for Linux.
- Translate images into a graphics format for facsimile transmission.
- Add photos to your e-mail.
- Create original art from your photographs.
- Snare images of three-dimensional objects, such as your coin collection.

What Kinds of Scanners Are There?

The short answer is one word: flatbeds. These devices, which look like mini-photocopiers, offer the best quality, the most flexibility, and the lowest prices of any other scanner alternatives. However, there are other types you might want to know about before picking out your dream flatbed scanner.

The most expensive kind of scanner is the drum scanner, a premium-priced, ultra-high-resolution scanner used for color separation in the graphic arts industry. If you work with one of these, you probably aren't using the GIMP, at least not to manipulate drum-scanned artwork.

Sheetfed scanners have a niche of their own. They originally gained attention because they cost less than flatbeds, but today they cost the same or more, and are used mainly for OCR or faxing. Their key advantage is that they have a built-in feeder for 10 or more sheets of paper, so you can drop in a stack of originals and let them rip (well, that might be a poor choice of words). There are also portable sheetfed scanners that you can take with you, and that will scan wherever you happen to be. (On the downside, sheetfed scanners handle only thin, regular-size sheets, and their roller feed makes it more difficult to align originals.)

Multifunction (or all-in-one) devices perform scanning, printing, copying, and perhaps fax functions. They do it all in a single, space-saving box. If you want the most versatility, multifunction devices may be a viable alternative to flatbed scanners.

You'll find other kinds of scanners available, such as consumer-oriented photo scanners that capture snapshots, and slide scanners for grabbing images from the transparencies that both pro photographers and vacationers favor.

How to Interface Your Scanner with the GIMP

Interfacing with a scanner has two aspects, hardware and software. From a hardware standpoint, unless you are very adventurous, you'll almost always want to use a SCSI scanner. Linux and its software are still in their infancy, and support for exotic hardware components will come eventually, but is not here just yet. You might be able to get a parallel port scanner to work with Linux. You might be able to use a SCSI-to-parallel converter (if you are one of those masochists who love challenges of that sort). If you're simply looking to connect up a scanner as quickly and painlessly as possible, go SCSI. SCSI lets you link up to other cool peripherals, such as mammoth, screaming-fast hard disk drives, and removable storage media, such as Iomega Zip drives. (But don't buy a SCSI card just so you can use removable media; get one for the scanner functionality.)

NOTE

> If you want to learn more about scanner hardware, you'll find some good information and links on my Web page at www.dbusch.com. My scanner page has links to most of the leading scanner vendors.

On the software side, for most GIMP users the best choice is to use the SANE (*Scanner Access Now Easy*) module, as it can be run either as a stand-alone program or within the GIMP itself as an add-on in the XTNS menu (much like TWAIN drivers used with Photoshop and other apps in the Mac and Windows worlds). SANE has an easy-to-understand GUI interface and includes all the controls you're likely to need; it certainly beats non-GUI scanner programs that can run from the Linux command line. You can find SANE included in your Linux distribution, or find it online at sites such as `ftp://metalab.unc.edu/pub/Linux/`; note that you will have to install it separately.

Appendix A includes some tips on compiling source code, installing RPM files, and other installation concerns; although the appendix deals solely with installing the GIMP itself, much of the information also applies to other modules, such as SANE.

You'll also find free scanner programs for specific brands of scanners, such as HP, Mustek, Epson, and Umax. Some commercial scanner software, sold for HP and other models, costs relatively little and can do a good job. The most important thing is to find and use some sort of calibration system, so that what you see on your monitor, what you output on your printer, and what you scan have a reasonable relationship to each other.

What Features You May Need

Before you purchase a scanner, you'll need to evaluate your needs and compare them to the feature list of the scanners you're considering. Not all scanners are the same, even in the flatbed realm. The following are some of the features to look at.

Size of Originals Scannable in One Operation

Sheetfed scanners may have no practical limit on the length of an original, but may be limited to flat documents no wider than 8.5 inches. Flatbed models, on the other hand, may handle originals no larger than 8.5 x 11 or 8.5 x 14 inches. It's relatively easy to scan bigger originals in pieces and to stitch them together.

Scanner Resolution

The resolution of scanners is a much-typed and often misleading feature. You'll see resolution expressed in pairs of numbers: 600 x 600, 600 x 1200, 400 x 800, and so forth. The first number is the optical resolution across the width of the scanner; it's generally determined by how many sensors are available, and is a relatively true representation of the scanner's capabilities. The second number, unfortunately, is subject to a bit of fudging; some vendors use hardware interpolation to calculate pixels, and present the result as the vertical resolution of the scanner. The second number may also represent the distance that the scanner sensor bar can be moved between scans of a line. In all cases, resolution alone doesn't indicate how sharp or finely detailed your scanned images will be; optical considerations, for example, can have as much of an impact on your final results as resolution does.

Physical Size

Make sure that your scanner fits in the space you have allotted for it!

Color Depth

Color depth is the number of different colors a scanner can capture, expressed in bit counts: 24 bits (16.7 million colors) or 30 bits (around 11 billion colors) or 36 bits (roughly 7 trillion colors). This is another spec subject to a lot of obfuscation. In practice, a 30-bit low-end scanner might not produce colors as true as those from a comparable 24-bit model. Rather than go by the numbers, you might want to compare a number of actual scanners with various depths.

Speed

Speed may be important to you if you make many scans, or if you scan large originals. The best test is to try some actual scans using a computer with approximately the same speed and memory complement as your own, even if it doesn't happen to be a Linux box.

Interface

Scanners have traditionally been designed to use the SCSI interface. Today, in the PC and Macintosh worlds, common scanner configurations generally involve Universal Serial Bus, FireWire, or even serial and parallel ports; support for these technologies is still spotty in the Linux community, though, so I recommend using a SCSI scanner until such time as scanners are shipped with Linux drivers or with Linux-specific installation instructions.

Scanner Nuts and Bolts for Scanner Nuts

There's not much to a scanner: it captures information the same way you read a book—line by line, using some sort of illumination, and converted to an intelligible form by your brain or the scanner's hardware. Scanners themselves are nothing new. Scanning was first proposed in 1850 as a method of transmitting photographs over telegraph lines (rather an advanced idea, when you consider that photography itself was invented only in 1839); a Catholic priest named Caselli actually pulled it off in 1863, sending an image between Paris and LeHavre, France. Since that breakthrough, we've had pre-television scanners (some others also dating to the nineteenth century), wirephotos since the mid-1920s, graphic arts scanners by the 1950s, and desktop scanners starting in the 1980s.

A scanner consists of several components. All scanners use some mechanism to hold the original reflective art or transparency, and bounce light off it or through it; the light then passes through a lens to a solid-state sensor. A device called a carriage has the moving parts, such as the light source and the optical system, which direct the image to a line of *CCD* or *CMOS* sensors, which grab the image one line at a time. The scanner may also contain memory to hold the scanned image, and some primitive intelligence to process the image, changing it from analog to digital format, adjusting brightness/contrast, and so on.

The sensor arrays in scanners are sensitive only to white light. To capture color, the scanner needs three separate images of an original, each representing the relative amounts of red, green, and blue for every pixel. Filters, multicolored light sources, and other techniques are used to provide these three images.

The resolution of the scanner is measured in spi (*samples per inch*), although you'll often see the misused dpi (*dots per inch*) spec used instead. Scanners don't display pixels, or use dots. Instead, they take samples of an array of positions on the original image, and translate the information into a format that your computer can use to create pixels for display, or dots for printing.

Your computer assigns each individual sample a color and a brightness value, based on its density and hue (for example, Red 128, Blue 63, Green 0). A scanned color image is nothing more than three different grayscale images, each one representing the amount of red, green, and blue in the original. Three 8-bit images (one for each color) are combined into one 24-bit file.

Many scanners now go beyond 24-bit color to capture 30, 36, or 48 bits of information per image. A 30-bit scanner, for example, grabs 10 bits per red, green, or blue color; a 36-bit scanner grabs 12 bits per color; and so forth. (Until recently there were few applications that could handle these ultra-color files, so scanners automatically converted them internally to 24-bit versions before they were stored on the computer.)

If you will end up with a 24-bit image, why grab 30- or 36-bit images in the first place? In theory, 24-bit color should provide plenty of colors for most images, as the human eye can't differentiate 16.7 million different hues. But, in real life, scanner electronics lose information to noise. The extra colors of a high-color scan allow discarding some information and still ending up with enough to produce a good-quality 24-bit scan.

Getting the Best Scans

Although modern scanners have automated features, you'll often find that a bit of manual tweaking, or making a few changes within the GIMP, may be necessary to get the very best scans. Here are some tips for improving your scans.

- Start with a good original. Scanners can't see information that isn't there. Don't use a small photo when a larger, sharper version is available. Use an original document rather than a photocopy.

- Preview your scan prior to making a final scan. This is a good way to evaluate an image, select the exact portion of the image to be scanned, and adjust the brightness or contrast.

- Perform sharpening with the scanner rather than in the GIMP. (You'll find that the results will usually be better if you let the scanner handle this.) Remember that sharpening increases contrast, so you may want to lower the contrast control when sharpening during a scan.

- Choose the right resolution. For text and line drawings, the resolution should be set to the printer's setting, up to no more than 600 dpi. For photographs, a resolution of 100 to 200 samples per inch should be sufficient. When you're scanning transparencies, scan at the maximum resolution offered by the scanner, but not more than 2000 samples per inch.

- Manipulate brightness and contrast in the scanner and in the GIMP in combination. Some scanner software displays histograms that you can use to tailor the distribution of light and dark tones (as you learned to do with the GIMP's Levels command); know when to leave adjustments such as color correction to the GIMP. You will have more flexibility and options within your image editor for adjusting color, so even if your scanner program has this capability, you might want to use the latter sparingly.

What's Next

In my book, scanning is the most fun you can have with a computer without engaging in virtual shooting and carnage. You'll find that a scanner can make the GIMP a lot more versatile, to the point that you may wonder how you ever got along without one. In the final chapter, I'll offer you an introduction to Script-Fu.

Chapter 14: Introducing Script-Fu

t is time for your introduction to the budo portion of your GIMP guerrilla training. Budo, as you may know, is a Japanese term for lots of different ways to coerce somebody against their will.

The GIMP equivalent of martial arts is known as Script-Fu, a tool you can use to bend your image editor to your will. Script-Fu lets you write and activate lists of commands that the GIMP will obediently carry out. You've already used Script-Fu from time to time as you worked your way through this book; many GIMP plug-ins and special effects are nothing more than Script-Fu scripts.

You can use Script-Fu in several different ways. Most of the time, you can content yourself with being an avid script collector. Hundreds or thousands of Script-Fu scripts are available for downloading. Odds are overwhelming that one that does what you want to do has already been written, debugged, improved upon, and perfected. In addition, if you nose around a bit, you'll discover a huge number of scripts that do things you never even thought of.

If what you need to do is very specialized, or you want to automate some repetitious or complicated tasks, you can write Script-Fu scripts of your own. But don't feel bad if you never get around to this. The new influx of GIMP guerrillas who just want to get things done are floating in the same boat with you.

This chapter will be a little like Bruce Lee's "art of fighting without fighting," in that you can learn to use Script-Fu scripts without actually doing any programming. As I said, most of the time you won't be writing your own scripts. In any case, I would not expect to teach you how to program in a single chapter. (Oddly enough, entire books and college courses have been devoted to that discipline.) However, I can tell you enough here to get you started on your journey towards Script-Fu proficiency.

NOTE

> If you really want to learn more about Script-Fu, I recommend the Web site www.script-fu.org. It contains tutorials, a code archive with useful examples you can learn from, more complete documentation than the skimpy material included with the GIMP, and book reviews.

If you're already a programmer (many Linux users are), you can be writing scripts faster than you can say "wax on; wax off." (Apologies to those who don't follow martial arts movies, and will be puzzled by some of the references.) Now, let's get started.

What Is Script-Fu

Most of the programs you use, including the GIMP itself, are compiled; that is, they are transformed from the instructions written in a higher-level language (such as C) into the machine code that a processor can run directly, and therefore can run very fast. As a program is compiled, the instructions, or source code, is converted into whatever form the particular platform requires. One set of easily modified source code can be compiled for any number of different machines.

Even if you haven't had the need to change any source yourself, you've probably had to compile some code from time to time: a new Linux kernel, perhaps, or the latest version of the GIMP. Script-Fu scripts are generally written in an interpreting programming language called SCHEME. Interpreted instructions are not in a form that can be executed directly by the computer; they must be translated into machine code each and every time you run them. Scripts are inherently slower than compiled programs for that reason, but modern computers are so fast that having a few dozen (or a few hundred) scripts that you run regularly doesn't really cost you much in terms of computing power and other resources. On the other hand, you can quickly make a change to a script and test it out immediately, without having to recompile it first. Win some, lose some.

SCHEME is an often maligned language, for reasons important mostly to programmers, who prefer more powerful and elegant languages such as Perl. However, SCHEME has a significant advantage: It's installed by default with every version of the GIMP used within memory. If you have a very new edition of the GIMP, you may find that Perl support has already been installed. If not, you can add it in the form of extensions that enable the GIMP to use that language. You'll find extensions for languages like Perl at `registry.gimp.org`.

What makes Script-Fu such a seamless and well-integrated tool is that scripts aren't executed as a mindless series of commands that play out on your screen beyond your control. Scripts can include dialog boxes and other graphical elements that let you interact with them. Unless you knew better, you probably would think that most Script-Fu components are part of the GIMP itself.

What Are Scripts

Scripts are nothing more than text files stored in a special directory, usually called `~/.gimp/scripts`, or `gimp/plug-ins/script-fu/scripts`, or some variation, depending on which version of the GIMP you are using and how it was installed. Scripts end in the .SCM file extension, so if you really don't know where your scripts are, you can use your file manager's Find feature to look for that type of file. It's useful to know where your script directory is, because you will want to be able to find them for editing, know where to put the scripts you write yourself, and know where to copy any scripts you download.

Finding the script you want once you're in the GIMP can also be tricky, but need not be. You'll usually find scripts that modify the image you're working on in the context menu that pops up when you right-click in an image. You can also find scripts in the Xtns menu of the toolbox, under Script-Fu.

What Scripts Can I Expect?

As I mentioned, there are thousands of scripts available. Many of the most popular are installed by default along with the GIMP. However, this list is constantly changing. As I worked with various developers' (unstable) versions, I noticed a constant influx of new ones, all vying to be included in the next official (stable) version of the GIMP. You can find details on some of the better ones, and tips on applying them to text or for special effects, in Chapters 11 and 12. But here is what you can expect:

- **Logos**. In the Logos menu, you will find about 30 great scripts for creating interesting logos from text you specify. All have descriptive names, like Frosty, Neon, and Starscape, which give you an idea of what kind of special effect the script produces. You can enter a text string (for example, Kitchen Table International), font size (in pixels, not points), the font you want to use, and the color of the logo.

- **Patterns**. The Patterns menu has some great scripts, with names like Camouflage and Swirly, which are very handy for generating interesting patterns for Web pages. You can enter your own parameters to create endless varieties of textures. Figure 14-1 shows one script's dialog box and a sample pattern.

- **Web Page Themes**. The Web Page Themes menu is where the scripts for creating Web page artifacts such as buttons and rules should go; you'll find scripts for producing "alien glow" objects, and other things built around a cohesive theme.

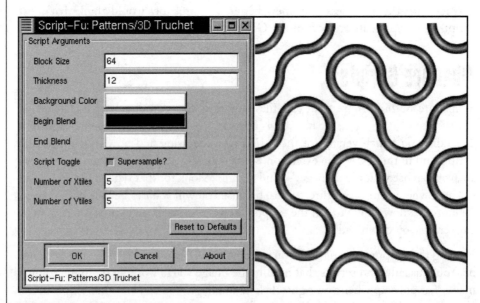

Figure 14-1 *Typical Pattern script*

- **Utils.** The Utils menu contains utility scripts, such as Font Map (which, as you might expect, produces a listing of all your installed fonts), and the Custom Gradient editor.

- **Buttons.** Scripts in the Buttons menu help you automate creation of beveled, round, and other buttons.

- **Make Brush.** The four scripts in the Make Brush menu give you the tools you need to create rectangular or elliptical brushes, with either a hard edge or a blurry, feathered edge.

- **Image Dependant Scripts.** Image-dependent scripts operate on the images you are working on. They're divided into nine different categories: Décor, Modify, Animators, Stencil Ops, Alchemy, Shadow, Render, Utils, and Selection. (Because these scripts operate much like the GIMP's filters, I covered their use in Chapters 11 and 12.)

- **Misc.** Any script that doesn't fit within the confines of one of the other menus goes in the Misc menu. An example is the Sphere script. You can control the size of the sphere, the illumination angle, background color, color of the sphere, and whether or not a shadow is produced. (See Figure 14-2.)

Using a Script

The first thing you need to do is to put a few scripts to work, so you can see how they operate. I'll provide an example here, and you can try a few more to get your feet really wet. The exact script you use is not important, but if you have a version of the GIMP that includes the same pre-packaged scripts I have, you can follow along with me.

In the toolbox, choose Xtns | Script-Fu, then select Chrome from the Logos fly-out menu. A dialog box appears. This box is a graphical way of entering parameters that the script will use to carry out the rest of the task. The arguments will vary from script to script, and occasionally won't be needed at all. (See Figure 14-3.)

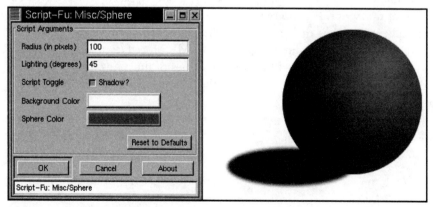

Figure 14-2 *A Script-Fu script for creating a cool sphere object*

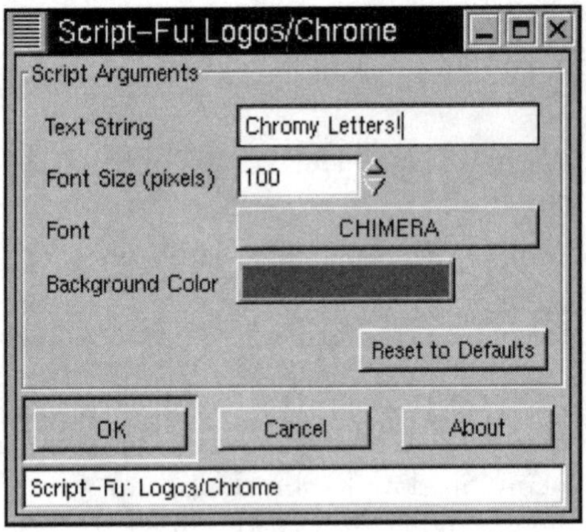

Figure 14-3 *Chrome-Logo dialog box*

An information box appears at the bottom of the dialog box. It displays the name of the script you're using, and will show the commands as they are being carried out. (Usually the commands will fly by faster than you can read them; they certainly did on my Celeron 433 computer.) In this case, you'll need to enter a string of text that you want to use to produce your chrome logo. You can also enter a size for the logo, click the Font box to select a font, and choose a background color. Click OK when finished, and the script will create a new graphic like the one shown in Figure 14-4.

The script performed steps you could have carried out yourself, although much faster than you could do them. The script kindly left the effects it produced in layers rather than as a flat image, so you are free to further modify each of the layers that make up the new image. If you weren't aware the image had layers, you'll find out quickly enough the first time you try to save it in a non-.XCF format; the GIMP's Export File dialog box pops up, offering to flatten the image for you before saving it.

I'm going to reproduce, in its entirety, the Chrome-Logos script, written by the GIMP's co-founders; this way, reading it closely, you can see exactly what's involved. As you look at this script, you can see that while it does nothing you could not have done manually, it performs each task in a rather unusual way: instead of using the mouse and menus, the script directly calls the GIMP procedure that performs the task. To use Script-Fu, you'll need to learn the names of functions, procedures, and classes that the GIMP can handle, as well as the commands in SCHEME (or Perl, or whatever) used to call them.

Figure 14-4 *Finished graphic*

```
; CHROME-LOGOS
(define (script-fu-chrome-logo text size font bg-color)
  (let* ((img (car (gimp-image-new 256 256 RGB)))
    (b-size (* size 0.2))
    (offx1 (* size 0.04))
    (offy1 (* size 0.03))
    (offx2 (* size (- 0.04)))
    (offy2 (* size (- 0.03)))
    (feather (* size 0.05))
    (text-layer (car (gimp-text-fontname img -1 0 0 text b-size TRUE size PIXELS
font)))
    (width (car (gimp-drawable-width text-layer)))
    (height (car (gimp-drawable-height text-layer)))
    (layer1 (car (gimp-layer-new img width height RGBA_IMAGE "Layer 1" 100
DIFFERENCE)))
    (layer2 (car (gimp-layer-new img width height RGBA_IMAGE "Layer 2" 100
DIFFERENCE)))
    (layer3 (car (gimp-layer-new img width height RGBA_IMAGE "Layer 3" 100
NORMAL)))
    (shadow (car (gimp-layer-new img width height RGBA_IMAGE "Drop Shadow" 100
NORMAL)))
    (background (car (gimp-layer-new img width height RGB_IMAGE "Background" 100
NORMAL)))
    (layer-mask (car (gimp-layer-create-mask layer1 BLACK-MASK)))
    (old-fg (car (gimp-palette-get-foreground)))
    (old-bg (car (gimp-palette-get-background))))
    (gimp-image-undo-disable img)
    (gimp-image-resize img width height 0 0)
    (gimp-image-add-layer img background 1)
    (gimp-image-add-layer img shadow 1)
    (gimp-image-add-layer img layer3 1)
    (gimp-image-add-layer img layer2 1)
```

```
(gimp-image-add-layer img layer1 1)
(gimp-palette-set-background '(255 255 255))
(gimp-selection-none img)
(gimp-edit-fill layer1)
(gimp-edit-fill layer2)
(gimp-edit-fill layer3)
(gimp-edit-clear shadow)
(gimp-selection-layer-alpha text-layer)
(gimp-layer-set-visible text-layer FALSE)
(gimp-layer-set-visible shadow FALSE)
(gimp-layer-set-visible background FALSE)
(gimp-palette-set-background '(0 0 0))
(gimp-edit-fill layer1)
(gimp-selection-translate img offx1 offy1)
(gimp-selection-feather img feather)
(gimp-edit-fill layer2)
(gimp-selection-translate img (* 2 offx2) (* 2 offy2))
(gimp-edit-fill layer3)
(gimp-selection-none img)
(set! layer1 (car (gimp-image-merge-visible-layers img CLIP-TO-IMAGE)))
(gimp-invert layer1)
(gimp-image-add-layer-mask img layer1 layer-mask)
(gimp-selection-layer-alpha text-layer)
(gimp-palette-set-background '(255 255 255))
(gimp-selection-feather img feather)
(gimp-edit-fill layer-mask)
(gimp-palette-set-background '(0 0 0))
(gimp-selection-translate img offx1 offy1)
(gimp-edit-fill shadow)
(gimp-selection-none img)
(gimp-palette-set-background bg-color)
(gimp-edit-fill background)
(gimp-image-remove-layer img text-layer)
(gimp-layer-set-visible shadow TRUE)
(gimp-layer-set-visible background TRUE)
(gimp-layer-set-name layer1 text)
(gimp-palette-set-foreground old-fg)
(gimp-palette-set-background old-bg)
(gimp-image-undo-enable img)
(gimp-display-new img)))
```

```
(script-fu-register "script-fu-chrome-logo"
     "<Toolbox>/Xtns/Script-Fu/Logos/Chrome"
     "Somewhat simplistic, but cool chromed logos"
     "Spencer Kimball"
     "Spencer Kimball & Peter Mattis"
     "1997"
     ""
     SF-STRING "Text String" "The GIMP"
     SF-ADJUSTMENT "Font Size (pixels)" '(100 2 1000 1 10 0 1)
     SF-FONT "Font" "-*-Bodoni-*-r-*-*-24-*-*-*-p-*-*-*"
     SF-COLOR "Background Color" '(191 191 191))
```

Writing Your Own Scripts

Writing your own scripts entails a recipe similar to the one for cooking elephant-under-glass. Step one: find an elephant. Once you've done that, everything else is easy. In the same vein, the first thing you need to do to write your own script is to learn SCHEME, its syntax (easy stuff, such as matching pairs of parentheses, as well as harder stuff), how to declare and use variables and functions, and working with lists. Once you've picked up enough SCHEME to begin writing your own scripts, you'll want to get started. You can access the GIMP's Script-Fu editing tool by choosing Xtns | Script-Fu | Console. A dialog box like the one shown in Figure 14-5 appears.

The center window, which displays a bunch of disclaimer stuff when you first load the console, displays the output of the commands you type. A script contains a number of elements, which you can see in the Chrome-Logo sample script earlier. For example, at the beginning of the script, you'll find a definition of the main function of the script. At the end is the registration information (although it can be anywhere in the script), which uses the *script-fu-register* function to register the script with the system's procedural database. Although it's not mandatory, Script-Fu scripts usually begin with the string `script-fu-`, so they'll all appear together when listed in the procedural database. (You can view your database using the DB Browser, which is available when you choose Xtns | DB Browser.) The registration information is interesting, even to non-programmers, because it provides some data about the script; this data includes some items needed to use the script.

One item is called `Name of the function(s) defined`. A script can contain more than one function, and you can call them individually. By registering the name of each function, the GIMP knows to enter the script at the point where the called function begins, whenever the script is executed.

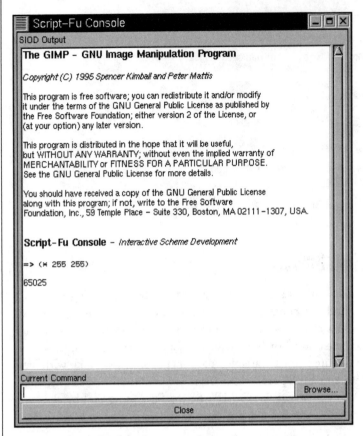

Figure 14-5 *Script-Fu Console*

Another item is called `Location`. This handy parameter determines where the GIMP will place your script in its menus. A standalone script that doesn't operate on a particular image should be placed in the Toolbox menu, using the path you want to use to access the script (for example, `<Toolbox>/Xtns/Script-Fu/Logos/Chrome`). Image-dependent scripts should be placed in the context menus that pop up when you right-click in an image (for example, `<Right-Click>/Script-Fu/MyFilters/Destroy`). Once the script has been installed and registered, the GIMP automatically creates the menu path for its scripts when it is launched.

Other information registered tells anyone who examines the script some things they need to know about it, including a description of the script, the name of the author, date it was created or last revised, copyright information, and the type of images (RGB, GRAY, and so on), if any, on which the script operates. Finally, the registration information provides a list of the parameters used by the script (marked with an `SF-` prefix), a description of what kind of information the parameter requires, and a default value that will be used if no value is entered interactively when the script is run.

Appendix A: Installation Tips

Finding the GIMP

Installing the GIMP

I f you've worked with Linux much, you have installed packages many times, and won't have much difficulty installing the GIMP. If you're new to Linux, then welcome to the wonderful world of installation! Don't panic, just yet.

This appendix provides tips on finding and installing the GIMP using the most common Linux distributions. If you read through the instructions here, you shouldn't have any trouble. I'm going to assume that you've mastered the rudiments of Linux; that is, you can navigate through subdirectories, create subdirectories, and perhaps use archiving programs like *tar*. I'll also assume that your Linux installation already has all or most of the supporting libraries which are needed for the GIMP, but which are not furnished with the GIMP itself. Finally, if you're going to compile the GIMP from source code, you must have the GNU C compiler installed.

Finding the GIMP

Your first step is to locate an installable copy of the GIMP. The application is available in one of two forms, as *binary* code and *source* code. Binary code is a version of the GIMP that has already been compiled for your particular platform and Linux/UNIX distribution. The binary code is ready to run after you've placed each module where it belongs and configured the application. Source code, on the other hand, is just the list of instructions used by the compiler to build an executable copy of the GIMP.

Binary installation is the easiest way to go, since all the hard work has been done for you. Compiling source code is not that difficult, because the instructions in the code take care of all the really tricky stuff. You're likely to run into problems only when your operating system distribution is missing some of the libraries needed to compile or run the application.

The first place to look for the GIMP is on a CD-ROM that you already have. Many Linux distributions already include the GIMP; they may even (as is the case with Red Hat Linux) install the GIMP files for you when the operating system is installed. If your distribution is one of those, you'll probably find the GIMP already listed in the Graphics menu of your desktop environment. Fire it up, allow the OS to install your personal files, and you're ready to go. If the GIMP isn't already installed for you, you may find copies of the files you need to install it on your distribution CD-ROM; instructions later in this appendix will help you install the application from the CD.

The chief problem with installing from an existing CD-ROM is that you probably don't have the latest version. Many distributions still have GIMP 1.0.4, which was the most stable version for a long time. Since then, however, GIMP 1.1.10 and later versions leading up to the newest stable release have been quite usable. If you have GIMP 1.0.4 and want to use a version more in line with the one used in the preparation of this book, you'll have to go hunting for a later edition.

Generally, that means hunting for the files on the Internet. The place to start is `www.gimp.org/`. There you'll find information about the most recent version and instructions for downloading both stable and developer's releases. You can use FTP to download the files you need for installation. (In the unlikely event that your Linux workstation does not have Internet access, you can still download the files to any Windows PC and transfer them over to your Linux box.)

You'll find the GIMP files on the Internet in one of several forms. You may find binary files for your particular platform. If you retrieve the files in this form, you'll need to follow the instructions included with their documentation to unpack the compressed archive they are packaged in (usually a tar.gz file) and place the files in the directories where they belong. This method is somewhat tedious, but can work well if the documentation furnished with the set of binary files is good.

You may also locate the binary files in RPM (*Red Hat Package Manager*) format. The *rpm* program, which works with this format, is included with Red Hat, Caldera, and SuSE distributions of Linux, and is available for other versions. *rpm* simplifies installation by taking care of unpacking and copying files to where they need to go. This is definitely the way to go, if you can. You may also find the GIMP in packages for other package managers, such as Debian's DEB format.

In some cases, you may need to work with the GIMP source code. This will be true if binary files are not available for your platform, or if you want to run a later version of the GIMP than is available in binary/RPM format. (During the course of writing this book, for example, I upgraded several times from GIMP 1.1.9 to 1.1.10 and beyond, and in all cases the source code was the only thing available.)

Navigate to an FTP site containing the GIMP files, locate the appropriate version, and download the files. You'll find all the files you need conveniently ensconced in a subdirectory of their own, so you won't have to worry about selecting the correct files. The archives will have names like `gimp-1.1.10.tar.gz` or `gimp-data-extras.1.0.4.i386.rpm`. The main GIMP application archive is all you really need. The "data-extras" and "plugins-unstable" archives contain extra files, patterns, and plug-ins not required to run the GIMP.

Installing the GIMP

Installation is different, depending on whether you'll be doing a binary or source code installation, so I'll cover each separately. The first thing to do is to copy the files to a subdirectory on your hard disk. You probably have a subdirectory already dedicated to the kind of installation you'll be making, such as `/usr/src/redhat/RPMS` for RPM source files, or `/usr/local/src` for standard source code. Choice of a directory is more of a housekeeping consideration than anything else.

Binary Installation with RPM

If you're using GNOME, you can use the *GnoRPM* application, but that's for sissies. Instead, log on as `root` and change to the directory containing the RPM files you downloaded or copied to your hard disk. Then type a command with the following form:

```
rpm -ivh packagename
```

For *packagename* substitute the name of the RPM file you'd like to install, such as `gimp-1.0.4.i376.rpm`. Repeat the process for any add-on GIMP packages you want to install. When you're finished, locate the GIMP executable file in your `.gimp` directory, and the application will automatically run its first-time installation routine to set up your personal version.

What Can Go Wrong

A few things can go awry, but they are often easily solved. The most common is that you'll have a *dependency error*. That means that a particular file or library required by the package being installed, but not part of the package itself, could not be located on your system. The GIMP may require a library you don't have, or (as is more likely) may need a later version than the one you have installed on your system. The *rpm* utility displays an error message labeled *failed dependencies* that clearly spells out which files are needed, and which components that you're trying to install are dependent on the missing files.

If that happens, trot off to the FTP site of your Linux distribution, and locate the missing file(s), preferably in RPM format. Download and install these packages using *rpm* as outlined above, or using the source code instructions below. Then try installing the GIMP again.

Here are some other error messages you might see:

```
Packagename is already installed
```

If you want to go ahead anyway, to force *rpm* to ignore the error, type:

```
rpm -ivh -replacepkgs packagename
```

If you see a message with the contents:

```
filename conflicts with file from packagename

error: packagename cannot be installed
```

this means that a file you are trying to install is already on your system. If you like, you can force *rpm* to ignore this error, and install your files on top of the old one, by typing:

```
rpm -ivh -replacefiles packagename
```

Source Code Installation

I've installed the GIMP from source code several times, and must say that the only hard part about it is waiting for the code to compile. Even on a fairly fast machine it can take an hour or more, and you'll have nothing to do but watch some interesting strings of commands that scroll by on your screen as the compiler does its job.

The first thing to do is to log in as root, and copy the source code archive to your hard disk. (I tend to put source code in the /usr/local/src directory, so I'll have the source code for all the programs I use in one place.) If this is a first-time installation and you don't have a current version of the GTK (GIMP Tool Kit), you'll need to install that first. Unarchive the toolkit, and then switch to the subdirectory created when you unarchive it. Substitute the name of the version of GTK that you're actually installing. Type something of this form:

```
tar -zxvf gtk-1.0.7.tar.gz

cd ./gtk-1.0.7
```

Then compile the toolkit by typing the following lines (you can relax a bit while the source code is compiled and installed):

```
./configure
make
make install
```

Repeat the process to compile and install the GIMP source code. The commands are almost identical. Substitute the name of the GIMP package you're installing for the example in the lines below.

```
tar -xvf gimp-1.0.7.tar
cd ./gimp-1.0.7
./configure
make
make install
```

Source Code Installation with *rpm*

If you must, you can create your own customized RPM files by compiling the GIMP source code into packages of your own. First, you'll need to locate the files, which will have names like `gimp-1.0.4-1.src.rpm`. You can hunt for them online. Then you'll need to carry out the following steps.

1. Decompress the source files from the directory where you've copied them to the `./SOURCES` and `./SPECS` directories, by typing as you did with the RPM binary files earlier:

   ```
   rpm -ivh packagename
   ```

2. Change to the `./SPECS` directory, and compile the source code into standard RPM packages, using the command:

   ```
   rpm -bb packagename
   ```

You'll end up with RPM packages you can install using the method described earlier in this appendix.

Appendix B: GIMP User Frequently Asked Questions

A number of questions related to pre-1.0 releases have been removed. You should really upgrade to the latest release if at all possible. If you really need an answer to a pre-1.0 question, e-mail the FAQ maintainer at meo@rru.com.

If your question isn't in this FAQ, it might be more of a developer FAQ than a user FAQ. Look there before you panic.

The latest version of this FAQ should always be available at http://www.rru.com /~meo/gimp /faq-dev.html.

General Questions

What is this GIMP?

Where do I get it?

Which version should I use?

Is there a user manual?

What about a Windows version?

Are there any Easter eggs in the GIMP?

What are layers?

Where do I find GIMP stuff?

Is there a mailing list?

Is there an IRC channel?

Do I need Motif?

Why does the GIMP complain about missing libraries?

Why does the GIMP complain "unresolved symbol: _gimp_message"?

Is XInput support available?

Does the GIMP support art tablets like the Wacom?

Does the GIMP have scanner support?

Can the GIMP install its own colormap?

The GIMP complains about MIT-SHM!

Where are the brushes, gradients, patterns, palettes?

What does "wire_read: unexpected EOF" mean?

Why doesn't GIMP configure find my (jpeg, tiff, pnm, etc.) libraries?

Do I have to have an X server? Even for batch mode?

Where can I get some icons for the GIMP?

What kind of system do I need to run GIMP?

The GIMP takes too long to load—how can I speed it up?

Is there a bug list somewhere?

Where should I report bugs? How?

Plug-Ins

What are plug-ins?

How do I add new plug-ins?

How do I build new plug-ins?

Is there a plug-in for . . . ?

Why did some plug-ins disappear for 0.99.19?

Script-Fu

What is Script-Fu?

Where can I learn about Script-Fu?

How do I call one Script-Fu script from another?

How do I call a plug-in from Script-Fu?

How do I execute Script-Fu from batch mode?

What does "procedural-database-error" in Script-Fu mean?

What is Net-Fu? Where is it?

Fonts

Where can I get the fonts I'm missing?

How can I change the GIMP font?

Why don't the Far Eastern fonts work?

What about TrueType fonts?

File Formats

What is GIMP's native graphics file format?

What other graphics file types are supported?

Why can't I save my image as a GIF (or whatever)?

Is there any way to keep the layers when I save?

Why can't I open or save JPEG/JPG files?

Why can't I open or save GIF files?

Why can't I open or save PNG files?

Why can't I open or save XPM files?

Why can't I open or save TIFF/TIF files?

Why can't I open or save PSD files?

Why can't I open or save SOME_FORMAT files?

Using the GIMP

How do I save a selected sub-image to a file?

How do I save an image with an alpha channel?

How do I merge an image from a file to the current image?

How do I get small fonts to look as nice as large ones?

How do I bind keys to menus for shortcuts?

How do I composite two layers, using a third layer as a mask? This worked in 0.54!

Is there a macro-recording interface?

How do I configure my X server to do global gamma correction?

How do I fill with transparent?

How do I draw in a different color?

Platforms

Why can't I get JPEG to work on my Digital Alpha/UNIX (4.0d) box?

Why won't GIMP compile on IRIX (SGI)?

Script-Fu won't compile on IRIX (SGI)

Why does GIMP complain about X Input Methods under Solaris?

How do I add fonts with Solaris?

Why won't the GIMP compile on Solaris?

How do I add fonts with SunOS?

Is there an RPM for Red Hat Linux?

Why won't my RPMs upgrade properly?

What is the gimp.wmconfig file?

Why does my Red Hat system get ___register_???? errors when I run GIMP?

Why don't GIF and JPEG work on Slackware Linux?

Why won't GIMP build for SuSE Linux 5.x?

Where can I get recent binaries?

Why does compiling on HP fail with notes about s%LIBXMU_LIB%-lXmu?

I get make errors on (Solaris, HP/UX, etc.)

Why do I see weird things when I use the GIMP with AcceleratedX?

Why is the selection marquee invisible using XFree3.3 with my S3 Virge graphics card?

InFrequently Asked Questions

Is there a history of the GIMP available?

What's this beavis.jpg image used in several scripts?

What lucky human does this adorable cat own?

General Questions

What is this GIMP?

The "GNU Image Manipulation Program" sired by Spencer Kimball & Peter Mattis.

In their own words, "The GIMP is our answer to the current lack of free (or at least reasonably priced) image manipulation software for Linux and UNIX in general."

Originally, GIMP stood for "General Image Manipulation Program."

Where do I get it?

The best bet is to check out the GIMP home page, which includes pointers to the latest source, as well as complete binaries for a variety of platforms, including at least Linux (a.out and ELF), FreeBSD-2.1, HP-UX, SunOS and Solaris 2.4, and SGI. More may be available by now; go check the Web page. Go on! Vamoose! You can come back here after you get it!

Which version should I use?

Version 1.0.0 is out, and very stable. Get the production version, and get rid of all your old developer versions!

Is there a user manual?

Yes. It is available at `http://manual.gimp.org/` in HTML form, and `ftp://manual.gimp.org/pub/manual/` in Frame, HTML, PDF and PS formats.

What about a Windows version?

Pointers to Windows projects are available on the official "About the GIMP" page.

A Windows version was announced on April Fool's Day, and those who missed the opportunity to download it should be sad, indeed; the announcement itself (a work of art!) follows (the URLs are no longer active):

"I got a little restless during spring break, so, besides sleeping a lot, and scaring squirrels in the yard, I did mad run of hacking and managed to create a surprising beast:

GIMP on Win32.

`www.gimp.org/gimp-win32.gif`

Yep, it really wasn't too hard, considering the way GTK abstracts out the underlying GUI. It clearly needs work though, but it's for the most part fully functional. Just crashes a lot. But you guys can take a look at it:

```
ftp://ftp.gimp.org/pub/gimp/win32/
```

-Yosh"

Are there any Easter eggs in the GIMP?

As of version 1.0, there is at least one Easter egg.

What are layers?

These are similar to the layers found in tools such as Adobe's Photoshop. Think of a stack of slides or filters, in a way that looking through them you see a sort of composite of their effects. For more information, check out the S&P introduction to layers.

Where do I find GIMP stuff?

Probably the prime GIMP resource page is maintained by Quartic at `www.nuclecu.unam.mx/~federico/gimp/el-the-gimp.html`.

A list of GIMP tutorials is available at `abattoir.cc.ndsu.nodak.edu/~nem/gimp/tuts` from Nem W. Schlecht.

The GIMP Documentation Project, spearheaded by Michael J. Hammel, is the central documentation point for users.

Is there a mailing list?

Send e-mail to **majordomo@scam.xcf.berkeley.edu** with the following command in the body (subject line is irrelevant):

```
subscribe gimp-user your-email-address
```

substituting your preferred e-mail address for the string "your-email-address."

Is there an IRC channel?

Zach Beane (xach@mint.net) maintains and tracks several IRC channels. The servers are in the following table:

Hostname	Port	Location
irc.canweb.net.net	6666	Toronto, CA
irc.mint.net	6666	Maine, USA
irc.coherent.net	6666	Chicago, USA
irc.eanut.org	6666	Texas, USA
rudolf.canberra.edu.au	6666	Canberra, AU
irc.giblets.com[down]	6667	Texas, USA
dazed.nol.net	6667	Texas, USA
irc.germany.gimp.org	6667	Bielefeld, Germany
irc.chillin.org	6667	Florida, USA

"All the excitement is in channel #GIMP." —Zach

Do I need Motif?

Some of the earliest versions needed Motif, but by the 0.60 (development) version, Motif was no longer necessary. S&P developed their own, very slick toolkit for the GIMP, called GTK. More information on GTK is available at www.gtk.org/.

Why does the GIMP complain about missing or wrong versions of libraries?

Probably because it can't find them.

There are a couple of solutions. The best one, if you have superuser access on your system, or a cooperative system administrator, is to add the GIMP's library directory to the system library configuration. To do this, edit:

/etc/ld.so.conf to include /usr/local/lib

and then type

ldconfig

and things should work from then on.

If you can't do this, add the directory to your LD_LIBRARY_PATH environment variable. Be sure you do this in your shell's startup scripts as well.

If you have old versions of the libraries, you will probably need to remove them first, especially if they are in standard system locations such as /usr/lib. Don't just delete them, though; move them somewhere safe, install the new ones, and try again. Then make sure everything else still works; you may have other programs on your system that require the old versions. The ideal response in such a case is to rebuild all the programs to use the new libraries. Where this isn't possible, you will just have to experiment with trying them in different locations, or statically linking them to one or more programs.

Why does the GIMP complain "unresolved symbol: _gimp_message"?

This is caused by attempting to use a pre-1.0 libgimp with GIMP 1.0. The gimp_message() was added in 1.0, and is required by 1.0 to operate. Remove old libgimp(s), and try again. (See previous question.)

Is XInput support available?

It's under development. For more information, see Owen Taylor's (**otaylor@gtk.org**) page about XInput support for GTK and the GIMP.

Does the GIMP support art tablets like the Wacom?

There is some support, but you have to do a little extra work to compile it in.

See `www.levien.com/free/linux_intuos.html` by Terry Mackintosh, or `www.gtk.org/~otaylor/xinput/` for details, but here's the quick overview from Juergen Schlag (**j.schlag@callisto.fulda.net**):

1. Run Linux with a X11 server which supports the Xinput-Section (my old S3-Board running under the XFree-Server works well, but the XSuSE- Server for PERMEDIA2-Boards doesn't work).

2. Install the Xinput driver for the Artpad (see the docs). I used a patched driver for the PenPartner.

3. Edit the Xinput-Section of your /etc/XF86Config to load the driver when X11 starts (see the main-pages for XF86Config and your X-server).

4. Recompile the GTK toolkit with the Xinput-support enabled. See the README and INSTALL file for the command switch to do this.

5. Restart your computer, start X11 and GIMP. If no error message occurred, your artpad should work well.

Does the GIMP have scanner support?

Yes. You can run xscanimage, the front end to SANE (Scanner Access Now Easy), either as a GIMP extension or in stand-alone mode. This supports Mustek and HP flatbed scanners, as well as the Connectix color QuickCam camera.

Further information is available at `www.mostang.com/sane/`

Can the GIMP install its own colormap?

Yes. In either the system-wide gimprc file or your personal gimprc file, uncomment the line that includes "install-colormap."

The GIMP complains about MIT-SHM!

If the GIMP gives you a message similar to either of these when you try to start it:

```
Xlib: extension "MIT-SHM" missing on display "198.51.29.58:0.0".
```

or

```
** WARNING **: XShmAttach failed!
```

then you need to run it with the —no-xshm option.

This happens for one of two reasons. Either your X display server does not have the shared memory option, or you are running the GIMP on a different system than the one on which it is displaying. In the former case, you may wish to look into different X servers, because shared memory can give you MUCH better performance. In the latter case, you will just have to live with it, since different systems can't generally share the same memory space.

Where are the brushes, gradients, patterns, palettes?

For a while, these were provided separately in the developer versions. For some time now a very good, "minimum" set of these has been shipping with the GIMP. More are available as "extra" data bundles from any of the download sites.

Others are available from various places. Adrian "Numerical Excess" Likins has a page with lots of gradients and palettes at `www4.ncsu.edu/~aklikins/gimp/AG.html`.

What does "wire_read: unexpected EOF" mean?

This error message should say something like "the plug-in (or the main GIMP app) I was talking to has exited before returning any results, so I assume that it has crashed."

Why doesn't GIMP configure find my (jpeg, tiff, pnm, etc.) libraries?

This should no longer be a problem, but if you insist on using older versions, read on for help. We recommend you try the latest version, though.

Somewhere around 0.99.16 or 0.99.17, configure stopped searching /usr/local for include files and libraries, at least for some of the common packages. Also, on some platforms (FreeBSd, for instance), things may get installed under /usr/X11R6/share instead of /usr/local. Running autoconf and automake might solve this, but for the rest of us, just set the following variables before running configure (substituting as necessary for /usr/local):

csh, tcsh, etc:

```
setenv CFLAGS -I/usr/local/include

setenv LDFLAGS -L/usr/local/lib
```

sh, ksh, bash, etc:

```
CFLAGS=-I/usr/local/include ; export CFLAGS

LDFLAGS=-L/usr/local/lib ; export LDFLAGS
```

On Solaris, you may need to set LDFLAGS to:

```
"-L/usr/local/lib -R/usr/local/lib"
```

The instructions state that these directories will be searched automatically, but in at least some cases, this is not correct.

Do I have to have an X server? Even for batch mode?

Yes, you have to have some form of X server—the GIMP is an X application! It needs an X server for image processing, and for font manipulation. However, if you wish to run in batch mode, you can run with a special, frame-buffer-less X server called Xvfb, which doesn't require a graphics card or mess with your screen:

```
Xvfb :1 -screen 0 10x10x8 -pixdepths 1 &
gimp —display :1.0 —no-interface —batch "commands" ... &
```

The first command starts the special X server; the second is an example of how to invoke the GIMP in batch mode. When you are done using the GIMP this way for a while, kill off Xvfb so it doesn't waste system resources. If you expect to use GIMP this way a lot, you might want to leave Xvfb running for better response time.

You should check the main page for Xvfb(1) for other options, such as whether to use shared memory.

Where can I get some icons for the GIMP?

www.cs.utexas.edu/users/mschaef/gimpicons/index.html

What kind of system do I need to run GIMP?

That depends on several factors, but in general, any UNIX-like system (Solaris, Irix, Linux, AIX, HP/UX, BSD, etc.) with an X server (preferably X11R5 or later) should work. You probably want at least 32MB of RAM. More RAM will help speed things up. I would prefer at least a decent 486 box, but even a 386 should work. And it really screams on higher-end workstations, like AIX, Solaris and Irix systems.

Like most graphics applications: the GIMP is resource intensive, which means it directly benefits from more memory, higher-end graphics cards, and faster disks. It's the nature of the beast (computer graphics) and not necessarily a problem with the GIMP (although there are probably areas in which it could use performance work— what program couldn't?).

The GIMP takes too long to load—how can I speed it up?

The main things are to make sure you are running at least version 1.0, and make sure you compiled with optimization on, debugging turned off, and the shared memory and X shared memory options tuned on.

Or, buy a faster system with more memory!

If it's still too slow for you, the easiest speedup is to invoke the GIMP with the "—no-data" option. This prevents the GIMP from loading patterns, brushes, and similar resources when it starts. You may benefit slightly from the "—no-splash" option as well; you might want to time that one to see if it really helps enough to be worthwhile.

On a Dell 100MHz 486 server box, the GIMP comes up in the following times:

Command	Time
gimp	18 seconds
gimp —no-data	11 seconds
gimp —no-data —no-splash	8 seconds
gimp —no-splash	16 seconds

Is there a bug list somewhere?

The original Seth Burgess's bug list has been replaced by the Wilberworks bug list at www.wilberworks.com/bugs.cgi.

Where should I report bugs? How?

Depends on what you find. If they seem to be plug-in problems, you definitely want to try to tell the plug-in authors (look in the offending plug-in's source or on the Plug-in Registry Web page).

For core functionality, you can report them at the Wilberworks bug list, or send e-mail to **bugs@gimp.org**.

Finally, if you need to discuss it with a wider developer audience (perhaps because it is really a feature request instead of a bug), send e-mail to the GIMP developer mailing list. It's a good idea to say something like "[bug]" or "[patch]" in the subject where applicable.

Always include the system type, OS, window manager, X version, and so on, as well as the GIMP version (and GTK version if known), and anything else that might be applicable. It's OK to send related problems in a single e-mail. Of course, patches are always welcome.

Plug-Ins

What are plug-ins?

Plug-ins are external modules that actually do the nifty graphics transformations. There is a plug-in registry with the latest plug-ins, maintained by Ingo Lütkebohle. (Special thanks to Adam Moss for the original registry!)

How do I add new plug-ins?

First, copy the plug-in(s) to your plug-in directory (typically /usr/local/lib/gimp/$VERSION/plug-ins/).

After copying the plug-in to its proper directory, just run the GIMP. It should automatically find new plug-ins.

How do I build new plug-ins?

You'll need a copy of the source directories. Build the GIMP. Place the new plug-in in the plug-ins directory. The docs with the new plug-in hopefully identify any special libraries it needs. Look for a plug-in with similar libraries (if all else fails, look at xpm and whirlpinch).

With newer versions, if the plug-in is contained in a single source file, you should just have to run the gimptool in the plug-in's directory:

```
gimptool -build plugin.c
```

For older versions, there are several methods. The first two walk you through a number of steps manually; these are the most thorough, but also require more work on your part. The last ones are scripts of one sort or another, and are easier on your part—if they work with your system. Go ahead and try—you can always fall back on the first methods.

The best way to proceed is to edit the Makefile. Pick a similar plug-in (such as whirlpinch). For the SRC and OBJ lines, just add entries similar to the others, but with the new plug-in's name. Now, find all the groups of lines with the other plug-in's name in them, duplicate them, and change the old name to the new name. The one exception is the huge set of lines that have a lot of paths that end in .h—do not bother with these. Now, just type

```
make
```

and it should build. Install it wherever your other plug-ins are installed.

A second choice for those who don't want to mess with the main Makefile is to build a file to create just the new plug-in. Start the same way—pick a similar plug-in. Now remove the binary and object files for the one you just picked. For instance, if you selected the whirlpinch plug-in, you will see the following files:

```
whirlpinch
```

```
whirlpinch.c
```

```
whirlpinch.o
```

In this case, you would remove the first and last files, leaving the whirlpinch.c file. Now type

```
make
```

to rebuild the old plug-in.

Copy the output (cut and paste it!) into a file. Edit the file and change all occurrences of "whirlpinch" (or whatever) to the name of the new plug-in. Execute the file you just edited. For instance, if the file is make_plug-in, just type

```
make_plugin
```

and it should work. Then copy the plug-in to wherever the others are installed on your system.

A Makefile

First, load Makefile-pi provided by Ciccio C. Simon. Change all occurrences of the word sharpen in Makefile-pi to the name of the new plug-in. Then type

```
make -f Makefile-pi
```

and watch it (hopefully) work.

If it doesn't work, try the next method.

A compile script

First, load the compile-pi script provided by Jeremy Dinsel. Change the permissions on compile-pi as follows:

```
chmod ugo+rx compile-pi
```

and type

```
compile-pi help
```

for instructions. Follow those instructions. If this one also fails, go back to the earlier, manual methods; you have too picky a configuration for the simple methods to work.

If you need more help, ask your system administrator or a handy programmer, or get a good book on make. You may want to join the GIMP developer's list as well (see the Developer FAQ).

Is there a plug-in for . . . ?

The plug-in registry referenced above is the place to check.

Why did some plug-ins disappear for 0.99.19?

Some of the plug-ins have proven unstable. These have been moved into a separate download, which should be available wherever you got the GIMP, in the file gimp-plugins-unstable-VERSION.tar.gz or gimp-plugins-unstable-VERSION.tar.bz2.

Because this list may change frequently, the unstable plug-ins are no longer listed here.

Script-Fu

What is Script-Fu?

In the words of S&P:

Script-Fu is the first GIMP scripting extension. Extensions are separate processes that communicate with the GIMP in the same way that plug-ins do. The distinction is that extensions don't require an active image to operate on, instead extending the GIMP's functionality. GIMP internals for version 1.0 have been completely over-hauled from version 0.54. In particular, the plug-in API has been made far more general with the advent of the procedural database (PDB). The PDB allows the GIMP and its plug-ins to register procedures which can then be called from anywhere: internally, from extensions, and from plug-ins. There are already over 200 internal GIMP procedures, and more being created all the time. Because all of these procedures can be easily invoked from extensions, the logical next step was to create a scripting facility; thus, Script-Fu was born.

Where can I learn about Script-Fu?

As with plug-ins, Web pages, COBOL, or anything else, one of the best things you can do is look at other peoples' code, and play with it. But it helps a lot if you know Scheme. Check out:

S&P's Script-Fu pages

Mike Terry's Black Belt School of Script-Fu

How do I call one Script-Fu script from another?

The trick to calling Script-Fu scripts from another script is to just reference the main define for the script and not to try to use the pdb call. All the scripts in Script-Fu share a common name space; you call other scripts just like a regular function / define / whatever you call those those things in_scheme.

For example, to call Script-Fu predator in a script, just use

```
(script-fu-predator img drawable 2 TRUE 3 TRUE TRUE)
```

For examples, see www.gimp.org/~adrian/scripts/test.scm.

How do I call a plug-in from Script-Fu?

The following examples assume the plug-in name is "plug_in_randomize_hurl," and the plug-in has four parameters specific to it, the first two of which are floats, and the next two ints. From the Script-Fu console, call a plug-in like this:

```
(plug-in-name 1 0 0 100.0 1.0 10 0)
```

The first parameter should always be a "1". The next two are the image number and drawable. Anything following these numbers will be plug-in parameters, which depend on the plug-in. Inside an actual script, call a plug-in like this:

```
(define (script-fu-fred img drawable)

(plug-in-randomize-hurl 1 img drawable 100.0 1.0 10 0)

(gimp-displays-flush)

)

(script-fu-register "script-fu-fred"

    "<Image>/Script-Fu/fred"

    "Randomize test"

    "Miles O'Neal <meo@rru.com>"

    "Miles O'Neal"

    "1998/May/1"

    "RGB*, GRAY*, INDEXED*"

    SF-IMAGE "Image" 0

    SF-DRAWABLE "Drawable" 0)
```

How do I execute Script-Fu from batch mode?

Invoke the script as non-interactive and add a pair of escaped quotes around each string just like you do in (script-fu-register). You DO NOT need to replace '-' with '_' in any names or registrations.

Example script:

```
(define (script-fu-famhist-link text filename)

  ;; code ommitted for brevity

  (file-gif-save 1 img 0 filename "" FALSE FALSE 0 0))

(script-fu-register "script-fu-famhist-link"

                "<Toolbox>/Xtns/Script-Fu/Family Historian/Link"

                "Family Historian Link"

                "John Johnson"

                "John Johnson"

                "1998"

                ""

                SF-VALUE "Text String" "\"Family Historian\""

                SF-VALUE "Base filename" "\"foo\""

                )
```

Example Invocation:

```
;; note the '1' as the first argument tell it to run non-interactivly

;; note the \" \" pairs around the strings

gimp -n -b  '(script-fu-famhist-link 1 "\"Introduction\"" \

    "\"intro.gif\"")' '(gimp-quit 0)'
```

For a detailed, step by step explanation, check out Adrian's Gimp Batch Mode how-to at adrian.gimp.org/batch/.

What does "procedural-database-error" in Script-Fu mean?

Normally it means that the script is trying to use a particular font that isn't available on your system—it's either not installed or not in your X server's FONTPATH. The base Script-Fu package makes extensive use of the freefont package, and at least one font (AlfredDrake) from the sharefont package.

What is Net-Fu? Where is it?

Net-fu is a Web-based interface to a Script-Fu server. The work is done at a remote site. To see Net-fu, point your Web browser at `scheme.XCF.Berkeley.EDU/net-fu/` or `www.cooltext.com/`. Any Web browser can read this page; the browser must be Java-enabled to actually run Script-Fu.

Fonts

Where can I get the fonts I'm missing?

The freefonts and sharefonts packages are both available from `ftp://ftp.funet.fi/pub/Linux/sunsite/X11/fonts/` or other Sunsite mirrors. If you get the sharefonts package, be sure and read the various licensing agreements, and abide by them.

How can I change the GIMP font?

You need to copy the gtkrc file that comes with the GIMP source (in the top level directory) into $HOME/.gimp/gtkrc. As of 0.99.10, this should be recognized. You then go in and edit the default font style, the one that looks like this:

```
style "default"

{

  font = "-adobe-helvetica-medium-r-normal—*-100-*-*-*-*-*-*"

}
```

I'm sure there's a lot of clever stuff that can be done here, and I'll try to track it down soon, but in the meantime, just change that "100" to something larger, like "120" or "140". (The number is points * 10, so 100 is a 10-point font).

Obviously, you could stick in any font you have available.

Why don't the Far Eastern fonts work?

These are 16-bit fonts, with thousands and thousands of characters. And the characters are more complex, which means (usually) more bits per character, which means more memory and more processing time.

This includes fonts such as kana, kanji, song ti, mincho and gothic. (If you look carefully at the fully qualified font name for gothic via xfontsel, you'll see clues. It's a daewoo font. The gothic name is misleading to western minds, but no doubt means something to its author(s).)

Check one of these out in a program that shows a font as pages (such as xfd). You can keep hitting Next page to see a new page of characters, almost forever.

What about TrueType fonts?

If neither your X server nor your X font server supports TrueType, you can try one of the TrueType font servers:

xfstt (`sunsite.unc.edu/pub/Linux/X11/fonts/`)

or

xfsft (`www.dcs.ed.ac.uk/home/jec/programs/xfsft/`)

xfstt supposedly has limitations on the font size.

File Formats

What is GIMP's native graphics file format?

XCF is the GIMP's "native" format. This will preserve all information about an image, including the layers.

What other graphics file types are supported?

All the common formats, and many more as well, including GIF, TIFF, JPEG, XBM, XPM, PostScript, and BMP. Plug-ins are used to load and save files, so adding new file types is very simple, compared to other graphics programs.

As of July 1, 1998, the list of supported types included BMP, CEL, FITS, FLI, GBR, Gicon, GIF, GIcon, HRZ, JPEG, PAT, PCX, PIX, PNG, PNM, PostScript, SGI, Sun Raster, TGA, TIFF, XPM, XWD, and XCF. Bzipped, Gzipped, and Xdelta'd files are understood, and URL support is provided.

Of course, plug-ins for other types may be available at the plug-in registry.

Why can't I save my image as a GIF (or whatever)?

The two most likely problems are related to image type and layers. For instance, your image type must be "Indexed" for GIF, but "RGB" for TIFF. Try a different image type (look under the "Image" menu). If you have more than one layer in your image, you probably need to merge the visible layers, and/or "flatten" the image. Both operations are available under the "Layers" menu or from the "Layers" dialog box. Flattening will destroy any background transparency.

Is there any way to keep the layers when I save?

Yes; the GIMP has a file format just for this—the XCF format. Don't flatten the image or merge the layers as you would to save to other formats! This will only work with the XCF type.

Why can't I open or save JPEG/JPG, GIF, PNG, XPM, TIFF/TIF, PSD, or SOME_FORMAT files?

There are several possibilities.

If the file type appears in the Save dialog box but is grayed out, you may need to change the image type. For instance, you can't save an RGB as a GIF (convert to indexed first) or an indexed image to JPEG (convert to RGB first).

The GIMP comes with full support for a few types built in. If the type you want doesn't appear in file type format of the Open and Save dialogs, you need to check the Plug-in registry to see whether you need to download an optional plug-in.

Some of the file types, such as JPEG and TIFF, require extra libraries (described elsewhere). Make sure you have the correct versions of these on your system.

Using the GIMP

How do I save a selected sub-image to a file?

Create a new image large enough to hold the selection. Copy the selection, then paste it into the new image. Crop the new image. Flatten, and so on, as necessary. Now save it.

The Script-Fu-selection-to image can also be used to cut a selection out of an image and create a new image with it.

How do I save an image with an alpha channel?

Before saving the image, select "Layers | Flatten Image." It would be more intuitive if it was called something like "Remove Alpha"… but that's generally not its primary function. It just happens to remove alpha.

How do I merge an image from a file to the current image?

Open the additional image via the File | Open menu. Then Select | Select all. Edit | Copy. Move the cursor to the edited image. Edit | Paste. This drops the new image (selection) into the middle of the edited image. Move it around as necessary, then anchor it.

How do I get small fonts to look as nice as large ones?

In general, small fonts won't ever look quite as nice as large ones. But there are a couple of things to try.

Make sure you are using an outline font as opposed to a bitmapped font. For details, check any book on using the X Window System.

"If your image is GRAYSCALE or RGB (i.e. not INDEXED) when there's a toggle button in the text tool which turns antialiased text on and off. It's on by default in GRAYSCALE or RGB modes, and forever off in INDEXED mode." —Adam Moss

How do I bind keys to menus for shortcuts?

Go to the menu selection you are interested in. Keeping it selected (hold the mouse's menu selection down if necessary), press the key sequence you wish to assign to the menu. It will appear on the right of the menu. The new binding will be saved and used in future GIMP sessions.

How do I composite two layers, using a third layer as a mask? This worked in 0.54!

0.54 is ancient history—it was an early, developer's release.

The equivalent method in 1.0 or later would be to have two layers, and create an alpha mask (add layer mask from the layer ops menu) and insert the "mask" layer into it.

Is there a macro-recording interface?

Not at this time. It's in the works for a future release.

How do I configure my X server to do global gamma correction?

Some servers have no facility for this; you may be able to adjust your monitor to correct it somewhat. Later versions of XFree86 allow these server options:

```
-gamma f              set gamma value (0.1 < f < 10.0) Default: 1.0

-rgamma f             set gamma value for red phase

-ggamma f             set gamma value for green phase

-bgamma f             set gamma value for blue phase
```

How do I fill with transparent?

If your image doesn't have an alpha channel, add one with Layers | Add Alpha Channel. Select the area you want to clear (if not the whole image). To change everything of a particular color transparent, pick Select | By Color... and click on the color in the image you want to replace. Then select Edit | Clear. That's it.

Any dithering, blurring, or related effects against the color you replace will be against the original color. This usually requires you to do some form of cleanup of the edge pixels. In cases likely to result in this, change the color to transparent as early as reasonably possible to preclude extra "cleanup" work.

How do I draw in a different color?

At the bottom of the toolbar there is a box with two smaller boxes and an arrow. The uppermost box displays the current foreground color; the lowermost box displays the current background color. You can single-click on the arrow to switch these two. You can also double-click on either of the color boxes (or single-click if that box is already selected) to pop up a color selection tool, with which you can elect any color you like for that box. That color then becomes the new foreground or background color. Subsequent drawing operations (including text and color fill) will now use these colors.

Platforms

Why can't I get JPEG to work on my Digital Alpha/UNIX (4.0d) box?

Even the JPEG libraries at the GIMP Web site may not work for all versions. If their JPEG-shared-6.a.tar.gz package doesn't work for you, try: `ftp://ftp.uu.net/graphics/jpeg/jpegsrc.v6b.tar.gz`

Why won't GIMP compile on IRIX (SGI)?

If you are using a 64-bit OS, you need to add the '-o32' option for the compiler, or use gcc. With the SGI compiler, you may also need to play with optimization. Some modules may have exhibit problems unless compiled with '-O1' or even '-O0'.

Script-Fu won't compile on IRIX (SGI)

Script-Fu requires the POSIX-compliant regex functions, which SGI only supports with IRIX 6.2 and later versions. The GNU version of regex should work just fine, though, and is available at: `wuarchive.wustl.edu/systems/gnu/regex-0.12.tar.gz`

Why does GIMP complain about X Input Methods under Solaris?

The GIMP is interacting in such a way with your system that it thinks you have XIM extensions when you don't. Run the configure script again, with the '—disable-xim' option, and recompile. You can also try compiling with '—disable-shared'. Or you can install a version of X11R6.

How do I add fonts with Solaris?

If you just want to use freefonts or sharefonts, you can copy these files into the appropriate directory (such as /usr/openwin/lib/fonts/freefonts/ or /usr/openwin/lib/fonts/sharefonts/), or merge them with the appropriate fonts.dir and fonts.scale files if you mixed in freefonts and sharefonts with existing fonts:

- freefonts fonts.dir
- freefonts fonts.scale
- sharefonts fonts.dir
- sharefonts fonts.scale

Or just try using fontadmin instead of mkfontdir.

I've never run into a Solaris system missing this, but according to Neil Corlett:

"The 'fontadmin' tool is a openwin demo program and sometimes does not exist. To properly add fonts the finagled directory requires fonts.dir, fonts.scale files to exist. mkfontdir does the first of these OK. For the second I built groff and downloaded type1inst-0.6.1 from an X contrib archive. type1inst (which needs groff) will build the fonts.scale file from the pfb files automatically."

Solaris 2.6 is supposed to include better font editor and admin tools.

Why won't the GIMP compile on Solaris?

There may be a number of reasons. Several answers are here. The most detailed answers, listed first, are the best bets with their noted versions.

According to resident GIMP on Solaris guru Jim Harmon, more recent versions (0.99.25 on) should compile easily, but you may need to make a change in /usr/graphics/gtk-config.in:

OLD:

```
-libs)

    echo -L${exec_prefix}/lib -L/usr/openwin/lib -R/usr/openwin/lib \

        -lgtk -lgdk -lglib -lXext -lX11 -lsocket -lnsl -lm

    ;;
```

NEW: (subs. your own GTK path for /usr/graphics)

```
-libs)

    echo -L${exec_prefix}/lib -L/usr/openwin/lib -R/usr/openwin/lib \

        -L/usr/graphics/gtk+-0.99.10/gtk/.libs \

        -R/usr/graphics/gtk+-0.99.10/gtk/.libs -lgtk \

        -L/usr/graphics/gtk+-0.99.10/gdk/.libs \

        -R/usr/graphics/gtk+-0.99.10/gdk/.libs -lgdk \

        -L/usr/graphics/gtk+-0.99.10/glib/.libs \

        -R/usr/graphics/gtk+-0.99.10/glib/.libs -lglib \
```

```
          -lXext -lX11 -lsocket -lnsl -lm

   ;;
```

Jim Harmon compiled GIMP 0.99.19 and GTK+ 0.99.5 on Solaris 2.5, SPARC 5. Here are the steps he took:

If you're installing a NEW VERSION, first:

```
cd <gtk install path>  (/usr/graphics/gtk+<ver>)

make uninstall clean

rm -r ~/.gimp
```

Then,

```
mkdir /usr/graphics

mv g*.tar.gz /usr/graphics

tar xvfz gtk+-0.99.5.tar.gz

   created  /usr/graphics/gtk+-0.99.5

cd gtk+-0.99.5

./configure, make, make install

   (executed successfully)

cd ..

tar xvfz gimp+-0.99.19.tar.gz

   created  /usr/graphics/gimp+-0.99.19

cd gimp+-0.99.18

./configure
```

Now, *** Edit "config.status" ***

```
vi config.status

          /LDFLAGS
```

Change:

(Note: the following are SINGLE LINES, remove any "\" characters and duplicate objects in the string if you cut/paste these into your config.status file)

```
s%@LDFLAGS@%   -L/usr/openwin/lib -R/usr/openwin/lib \

              -lgtk -lgdk -lglib \

              -lXext -lX11 -lsocket  -lnsl -lm%g
```

To:

```
s%@LDFLAGS@%      -L/usr/local/lib -R/usr/local/lib \

                  -L/usr/openwin/lib -R/usr/openwin/lib \

                  -L/usr/graphics/gtk+-0.99.5/gtk/.libs \

                  -R/usr/graphics/gtk+-0.99.5/gtk/.libs -lgtk \

                  -L/usr/graphics/gtk+-0.99.5/gdk/.libs \

                  -R/usr/graphics/gtk+-0.99.5/gdk/.libs -lgdk \

                  -L/usr/graphics/gtk+-0.99.5/glib/.libs \

                  -R/usr/graphics/gtk+-0.99.5/glib/.libs -lglib \

                  -lXext -lX11 -lsocket -lnsl -lm%g
```

To SAVE SPACE in compiling, in the config.status file, REMOVE the "-g" option from the CFLAGS line:

```
[was] s%@CFLAGS@%  -g -I/usr/openwin/include -O2 -Wall%g

[is]  s%@CFLAGS@% -I/usr/openwin/include -O2 -Wall%g

   ./config.status, make, make install
```

(In other words, where "-lgtk -lgdk -lglib" appear on the LDFLAGS line, add the GTK+ path to the libs with the format of "-L/usr/graphics/gtk+-0.99.3//.libs -R/usr/graphics/gtk+-0.99.3//.libs -l", substituting gtk/gdk/glib for)

Also bear in mind that "/usr/local/lib" won't exist if not added as shown to LDFLAGS.

Caveats

I'm using the precompiled GCC 2.7.2.3 for Solaris 2.6, and gmake instead of make. To get GCC and GMAKE working, I had to set the paths to /usr/xpg4/bin and /usr/ccs/bin to the PATH variable, so that different compiler tools could be found. (ar, bison, cpp, etc.)

Jim Harmon compiled GIMP 0.99.18 and GTK+ 0.99.3 on Solaris 2.5, SPARC 5. Here are the steps he took:

```
mkdir /usr/graphics

mv g*.tar.gz /usr/graphics

tar xvfz gtk+-0.99.3.tar.gz

    created  /usr/graphics/gtk+-0.99.3

cd gtk+-0.99.3

./configure, make, make install

    (executed successfully)

cd ..

tar xvfz gimp+-0.99.18.tar.gz

    created  /usr/graphics/gimp+-0.99.18

cd gimp+-0.99.18

./configure
```

Now: *** Edit "config.status" ***

```
vi config.status

    /LDFLAGS
```

Change:

(Note: the following are SINGLE LINES, remove any <CR> characters in the string if you cut/paste it into your config.status file)

```
s%@LDFLAGS@%    -L/usr/openwin/lib -R/usr/openwin/lib -lgtk -lgdk -lglib

-lXext -lX11 -lsocket  -lnsl -lm%g
```

To:

```
s%@LDFLAGS@%    -L/usr/openwin/lib -R/usr/openwin/lib
```

```
-L/usr/graphics/gtk+-0.99.3/gtk/.libs
```

```
-R/usr/graphics/gtk+-0.99.3/gtk/.libs -lgtk
```

```
-L/usr/graphics/gtk+-0.99.3/gdk/.libs
```

```
-R/usr/graphics/gtk+-0.99.3/gdk/.libs -lgdk
```

```
-L/usr/graphics/gtk+-0.99.3/glib/.libs
```

```
-R/usr/graphics/gtk+-0.99.3/glib/.libs -lglib -lXext -lX11 -lsocket
```

```
-lnsl -lm%g
```

```
    ./config.status, make, make install
```

(In other words, where "-lgtk -lgdk -lglib" appear on the LDFLAGS line, add the GTK+ path to the libs with the format of "-L/usr/graphics/gtk+-0.99.3/<lib>/.libs-R/usr/graphics/gtk+-0.99.3/<lib>/.libs -l<lib>", substituting gtk/gdk/glib for <lib>)

I'm using the precompiled GCC 2.7.2.3 for Solaris 2.6, and gmake instead of make. To get GCC and GMAKE working, I had to set the paths to /usr/xpg4/bin and /usr/ccs/bin to the PATH variable, so that different compiler tools could be found. (ar, bison, cpp, etc.) According to Keyly Price, here's a major one for 0.99.10:

"If you do a -lX11, you must also include -lsocket, or it won't compile anything of X on Solaris 2.5. X doesn't have the socket lib. Which means you'll need to setenv LIBS -lsocket while running configure if you run Solaris 2.5."

Will Lowe did the following to get the GIMP compiled for Solaris 2.5.1: (You should replace /usa/lowe/usb_lowe/gimp in each "-L" part with wherever you are compiling GIMP, and replace /usa/lowe/gimp/lib in the "-R" parts with wherever you're going to install GIMP. -Will)

Get gimp source (gimp-0.99.9). Uncompress and untar the source.

```
./configure —without-libtiff
```

```
rm docs/pdb.info
```

```
gimp/gtk+/gdk/gdkimage.c
```

Remove these three lines:

```
#if defined (HAVE_IPC_H) && defined (HAVE_SHM_H) && defined (HAVE_XSHM_H)

#define USE_SHM

#endif
```

gimp/gtk+/gdk/Makefile:

> change the variable "libgdk_la_LDFLAGs" to include:
>
> -L/usa/lowe/usb_lowe/gimp/gtk+/glib/.libs -R/usa/lowe/gimp/lib
>
> before "-lglib"

gimp/gtk+/gtk/Makefile:

> change the variable "libgtk_la_LDFLAGS" to include:
>
> -L/usa/lowe/usb_lowe/gimp/gtk+/gdk/.libs -R/usa/lowe/gimp/lib
>
> before "-lgdk"

gimp/libgimp/Makefile:

> change the variable "libgimp_la_LDFLAGS" to include:
>
> -L/usa/lowe/usb_lowe/gimp/gtk+/glib/.libs -R/usa/lowe/gimp/lib
>
> before "-lglib"

change "libgimpui_la_LDFLAGS" to include

> -L/usa/lowe/usb_lowe/gimp/gtk+/gtk/.libs -R/usa/lowe/gimp/lib
>
> before "-lgtk"

gimp/plug-ins/dgimp/dgimp.c

> move "#include <sys/types.h>" to above "#include <sys/socket.h>"

gimp/plug-ins/dgimp/lpg.c

> same as dgimp.c

For 0.99.pre11, Sheldon E. Newhouse suggests the following change to the libtool files:

```
#archive_cmds='$LD -G -z text -h $soname -o $lib$libobjs$deplibs'
archive_cmds='$LD -G -h $soname -o $lib$libobjs$deplibs'
```

How do I add fonts with SunOS?

SunOS ships with an X11R4 server, which does not handle either scaleable fonts or communications with the X font server. If you want to use the freefonts (or any scalable fonts) on SunOS, you need to install your own, newer X server, preferably X11R6.4 (which will be much faster than the server shipped with SunOS).

If you do this, you will no longer have PostScript capability directly in your X server; you will need to use ghostscript. You may well want to keep both servers around, and use each when you need its features.

Of course, you could always try to find a PS version of the font you need and make a bitmap for the size you need and add that to the X11R4 server's font path, but if you need more than one or two font/size combinations over all the time you use GIMP, this is an obnoxious solution.

Is there an RPM for Red Hat Linux?

Yes. Try the following:

```
ftp://ftp.gimp.org/pub/gimp/binary/RPMS/
ftp://s9412a.steinan.ntnu.no/pub/gimp/
```

Why won't my RPMs upgrade properly?

According to Rob Payne,

"there are old .src.rpm's on ftp.redhat.com for GIMP and gtk that if used to build new gtk+ and GIMP will create all kinds of headaches for the builder.

The gtk SPEC file manually moves header files from gtk default installation place, and then the CFLAGS returned by gtk-config are incorrect when it comes time to build/install GIMP. I was successful in bringing the gtk+ SPEC file up to date by removing the following lines from (gtk-970925.spec) to build 0.99.7 and 0.99.8:

```
(cd $RPM_BUILD_ROOT/usr/local/include

 mkdir glib

 mv glib.h glibconfig.h glib)
```

Of course, the %files section of that SPEC need to be changed, as well to include the differences in places for the header files, and to include gtk-config.

I hope that information is useful to someone. If you have any questions about any of this, please let me know."

What is the gimp.wmconfig file?

It's a Red Hat RPM-related file, related to their desktop and window manager.

Why does my Red Hat system get ___register_???? errors when I run GIMP?

This is due to incompaitble RPMS. If (for example) gtk was compiled with egcs, GIMP must be compiled with egcs. There is no easy way to tell what is compiled with what, so getting both GIMP and gtk off a GIMP mirror would be a good idea.

Another possibility for this error (far less common) is that there is an old library compiled with the other hanging around somewhere on the system. Remove old copies of libgimp.

Why don't GIF and JPEG work on Slackware Linux?

You need to manually get libgif and libjpeg and compile and install them on your system. They will install by default in /usr/local/lib, so once they're installed, you have to make sure that LD_LIBRARY_PATH=/usr/local/lib or put /usr/local/lib in your ld.so configuration file. In addition, you also have to remove libgif.* and libjpeg.* from your /usr/lib directory, as these will be found first (and even if you finagle ld.so to find the other libs first, they're still broken, so remove them anyway). I think that if you go to ftp.gimp.org there's a "support" type subdirectory that has the gif, jpeg, png, and mpeg libraries, though I've never gotten the mpeg stuff to compile.

Why won't GIMP build for SuSE Linux 5.x?

You probably just installed the graphics libraries. You also need to install the development portion as well; it's called the libgr source package. After installing that, GIMP should compile easily.

Where can I get recent binaries?

Irix: `www.easysw.com/~mike/gimp` or its mirror site, `ftp://ftp.funet.fi/mirrors/ftp.easysw.com/pub/gimp`

Digital UNIX 4.0D: `ftp://finwds01.tu-graz.ac.at/pub/gimp/`

"This version does not need the colormap workaround on DEC3000 machines. The JPEG plug-in is included as well."

Why does compiling on HP fail with notes about s%LIBXMU_LIB%-lXmu?

From the Sun | HP porting guide...

"Some of the X include files and libraries are not in /usr/include/X11 and /usr/lib/X11 as you may expect. This is because HP allows support for X11R4 and X11R5 on the same machine. You must modify a configuration file so that the Makefile created by imake looks for these files and libraries in an alternate location. See 'Motif and Xt' on page A-5 and 'Xaw and Xmu' on page A-6 for details on installation of OSF/Motif, Xt, Xaw and Xmu....

"HP does not ship or support these widget libraries; however, they are widely used for X public domain software. Binaries and header files are available from the Interworks library. Source is available from public domain archives. The name of the binary package in the Interworks library is x8.0s700.tar.Z. You may also be able to locate these files on another machine and copy them to your machine."

The ref'd package is at:

   `ftp://www.interworks.org/pub/comp.hp/`

Look for the x8.0s[378]00.tar.Z files.

I get make errors on (Solaris, HP/UX, whatever)

You are probably not using the GNU make. Most, if not all, non-GNU makes will fail on the GIMP makefiles. Get the GNU make package.

Why do I see weird things when I use the GIMP with AcceleratedX?

It's a bug in AcceleratedX with shared memory. Turn off shared memory when you start the GIMP (—no-xshm) or pick up the patch to AcceleratedX's X server from `ftp://ftp.xinside.com/pub/update/`.

At least one person has found this bug (or another one with the same symptoms) to still be present in 4.1.

Why is the selection marquee invisible using XFree3.3 with my S3 Virge graphics card?

This is a bug in XFree. You need to upgrade to XFree3.3.2.

InFrequently Asked Questions

Is there a history of the GIMP available?

Seth Burgess has written a brief history of the GIMP. It's available at students.ou.edu/B/Seth.J.Burgess-1/gimp-history.html.

What's this beavis.jpg image used in several scripts?

(/usr/local/share/gimp/scripts/beavis.jpg is the B/W image in question.)

The image (of a kitten playing with Gumby) is used as "sorta random, sorta not" data to generate (for example) the crystal bands, or other texture maps. There are other ways to produce this data as well, but the author stuck with this one, found in a tutorial somewhere.

What lucky human does this adorable cat own?

One of the original GIMP authors, Spencer Kimball or Peter Mattis, we forget which.

Contributors

Spencer Kimball & Peter Mattis, Thomas Bahls, Zach Beane, Brandon Beattie, Seth Burgess, Mats H. Carlberg, Neil Corlett, Christopher Curtis, Jeremy Dinsel, Robert Dinse, Ian Donaldson, Bert Driehuis, Pat Dunn (?), Stephen Eglen, Eugene Filippov, Rial Fletcher, Trond Eivind Glomsrød, Michael J. Hammel, Pete Harlan, Jim Harmon, Thimo Jansen, John Johnson, Christoph Kukulies, Philippe Lavoie, Marc Lehmann, Adrian Karstan Likins, Will Lowe, Ingo Lütkebohle, T. Paul McCartney, Wenxin Mao, Adam Moss, Sven Neumann, Sheldon E. Newhouse, Miles O'Neal, Rob Payne, piranha (alix albert), Kelly Price, Quartic (Federico Mena), Raphael Quinet, Deon Ramsey, Donovan Rebbechi Juergen Schlag, William L. Sebok, Terrelle Shaw, Ciccio C. Simon, Yosh (Manish Singh), Phil Stracchino, Mike Sweet, Owen Taylor, Mike Terry, Tyzen

Copyright 1996-1998 Miles O'Neal, (meo@rru.com) Austin, TX. All rights reserved. You may freely redistribute this FAQ so long as you redistribute it in its entirety, including this notice and the Web location of the latest version. You are not required to redistribute the graphics with this FAQ. It would be much appreciated if you let the FAQ maintainer (Miles O'Neal) know if you redistribute this FAQ. Web service donated by Net Ads as a community service.

GIMP Graphics Glossary

In this glossary, you'll find short definitions of many of the graphics- and Web-oriented terms used in this book—plus many that are not. This lexicon can be a shortcut to refamiliarizing yourself with terms when you don't want to hunt for the definition provided when they were first used. I'm also defining words not covered in this book, but which are commonly encountered when carrying out imaging, prepress, and scanning tasks. I've avoided providing definitions for every single GIMP feature or plug-in, but do cover nearly every other common word or phrase you need to understand to use the program successfully.

absolute URL: A full and complete uniform resource locator (URL) that unambiguously points to a specific location. *See also* URL

achromatic color: An unsaturated color, such as gray.

acquire: A way of importing a file into GIMP using a special plug-in module, such as SANE.

active hyperlink: The link currently selected in a browser, often differentiated from other links on the same page by a change of color.

additive colors: The red, green, and blue (RGB) colors used to display images on a monitor (and therefore by browsers); all three colors added together produce white. Web graphics are usually prepared in an image editor's RGB mode.

address: An informal name for a URL.

airbrush: Originally an artist's tool that sprays a fine mist of paint to create soft-edged effects. The digital version in most image editors includes user-configurable brushes that can apply a spray of a selected tone at adjustable "pressure" levels to an area.

alignment: The position of type or an object in an image; for example, left, center, or right.

alpha channel: A grayscale layer of an image used to store selections. They may be copied from one image to another, saved with an image in formats like TIFF, recalled, and combined with other selections.

ambient lighting: A diffuse nondirectional lighting caused by light bouncing off the surroundings, used to fill in the dark areas not illuminated by one of the main light sources.

anchor: A tagged element, either text or graphics, which serves as the destination of a hyperlink.

animated GIF: A GIF file that contains the multiple images of an animation, which are displayed one after another by a Web browser to produce the illusion of movement.

animation: Computer graphics used to prepare moving sequences of images. On the Web, you'll find animations in the form of animated GIFs, QuickTime movies, and other formats.

anonymous FTP: A protocol for retrieving files from a server remotely, without the need for a special user name or password.

anti-aliasing: A process that minimizes jaggy diagonal lines by using in-between tones to smooth the appearance of the line. Anti-aliasing helps produce smoother images for Web graphics, even at relatively low resolutions.

applications program interface (API): A shared intermediate interface that allows a broad range of hardware and software products to communicate. Plug-ins use APIs to integrate filters with image editors or to link a program to scanners and digital cameras.

archive: To store files that are no longer active, usually on a removable disk or tape.

ascender: The portion of a lowercase letterform that rises above the top of the main portion of a lowercase letter.

aspect ratio: The proportions of an image—for example, 1024 by 768-, 800 by 600-, and 640 by 480-pixel Web pages all have the same 4:3 aspect ratio or proportions.

attribute: Characteristics of a page, character, or object, such as line width, fill, underlining, boldface, or font. In HTML, attributes are entered within the tag to which they apply.

backbone: A network that connects other networks.

background: The bottom layer of a GIMP image, or, the color or pattern of a Web page on which text and images are displayed.

backlighting: Lighting effect produced when the main light is located behind the subject.

bandwidth: The amount of information that a communications link can carry at one time.

baseline: The imaginary line on which the main part of each character of text rests.

Bézier curve: An editable curved line like those produced by GIMP's Paths tool.

bicubic: The most preferred of three common resampling algorithms, which uses sophisticated formulas to calculate new pixels based on the pixels above, below, and to either side. See also *bilinear* and *nearest neighbor*.

bilinear: One of three common resampling algorithms, which bases its calculations on the values of the pixels on either side of the target pixel. See also *bicubic* and *nearest neighbor*.

bilevel: An image that stores only black-and-white information, with no gray tones; GIMP calls such images bitmaps.

bitmap: A description of an image that represents each pixel as a number in a row and column format.

bit: A binary digit—either a 1 or a 0. Image files typically use multiple bits to represent information about each pixel of an image. A 1-bit image can store only black or white information about a pixel. There are also 8-bit (256 hues), 16-bit ("thousands of colors", or 65,535 hues); and 24-bit color ("millions of colors" or 16.8 million hues) systems.

black printer: A printing plate used to add black ink to a cyan-magenta-yellow image, emphasizing neutral tones and adding detail to shadows. A skeleton black printer adds black ink only to darker areas; a full-range black printer adds at least some black to all of an image.

black: The color formed by the absence of reflected or transmitted light—for example, the combination of 100 percent values of cyan, magenta, and yellow ink (in the subtractive color system) or 0 values of red, green, and blue light (in the additive color system).

bleed: A printed image that extends right up to the edge of a page, often accomplished by trimming a larger image down to a finished size.

blend: To merge portions of an image smoothly.

blur: To reduce the contrast between pixels that form edges in an image, softening it.

BMP: A Windows graphics format.

brightness: The amount of light and dark shades in an image. The relative lightness or darkness of the color, usually measured as a percentage from 0% (black) to 100% (white).

bucket fill: GIMP tool for filling an area with color.

buffer: An area of computer memory set aside by a computer or an application to store information meant for some sort of input or output, such as printing or writing to disk.

bump map: A file which contains information used to build the texture of a selection.

burn: To darken part of an image.

BZIP: Files compressed using the Bzip compression scheme.

cache: A fast memory buffer used to store information that has been read from disk or from slower RAM to allow the operating system to access it more quickly.

calibration: Adjusting a device such as a scanner, monitor, or printer so its output represents a known standard.

camera ready: Artwork in a form usable for producing negatives or plates for printing.

cascading style sheet: Formatting information for Web pages that provide precise control over fonts, position, and other content attributes. Style sheets can be applied to paragraphs, parts of pages, or entire pages. The term *cascading* is used because several sheets can apply to a single page, and the formatting is applied to individual opponents according to a hierarchy of precedence.

cast: A tinge of color in an image, particularly an undesired color.

CEL: A format used by KISS Software International programs.

channel: One of the layers that makes up an image, such as the red, green, and blue channels of an RGB image, or the cyan, magenta, yellow, and black channels of a CMYK image. Alpha channels are additional layers used to represent masks or selections.

chrome: A color transparency such as Kodachrome, Ektachrome, or Fujichrome.

clickable image: A graphic or image map in an HTML document that can be clicked on to retrieve associated URLs and their contents.

client-side image map: A clickable image map that includes the URLs available for access, and their coordinates on a page, directly on the page itself, so a Web browser supporting this feature can follow the designated hyperlinks without intervention by the server.

clipping path: A path exported with an image when the image is intended to be silhouetted when placed in a page layout program.

clone: To copy pixels from one part of an image to another with GIMP's rubber stamp tool.

CMYK color model: A model that defines all possible colors in percentages of cyan, magenta, yellow, and black.

color cast: An overall tone that dominates a color image, such as excessive magenta or blue.

color correction: Changing the color balance of an image to produce a desired effect, usually a more accurate representation of the colors in an image.

color depth: The number of bits of information used to represent color values in an image; the higher the number of bits, the greater the number of colors (and shades) that can be represented.

colorizing: To add color to a monochrome image.

color picker: A dialog box used to choose colors for painting, filling, and other tasks.

color separation: The process of converting an image to its four separate color components—cyan, magenta, yellow, and black—for printing.

color wheel: A circle representing the spectrum of visible colors.

complementary color: Generally, the opposite hue of a color on a color wheel, which is called the direct complement. For example, green is the direct complement of magenta.

compression: Reducing the size of a file by encoding using smaller sets of numbers that don't include redundant information. Some kinds of compression, such as JPEG, can degrade images, while others, including GIF and PNG, preserve all the detail in the original.

compile: To translate computer source code written in a higher level language, such as C, into the code a computer can execute.

constrain: To limit a tool in some way, such as forcing a brush to paint in a straight line, or an object being rotated to a fixed increment.

continuous tone: Images that contain tones from the darkest to lightest with an infinite range of variations in between.

contrast: The range of individual tones between the lightest and darkest shades in an image.

convolve: A process used by imaging filters, which takes the values of surrounding pixels to calculate new values for sharpening, blurring, or creating another effect.

crop mark: A mark placed on a page showing where the page should be trimmed to produce its final size.

crop: To trim an image or page by adjusting the boundaries.

darken: The process of selectively changing pixel values to darker ones.

default: A preset option or value that is used unless you specify otherwise.

defloat: To merge a floating selection with the underlying image.

defringe: To remove the outer-edge pixels of a selection, often when merging a selection with an underlying image.

densitometer: An electronic device used to measure the density of an image.

desaturate: To reduce the purity or vividness of a color, as with GIMP's Sponge tool. Desaturated colors appear washed out and diluted.

descender: The portion of a lowercase letter that extends below the baseline, such as the tail on the letter y.

deterministic dithering: A way of dithering colors to arbitrary palettes.

diffusion: The random distribution of tones in an area of an image, often used to represent a larger number of tones.

digitize: To convert information, usually analog information, such as that found in continuous tone images to a numeric format that can be accepted by a computer.

displace: To offset an image or pixels by a certain amount, based on user input or a file called a displacement map.

dithering: A method of simulating full-color tones on monitors that can display only 256 colors by grouping the dots into larger clusters of varying size. The mind merges these clusters and the surrounding background into different tones.

dodge: A photographic term for blocking part of an image as it is exposed, lightening its tones.

dot gain: The tendency of a printing dot to grow from the original size when printed, as ink is absorbed and spread into the paper.

dot: A unit used to represent a portion of an image, especially on a printer.

dots per inch (dpi): The resolution of an image, expressed in the number of pixels or printer dots in an inch. Scanner resolution is also commonly expressed in dpi, but, technically, scanners use an optical technique that makes *samples per inch* a more accurate term.

download: To receive something, such as a file retrieved from the Internet, or a font received by a printer.

Drag and Drop: A new GIMP capability for dragging layers, colors, brushes, and patterns to new locations.

duotone: A printed image, usually a monochrome halftone, which uses two different colors of ink to produce a longer range of tones than would be possible with a single ink density and set of printer cells alone.

edge detect: To find the transitions between portions of an image by examining the contrast of the pixels.

elasticity: Tolerance of the GIMP's Intelligent Scissors tool.

emboss: A filter technique that makes an image appear to be raised above the surface in a 3-D effect.

emulsion side: The side of a piece of film that contains the image, usually with a matte, nonglossy finish.

encapsulated PostScript (EPS): An image format for PostScript printers, which can include a bitmap description of an image file, or an outline-oriented image of line graphics and text. GIMP can import both bitmap and line-oriented EPS files, but can export only the bitmapped version.

export: To transfer text or images from a document to another format, using an image editor's Save As or Export functions.

extrude: To create a 3-D effect by adding edges to an outline shape as if it were clay pushed through a mold.

FAXG3: The most common fax file format.

feather: To fade the edges of a selection to produce a less-obtrusive transition.

file format: A defined way in which applications store information on a disk, such as JPEG or GIF for Internet graphic images.

fill: To cover a selected area with a solid, transparent, or gradient tone or pattern.

filter: A GIMP feature that changes the pixels in an image to produce blurring, sharpening, and other special effects.

FITS: Flexible Image Transport System, or FITS, is the format adopted by the astronomical community for data interchange and archival storage

FLI/FLC: Common animation formats, for 320 by 320 pixels at 64 colors and 64K by 64K pixels at 256 colors, respectively.

font: A group of letters, numbers, and symbols in one size and typeface. Garamond and Helvetica are typefaces; 11-point Helvetica Bold is a font.

four-color printing: Another term for process color, in which cyan, magenta, yellow, and black inks are used to reproduce all the hues of the spectrum.

FPO: For Position Only. Artwork that is not good enough for reproduction, but can be used in a page layout to make it easier to visualize how the document will look.

frequency: The number of lines per inch in a halftone screen.

FTP: File Transfer Protocol is an Internet protocol used to provide network file transfer between any two network nodes for which a user has file access rights (especially a remote host and your local host or desktop machine).

gamma correction: A method for changing the brightness, contrast, or color balance of an image by assigning new values to the gray or color tones of an image. Gamma correction can be either linear or nonlinear. Linear correction applies the same amount of change to all the tones. Nonlinear correction varies the changes tone by tone, or in highlight, midtone, and shadow areas separately to produce a more accurate or improved appearance.

gamma: A numerical way of representing the contrast of an image's midtones. Gamma is a method of tonal correction that takes the human eye's perception of neighboring values into account.

gamut: A range of color values; those present in an image that cannot be represented by a particular process, such as offset printing or CRT display, are said to be out of gamut.

Gaussian blur: A method of diffusing an image using a bell-shaped curve instead of blurring all pixels in the selected area uniformly.

GBR: The format used by the GIMP to store brushes.

GICON: The format used by the GIMP to store Toolbox icons.

GNOME (GNU Network Object Model Environment): An easy-to-use graphical desktop environment that runs under X Windows.

GNU Project: An effort started in 1984 with the goal of producing a completely free UNIX-like operating system.

GPL (GNU General Public License): An agreement intended to guarantee the right to share and change free software, and insure software distributed under the license is available to everyone.

gradient: Colors that evenly merge from one to another.

gray component removal: A process in which portions of an image that have a combination of cyan, magenta, and yellow are made purer by replacing equivalent amounts of all three with black. Similar to *undercolor removal*, except that GCR uses more black.

gray map: A graph that shows the relationship between the original brightness values of an image and the output values after image processing.

grayscale: The range of different gray values an image can have.

guides: Grid lines that can be used to help position objects in an image.

GZIP: Files compressed using the Gzip compression scheme.

halftoning: A way of simulating the gray tones of an image by varying the size of the dots used to show the image.

HEADER: The C programming language header format, used for embedding images in C program files.

highlight: The brightest values in a continuous tone image.

histogram: A barlike graph that shows the distribution of tones in an image.

HRZ: An older 256- x 240-pixel slow-scan TV format.

HSB color model: A model that defines all possible colors by specifying a particular hue and then adding or subtracting percentages of black or white.

hue: A pure color.

image map (also called clickable image, or clickable map): A graphical image that has an associated sever-side or client-side map file that lets users select links by clicking on certain portions of the image.

inline image: A graphic that can be viewed in the same browser window as the text, as opposed to with a separate viewing helper program.

interlaced GIF: See *interlacing*

interlacing: A way of displaying a GIF image in two fields: odd-numbered lines first, then even-numbered lines, thereby updating or refreshing half the image on the screen at a time, allowing visitors to view a rough version of an image even before the entire file has been downloaded from a Web page.

interpolation: A technique used to calculate the value of the new pixels required whenever you resize or change the resolution of an image, based on the values of surrounding pixels.

invert: To change an image into its negative; black becomes white, white becomes black, dark gray becomes light gray, and so forth. Colors are also changed to the complementary color; green becomes magenta, blue turns to yellow, and red is changed to cyan.

jaggies: Staircasing of lines that are not perfectly horizontal or vertical. Jaggies are produced when the pixels used to portray a slanted line aren't small enough to be invisible.

Java: A programming language created by Sun Microsystems, now most commonly used to create Java applets, which can be downloaded from a Web server and executed by a visitor's browser. *See also* applet.

JavaScript: A cross-platform scripting language that can be inserted directly into an HTML page, and executed by browsers, which support it. Originally developed by Netscape Communications.

JPEG compression: Reducing the size of an image through algorithms specified by the Joint Photographic Experts Group. The image is divided into blocks, and all the pixels within the block are compared. Depending on the quality level chosen by the user, some of the pixel information is discarded as the file is compressed. For example, if all the pixels in a block are very close in value, they may be represented by a single number rather than the individual values.

justified: Text aligned at both right and left margins.

KDE (K Desktop Environment): A graphical user interface for Linux, UNIX, and similar operating systems.

kern: To adjust the amount of space between two adjacent letters.

lasso: A tool used to select irregularly shaped areas in a bitmapped image.

layer: A virtual "acetate overlay" that is initially transparent, but can be used to store portions of an image for separate manipulation until you "flatten" the image back to a single layer for output.

layer mask: A grayscale mask applied only to one layer of an image.

leading: The amount of vertical spacing between lines of text measured from baseline to baseline.

lens flare: The effect used by spreading light as if it were being reflected by the internal elements of an optical lens.

LHS color: A system of color based on the luminance, hue, and saturation of an image.

lighten: An image-editing function that is the equivalent to the photographic darkroom technique of dodging. Gray tones in a specific area of an image are gradually changed to lighter values.

line art: Usually, images that consist only of white pixels and one color.

line screen: The resolution or frequency of a halftone screen, expressed in lines per inch.

lines per inch (lpi): The method used for measuring halftone resolution.

lithography: Offset printing.

luminance: The brightness or intensity of an image.

Lynx: One of the original UNIX, text-based browsers.

LZW compression: A method of compacting TIFF files using the Lempel-Zev Welch compression algorithm. It produces an average compression ratio of 2:1, but larger savings are produced with line art and continuous tone images with large areas of similar tonal values.

magic wand: A tool used to select contiguous pixels that have the same color value or range you select.

map file: File on the server that includes pixel coordinates of hotspots on an image map.

mapping: Assigning colors or grays in an image.

marquee: A selection tool used to mark rectangular and elliptical areas.

mask: To protect part of an image so it won't be affected by other operations.

midtones: Parts of an image with tones of an intermediate value.

Moiré: An objectionable pattern caused by the interference of halftone screens, frequently generated by rescanning an image that has already been halftoned.

monochrome: Having a single color.

MS-DOS: An operating system like Linux, except unencumbered by useful features.

nearest neighbor: One of three common resampling algorithms, which examines the nearest pixel in the position where a new pixel will go, and bases the value of the pixel on that. See also *bilinear* and *bicubic*.

negative: A representation of an image in which the tones are reversed. That is, blacks are shown as white, and vice versa.

neutral color: In RGB mode, a color in which red, green, and blue are present in equal amounts, producing a gray.

noise: Random pixels added to an image to increase apparent graininess.

NTSC: National Television Standard Code, the standard for video in the United States. Critics sometimes refer to the acronym as Never Twice the Same Color.

opacity: The opposite of transparency: the degree to which a layer obscures the view of the layer beneath. High opacity means low transparency.

Open Source: A trademark of Software in the Public Interest Inc., a non-profit organization that was founded to help organizations develop and distribute open hardware and software. SPI encourages programmers to use the GNU General Public License or other licenses that allow free redistribution of software, and hardware developers to distribute documentation that will allow device drivers to be written for their product. Open Source is managed by the Open Source Initiative.

palette: Tones available to produce an image, or a row of icons representing the available tools.

PAT: The format used by the GIMP to store patterns.

PCX: A 24-bit format widely used by Windows painting programs.

Photo CD: A special type of CD-ROM developed by Eastman Kodak Company that can store high quality photographic images in a special space-saving format, along with music and other data.

PIX: A format used by Alias/Wavefront on Silicon Graphics workstations.

pixel: A picture element of a screen image; one dot of the collection that makes up an image.

plate: A thin, light-sensitive sheet, usually of metal or plastic, which is exposed and then processed to develop an image of the page, then placed on a printing press to transfer ink to paper.

plug-in: A filter or some other added feature, which is not an integral part of the program itself.

PNM: The Portable aNyMap format, used by PBM programs.

point: Approximately 1/72 of an inch outside the Macintosh world, exactly 1/72 of an inch within it.

Portable Network Graphics: A new RGB file format which offers progressive, interleaved display, like GIF and progressive JPEG, for gradual display of images on Web pages, but is lossless (unlike JPEG, which can discard some image information).

portrait: The orientation of a page in which the longest dimension is vertical; also called *tall orientation.*

posterization: A GIMP effect produced by reducing the number of tones in an image to a level at which the tones are shown as posterlike bands.

PostScript: A page description language developed by Adobe, which allows any printing device to output a page at its highest resolution.

prepress: The stages of the reproduction process that precede printing, when halftones, color separations, and printing plates are created.

process colors: Cyan, magenta, yellow, and black—the basic ink colors used to produce all the other colors in four-color printing.

progressive JPEG: A type of JPEG image in which increasingly detailed versions of an image are displayed, allowing a visitor to a Web site to view a graphic in rough form before it is completely downloaded.

PSD: The native format used by Adobe Photoshop.

quadtone: An image printed using black ink and three other colored inks.

QuickMask: GIMP's new capability for painting masks with any of the brush tools.

raster image: An image defined as a set of pixels or dots in row and column format.

ray tracing: A method for producing realistic highlights, shadows, and reflections on a three-dimensional rendering by projecting the path of an imaginary beam of light from a particular location back to the viewpoint of the observing.

reflection copy: Original artwork that is viewed by light reflected from its surface, rather than transmitted through it.

register marks: Small marks, also known as registration marks, placed on a page to make it possible to align different versions of the page precisely.

register: To align images, usually different versions of the same page or sheet. Color separation negatives must be precisely registered to one another to ensure that colors overlap in the proper places.

registration marks: Bull's-eye marks that are placed in the margins of a printed CMYK image to make sure that printing plates align properly.

relative URL: A link that is relative to the current page's URL. For example, the page `http://www.dbusch.com/CCS/index.htm` might include a reference to page2.htm, which tells the browser to look for it in `http://www.dbusch.com/CCS/`.

rendering: To produce a realistic 3-D image from a drawing or other data.

resampling: The process of changing the size or resolution of an image, by replacing pixels with additional pixels or fewer pixels calculated by examining the value of their neighbors.

rescaling: The operation of changing the dimensions of an image by reducing the height and width in proportion to its overall dimensions.

resolution: A measure of the amount of detail in an image as expressed in units per inch. See specific resolutions—ppi, dpi, or lpi.

retouch: To edit an image, most often to remove flaws or to create a new effect.

RGB color correction: A color-correction system based on adjusting the levels of red, green, and blue.

RGB color model: A way of defining all possible colors as percentages of red, green, and blue.

right-reading image: An image, such as a film used to produce a printing plate, that reads correctly, left to right, when viewed as it will be placed down for exposure.

rubber stamp: A GIMP tool that copies or clones part of an image to another area or image.

sample: A picture element captured by a scanner.

SANE: A scanner driver for capturing images directly into the GIMP.

saturation: The purity of color; the amount by which a pure color is diluted with white or gray.

scale: To change the size of a piece of an image.

scanner: A device that captures an image of a piece of artwork and converts it to a bit-mapped image that the computer can handle.

screen angle: The alignment of rows of halftone dots, measured from the horizontal (which would be a 0-degree screen angle).

screen: The halftone dots used to convert a continuous tone image to a black-and-white pattern for output on printers or printing presses.

script: Instructions that can be executed by a program that understands the script's language. Script-Fu is an example of scripting language.

secondary color: A color produced by mixing two primary colors, such as yellow and cyan inks to create blue, or red and green light to create magenta.

selection: An area of an image chosen for manipulation, usually surrounded by a moving series of dots called a selection border.

separations: Film transparencies representing each of the primary colors (cyan, magenta, and yellow) plus black, used to produce individual printing plates.

serif: Short strokes at the ends of letters.

server side image map: A way of navigating a Web page using an image map that transfers the coordinates of the user's mouse on a Web page back to the server, where a CGI program determines which URL to direct you to.

SGI: The graphics format used by Silicon Graphics workstations.

shade: A color with black added.

shadows: The darkest part of an image holding detail.

sharpening: Increasing the apparent sharpness of an image by boosting the contrast between adjacent tones or colors.

smoothing: To blur the boundaries between edges of an image, often to reduce a rough or jagged appearance.

smudge: A tool that smears part of an image, mixing surrounding tones together.

snap: A feature that causes lines or objects being drawn or moved to be attracted to a grid or guides.

SNP: An animation format used by MicroEyes.

spot color: Individual colors, often just one or two in addition to black, used on a page as an accent, rather than to provide an accurate representation of a color image.

spot: The dots that produce images on an image setter or other device.

staircasing: The jaggy effect produced by lines that are not perfectly horizontal or vertical, especially when they are scaled up or down. Jaggies are produced when the pixels used to portray a slanted line aren't small enough to be invisible.

subtractive colors: The primary colors of pigments. When two subtractive colors are added, the result is a darker color, which further subtracts from the light reflected by the substrate surface.

SunRas: Sun rasterfile format, used by Sun workstations.

threshold: A predefined level used to determine whether a pixel will be represented as black or white.

Targa: A graphics format developed by TrueVision.

thumbnail: A miniature copy of a page or image that provides a preview of the original.

TIFF (Tagged Image File Format): A standard graphics file format that can be used to store grayscale and color images plus selection masks.

tint: A color with white added to it.

tolerance: The range of color or tonal values that will be selected (when using a tool like the magic wand) or filled with paint (when using a tool like the paint bucket).

trim size: Final size of a printed publication.

tritone: An image printed usually with black ink (or another color) plus two other colored inks.

undercolor removal: A technique that reduces the amount of cyan, magenta, and yellow in black and neutral shadows by replacing them with an equivalent amount of black. See also *gray component replacement.*

unsharp masking: The process for increasing the contrast between adjacent pixels in an image, increasing sharpness.

URL (Uniform Resource Locator): The complete address of a file or some other destination on the Internet.

vector image: An image defined as a series of straight-line vectors. The beginning and ending points of each line are stored and later adjusted as the image is sized.

vector image: An image defined as a series of straight-line vectors and curves.

wire frame: A rendering technique that presents only the edges of a 3-D object, as if it were modeled from pieces of wire. This is much faster than modeling the entire object, including all surfaces.

wrong-reading image: An image that is backward relative to the original subject—that is, a mirror image.

WYSIWYG: Any editing program that displays a document more or less exactly as it will appear to the end user when printed out, or displayed on a Web page.

XCF: The native file format of the GIMP.

x-height: The height of a lowercase letter, such as the letter x, excluding ascenders and descenders.

XPM: X PixMap, a format used by X Windows icons.

XWD: X Window Dump, a format used by X Windows *screendump* utility.

X Windows: A graphical user interface for Linux, UNIX, and similar operating systems.

zoom: To enlarge part of an image so that it fills the screen, making it easier to work with that portion.